For Marti..

Happy

Bro!

All the Best

Steve

THE AUTHOR WHO
OUTSOLD
DICKENS

'How do you like Forster's *Life of Dickens*? I have only dipped into the book, but I see he only tells half the story.'

W.H. Ainsworth, letter to James Crossley,
25 January 1872.

THE AUTHOR WHO
OUTSOLD
DICKENS

The Life and Work of W.H. Ainsworth

STEPHEN CARVER

PEN & SWORD
HISTORY

AN IMPRINT OF PEN & SWORD BOOKS LTD.
YORKSHIRE – PHILADELPHIA

First published in Great Britain in 2020 by
PEN AND SWORD HISTORY
An imprint of
Pen & Sword Books Ltd
Yorkshire – Philadelphia

ISBN 978 1 52672 069 6

Typeset in Times New Roman 11.5/14 by
Aura Technology and Software Services, India.
Printed and bound in the UK by TJ International.

Pen & Sword Books Limited incorporates the imprints of Atlas, Archaeology,
Aviation, Discovery, Family History, Fiction, History, Maritime, Military, Military
Classics, Politics, Select, Transport, True Crime, Air World, Frontline Publishing,
Leo Cooper, Remember When, Seaforth Publishing, The Praetorian Press,
Wharncliffe Local History, Wharncliffe Transport, Wharncliffe True Crime and
White Owl.

For a complete list of Pen & Sword titles please contact
PEN & SWORD BOOKS LIMITED
47 Church Street, Barnsley, South Yorkshire, S70 2AS, England
E-mail: enquiries@pen-and-sword.co.uk
Website: www.pen-and-sword.co.uk

Or
PEN AND SWORD BOOKS
1950 Lawrence Rd, Havertown, PA 19083, USA
E-mail: Uspen-and-sword@casematepublishers.com
Website: www.penandswordbooks.com

For Professor Victor Sage, to whom I owe so much

Other books by Stephen Carver

The Lancashire Novelist

The 19th Century Underworld: Crime, Controversy & Corruption

Shark Alley: The Memoirs of a Penny-a-liner

Contents

Acknowledgements

Special thanks, as ever, go to the team at Pen & Sword – to Jonathan Wright and Laura Hirst for commissioning this book, and Alice Wright and Emily Robinson for all their editorial and marketing support, not to mention patience; also, to Linne Matthews, my trusted editor, and Jon Wilkinson for another brilliant cover. I'd also like to thank Derek Wright at Wordsworth Editions, and the historians Jessica Cale and Geri Walton for their continued interest and support, and Dr Stephen Basdeo for sharing his excellent work on Dick Turpin and Wat Tyler. Many thanks and respect also to Professors Victor Sage, William Hughes, David Punter and Roger Sales who helped me so much during the early stages of this research; and likewise Dr Glyn White, University of Salford, Dora Rayson and her colleagues at the Archives Section, Local Studies Unit, Manchester Central Library, and D.W. Riley F.L.A., Keeper of Printed Books at the John Rylands Library, who all did the same. Love, finally, to my dear wife, Rachael, for her belief, encouragement, and genealogical and proofreading skills; and my son, Vincent, for forgiving me the time this took when we should've been doing fun stuff, and for being so proud of me when I finished. I couldn't do any of this without you.

Table of Illustrations

Prologue

Man of La Manchester

On the evening of Thursday, 15 September 1881, the man they called the 'Lancashire Novelist' attended a mayoral banquet in his honour at the new Manchester Town Hall, 'as an expression of the high esteem in which he is held by his Fellow-townsmen and of his services to literature'. William Harrison Ainsworth, the author of the bestselling novels *Rookwood*, *Jack Sheppard*, *The Tower of London*, *Old St Paul's*, *Windsor Castle* and *The Lancashire Witches*, was seventy-six years old. Four decades before, he had sat at a similar table at another public dinner in the city, sharing the laurels with his close friend, Charles Dickens.

Back then, reviewers had called Ainsworth the 'English Victor Hugo' and the 'Defoe of his day', fit to fill the shoes of Sir Walter Scott, who had died in 1832 without an obvious successor. But the glory days were long past now. Although *Jack Sheppard* had eclipsed even Dickens's *Oliver Twist* in its day, his current serial, *Stanley Brereton*, could only find a place in the *Bolton Weekly Journal*. Now, a new generation of writers like Henry James, George Eliot and Thomas Hardy were redefining the English novel, laying the foundations for the Modernist revolution that was to come with the new century. Ainsworth's epic historical adventures, replete with ghosts, outlaws and scheming English monarchs, now felt hackneyed and melodramatic. He had made some powerful enemies as well. His legacy would not survive the century in any meaningful way. Ainsworth was destined to become a footnote, at best, in the history of English literature.

But they still loved him in Manchester. The great Gothic banquet hall was packed with civic dignitaries, captains of industry, old soldiers, spiritual leaders, journalists, novelists, family and friends. Although seven years younger than Ainsworth, Dickens had died, 'exhausted by fame', in 1870. Were he still alive, however, it is unlikely that he would have attended. Their friendship had not stood the test of time.

After an extravagant meal, the Lord Mayor, the Right Honourable Thomas Baker, rose to toast Her Imperial Majesty Queen Victoria, before delivering his welcoming address to Ainsworth. It was an expansive eulogy, in which the mayor spoke with great civic pride of the Manchester-born novelist's prolific bibliography, over three-dozen historical novels, several of which were set in his beloved home county of Lancashire. He allied him, too, with many of the great writers of his generation, all of whom Ainsworth had known well. But that generation had all but gone. Ainsworth had outlived them all, friends and foes alike. The mayor had managed to trace three surviving friends from the Manchester Free Grammar School, but all were too infirm to attend. 'We may congratulate ourselves', he said, having explained this, 'that Mr Ainsworth is in a sufficiently hale state of body and mind to be with us to-night to receive our recognition of his great literary abilities.'[1]

Four months later, Ainsworth would be dead. But this was a good night. With cheers ringing in his ears, he accepted the mayor's toast and rose to speak...

In the history of English literature, William Harrison Ainsworth is the national treasure that most people haven't heard of. Literary journalist, magazine editor and proprietor, and, most of all, novelist, Ainsworth was a member of the early Victorian publishing elite, and Charles Dickens's only serious commercial rival until the late 1840s. He counted among his friends the literary lions, political giants and great artists of his age, both Regency and Victorian. He was in the Dickens circle before it was the Dickens circle, and he worked closely with the most prominent publishers in London. In an illustration of the *Fraser's Magazine* 1835 New Year dinner, for example, he can be seen seated next to Coleridge. At various times throughout the century, he owned and edited *Bentley's Miscellany* (whose editorship he assumed after Dickens), the *New Monthly Magazine* and *Ainsworth's Magazine*. An energetic and prolific author, Ainsworth wrote and published well over a hundred literary articles and short stories, two volumes of poetry, and forty (mostly) historical novels, fictionalising four centuries of British history. In his heyday, Ainsworth commanded a massive audience, if not always critical acclaim, his novels multiply adapted for the stage and plagiarised by the penny-a-liners.

As a popular writer and publisher whose life ran the course of the century, from Romantic innocence to Victorian experience, Ainsworth's story is very much also the story of the development of the English novel, perhaps just as much as that story belongs to Dickens and his other more famous contemporaries.

But it is a story rarely told, at least until now.

Introduction

The Ghosts of Critics Past

As anyone who has ever written professionally knows, success is largely a matter of luck. Drive, craftsmanship, originality and talent will only get you so far. After that, the cards fall as they may. In Ainsworth's case, were he born a generation sooner, placing his work more firmly in the era of the Gothic romance, this might be a very different story. Similarly, had he concentrated on publishing and magazine editorship as his sole occupation, his name would in all probability be enshrined in the pantheon of great Victorian publishers. As it is, he is no more than a passing reference in the histories of his better-known contemporaries, his brief entry in *The Oxford Companion to English Literature* concluding, 'His swift narrative and vivid scene setting made him extremely popular, with enormous sales in the mid-century, but his reputation has not been sustained.'[1] Thus, there have been no scholarly editions of his novels, no costume dramas, no movies, no stage revivals, and his work is seldom read either in or outside the academy. And if he does get a mention, it will invariably be cursory, his life's work dismissed in a couple of sentences on turgid historical fiction, provincial melodrama and Newgate novels. In his recent *History of Supernatural Fiction*, for example, S.T. Joshi bats away the work of the author of *The Lancashire Witches* as an 'appalling array of dreary and unreadable historical novels'.[2]

Joshi is here paraphrasing a very long line of critical voices that warn potential readers away with the curt response of a Transylvanian peasant who has just been asked the way to Dracula's castle. Ainsworth, we are advised, was a second-rater in his own day and deserves his place in the dustbin of history. Yet when he succeeded Dickens as the editor of *Bentley's Miscellany* in 1839, he was the obvious choice – a bestselling novelist of established and increasing reputation, with experience and talent for editorial work, having been active as a literary journalist since the Regency. Like Dickens, Ainsworth was both the editor and the primary contributor to the *Miscellany*, supplying the monthly serial that was its principle feature. This was a revolutionary new development in magazine publishing, in which the work and reputation of an individual author became the main selling point. Ainsworth's *Jack Sheppard* was following Dickens's *Oliver Twist*.

Something clearly went wrong somewhere. But as the critical establishment and television dramatists alike still revere many popular Victorian novelists that are neither literary giants nor the easiest reads, perhaps literary style was not the true reason that Ainsworth was edited out of our cultural history. As is often the case with fame and fortune, Ainsworth made some powerful enemies in his own industry, and their critical annihilation has been so absolute that later literary critics often do no more than paraphrase the original attacks, with little apparent attention paid to his actual writing. There is often scant evidence, in fact, that they have read him at all.

In a collection of critical essays intended to capture the new Victorian literary zeitgeist, for example, *A New Spirit of the Age* (1844), Dickens's friend and collaborator R.H. Horne described Ainsworth as a 'reviver of old clothes', whose novels were 'generally dull, except when they are revolting'.[3] A generation on, the critical tone had still not moderated. In J. Hain Friswell's collection of critical essays, *Modern Men of Letters Honestly Criticised* (1870), the chapter devoted to Ainsworth begins:

> Let us start with an opinion, fearlessly expressed as it is earnestly felt, that the existence of this writer is an event to be deplored; and the fact that he is able to assume that he is a Man of Letters who has been of service to his country, and that he has received from the hands of a Prime Minister, himself a Man of Letters, the reward of £100 a year pension for literary services, is a disgrace to this bewildered and Philistine nation.[4]

So closely, in fact, does Friswell follow Horne's model that the 'romance of old clothes' is regurgitated, unacknowledged, as 'a mere list of the frippery of the wardrobe'.[5] And so it goes on. In Andrew Sanders's study,

The Victorian Historical Novel, 1840–1880 (1978), Ainsworth is summarily dismissed with:

> In Horne's terms, Ainsworth was little more than a reviver of old clothes, and his novels were destructive of the real potential of historical fiction. In considering whether or not that potential was ever realised in the Victorian novel, it is essential to look beyond the model that Ainsworth left.[6]

And so is Ainsworth made a ghost, a phenomenon without substance, his reputation abstracted to fleeting celebrity, sales and controversy, rather than by direct engagement with the books on which these attributes ultimately rest, a writer stripped of his writing. Paradoxically, his reputation *has* been sustained, only it is not the reputation he deserves. Perhaps it is equally essential to look beyond the model that the critics have left.

Chapter 1

The Publisher's Apprentice

Manchester was a very different place to the grim megacity of 1881 when Ainsworth was born there on 4 February 1805, George III still on the throne. Although already committed to the English industrial project that would define the coming century, Manchester was still a small town of quaint timber buildings surrounded by wild countryside.

As a commercial and manufacturing centre, Manchester grew quickly, attracting workers whose traditional livelihoods had been disrupted if not destroyed by the pace of industrialisation, or who simply saw a better wage in the factories than the fields. Local manufacturing diversified on the back of textile production. Engineering works sprang up to produce and service factory machinery, branching out into general manufacture. Chemical works provided the mills with bleaches and dyes, and then expanded into adhesives, paint, solvents and pharmaceuticals. Financial services grew alongside commerce, leading to a proliferation of banks and insurance brokers. To keep the engines of trade and its workforce fed, the canal system was extended and, in 1830, the first steam railway in the world opened, linking Liverpool and Manchester. The population exploded, and slums grew like cancer, rivalling the ancient rookeries of London.

But Ainsworth's world was a long way from this one. He was born at the family home, No. 21, King Street, a three-storey Georgian house in an affluent residential area populated by a growing mercantile class that had yet to abandon the city centre to the industrial poor. He was the first child of Thomas Ainsworth, solicitor, and Ann Harrison, the daughter of a Unitarian minister, the couple having married in the summer of 1802. A brother, Thomas Gilbert, was born on 4 October the following year. King Street was a stone's throw from the medieval town centre, the fifteenth-century Collegiate Church (now Manchester Cathedral, where Thomas and Ann had married), and Chetham's Library, established in 1653, the oldest free public reference library in Britain.

This was an environment for men of business, but young William Ainsworth was a dreamer. A child of the Romantic era, he was in love with tales of history, adventure and the supernatural as far back as he could remember. He was particularly enamoured with the tortured protagonists of Byron and Coleridge, the historical novels of Sir Walter Scott, and the brooding Gothic romances of Ann Radcliffe and Matthew Lewis, which he would devour in the reading room of the Chetham's Library. And before he could read himself, his youthful imagination had been fuelled by fireside tales from his father. Thomas Ainsworth was a successful lawyer, and thus a great talker, who could keep William and his brother enthralled for hours. His best stories were decidedly picaresque, and he regaled his boys with tales of daring outlaws and bloodthirsty brigands, just as his wife's elderly relatives filled their heads with anecdotes about the Jacobite rebellion and the Manchester Rebels of 1745, the most romantic of lost causes.

There was one character plucked from relatively recent history that his eldest son loved most of all, the Georgian highwayman Dick Turpin. Already a figure of legend rather than fact, Turpin in Ainsworth's young mind came to embody all the qualities of his favourite stories, a 'gallant robber' in a stylised Gothic setting. 'Turpin was the hero of my boyhood,' he later wrote. 'I had always a strange passion for highwaymen, and have listened by the hour to their exploits, as narrated by my father.' Visits to his mother's family in Rostherne put Ainsworth in the same wild countryside where Turpin had pulled off some of his final robberies, once, according to folklore, riding hell for leather to Hough Green to establish an alibi. Ainsworth was captivated by this story, later writing that:

> When a boy, I have often lingered by the side of the deep old road where this robbery was committed, to cast wistful glances into its mysterious windings; and when night deepened the shadows of the trees, have urged my horse on his journey, from a vague apprehension of a visit from the ghostly highwayman.[1]

Playing highwaymen was a favourite game between the brothers, especially after their father bought a country house in Cheetham Hill as a summer residence in 1811. 'Beech Hill' had a large and untidy garden overlooking the hills and woodland of Crumpsall and Heaton Park, an ideal space for dens and ambushes, with big brother William always assuming the part of the 'Captain of Banditti'.

Ainsworth's other major influence was James Crossley, the second son of a Halifax wool merchant, who joined the legal firm of Thomas Ainsworth and John Sudlow as an articled clerk in 1817. Crossley was five years older than Ainsworth, who was then twelve, but the two bonded quickly over a shared passion for literature and history. Crossley was an avid book collector, and already contributing to literary journals like *Blackwood's Edinburgh Magazine* and the *Quarterly Review*. This early promise was never really fulfilled, although he later edited numerous volumes for The Chetham Society, which he co-founded in 1843 to preserve and publish historical and literary documents from Lancashire and Cheshire, eventually becoming President. This was the beginning of a lifelong friendship. And although Crossley rarely left Manchester, the two men regularly corresponded for the rest of their lives from the moment Ainsworth decamped for London. As Ainsworth's lawyer, Crossley managed to keep his friend's finances reasonably stable, managing property and often lending him money against future publications. He never married and was as devoted to Ainsworth as the mercurial journalist John Forster was to Dickens. It is through his diligence, or at least his tendency to hoard, that Ainsworth's letters have survived, although regrettably, Crossley's side of the correspondence has not been preserved.[2]

Under Crossley's tutelage, the young Ainsworth became even more well read, a process that continued throughout his subsequent career. In their correspondence, Ainsworth constantly defers to his friend's historical and literary knowledge, frequently consulting his ever-expanding library for project ideas and historical details for works in progress. In a way, Crossley wrote through Ainsworth, providing raw material that he was apparently unable to creatively shape himself, being by nature an editor rather than a storyteller. As a writer, Crossley also swung between procrastination and meticulous attention to scholarly detail, neither trait conducive to literary productivity, whereas Ainsworth could bang out a book a year. Professionally, Crossley was also perhaps too prudent to choose the precarious life of letters over the law, and in that sense represents what Ainsworth would have become had he followed in his father's footsteps, a successful lawyer active in public life and the cultural development of Manchester.

The same year Ainsworth met Crossley, he began attending the Manchester Free Grammar School, Gilbert following a couple of years later. Founded in 1515, the curriculum in the brothers' day remained essentially classical, and was intended to prepare pupils for university with a view to entering either the Church or the Law. Many of the boys' paternal ancestors had attended the school, and the expectation was that Gilbert was destined for the clergy while William would join his father in the family law firm. This 'great school on an ancient foundation' was the same one that the other famous literary rebel, Thomas De Quincey, had fled in 1802.[3] The brothers both distinguished themselves academically, especially Gilbert, who won a scholarship to St John's College, Cambridge. Ainsworth wrote about this period with great affection in his semi-autobiographical novel *Mervyn Clitheroe*, painting a picture of a confident and slightly mischievous kid. Of the second master, Dr Robinson Elsdale, who was a firm believer in corporal punishment, Ainsworth wrote, 'We notched his canes so that they split when he used them; put gravel into the keyhole of his drawer; mingled soot with his ink; threw fulminating balls under his feet; and even meditated blowing him up with gunpowder.' The High Master, Dr Jeremiah Smith, who took a particular shine to Gilbert, was more popular. 'He aspired to make his pupils gentlemen as well as good scholars,' wrote Ainsworth, and 'he never used the cane'.[4] Dr Smith noted William's 'imaginary powers' in his reports, and supported Gilbert in his application to Cambridge.

Despite the professional roles to which the brothers seemed fated, both were still drawn to storytelling. In 1820, when William was fifteen and Gilbert thirteen, their childhood games progressed to amateur dramatics. They built a stage, sets and a drop curtain in the cellar of the family house and proclaimed it a 'Private Theatre', performing plays for friends and family in costumes of their own making, acting alongside cousins and schoolmates. William wrote the plays. Of the first production, *The Brothers*, only the title survives, but its sequel has endured, including the original handwritten playbill carefully preserved by Crossley, which proclaims that 'This present Monday, October 1st, will be presented for the first time a new Melo-Dramatic Spectacle by W.H. Ainsworth called *Giotto; or The Fatal Revenge*'. Uncle John Harrison provided musical accompaniment with his violin. William acted in everything in the programme and provided a comic song in the interlude.

4

Giotto is a simple revenge tragedy, a pastiche of the Jacobean dramatic form refined by Shakespeare and the foundation of the eighteenth-century Gothic novel. Conventions include madness, murder, cannibalism, and the ghost of a murdered victim seeking vengeance. While his parents smiled indulgently upon this childish endeavour, Ainsworth was taking his first steps towards becoming a serious professional writer, not the provincial lawyer expected by his elders. The play also clearly indicates its author's literary influences, containing Gothic motifs that would thereafter recur in almost everything he wrote, a taste for horror and the supernatural that would stay with him for life.

The 'theatre' was opened with a florid prologue written and delivered by Crossley, which was subsequently published in *Blackwood's*. The audience comprised of family, legal clerks and servants seated on dining chairs. The stage lit by candles reflected off polished pots and pans, the play then began...

The curtain opened on the medieval aristocrat Giotto (played by Ainsworth) plotting the downfall of a rival:

> But Manfred, cursed Manfred, still survives
> The cause of all my shame, my hated cousin.
> By hell, he lives not long; this villain here,
> Orsino, with his comrade Hugo, shall destroy him.[5]

Set in the Spanish court, the two-act play concerns the rivalry of the cousins Giotto and Manfred (played by Gilbert), for political power and the hand of the Lady Isabinda. Giotto plots to have Manfred banished by telling the King that he's a Portuguese spy and then murdered, but the inept Orsino mistakes Hugo for Manfred in the dark and mortally stabs his accomplice instead. Unaware his plot has gone awry, Giotto receives a royal visit, closely followed by the dying Hugo, who confesses everything. Orsino attempts to deflect the accusation but is struck by lightning before he can swear to his master's innocence. When Giotto rejects Hugo's final words with 'By the blue heaven he lied!' the lights go out and Manfred challenges him to swear his innocence upon the corpse. Giotto reluctantly complies, but when he touches Hugo, fresh blood begins to flow from the wound and the corpse opens its eyes and stares at him in mute accusation. Unlike Banquo's ghost, everybody sees this, and Giotto is immediately condemned. He cheats his executioners by killing himself in his cell with a concealed dagger, cursing his nemesis with his dying breath. In a preachy denouement, Manfred explains that his cousin's fatal flaw was 'ambition and desire of greatness'.[6] 'The applause of select company', wrote Crossley, 'was, as might be expected, enthusiastic.'[7]

Years later, Crossley came across the playbill for *Giotto* and sent it to Ainsworth, prompting a flood of memories. Most poignantly, he wrote that 'Poor Gilbert took a great interest in the performance,' adding, 'On looking back, I almost think this was the happiest moment in his life.'[8] Not long after the play, Gilbert fractured his skull in a riding accident. Although he seemed to recover, his promising academic career came to an abrupt end in his first year at Cambridge, when he was stricken with what was then diagnosed as 'brain fever'. This was a common medical term that covered encephalitis, meningitis, and cerebritis, as well as varying levels of mental illness. William later described a 'melancholy expression' in his brother's 'fine dark eyes' and characterised him as 'reserved' as a child, which might indicate a depressive personality, but the family certainly connected the accident with the drastic change in Gilbert's temperament at university.[9] The accompanying loss of memory suggests some sort of brain injury. Once more, Gilbert seemed to rally at home, but a second episode left him mentally disabled for the rest of his life.

The next logical move was publication, and it seems likely that Crossley encouraged Ainsworth in this direction. The problem was that Ainsworth was not only unknown, he was still a schoolboy. Exploiting the common practice of literary pseudonym and anonymity, he targeted the *Pocket Magazine of Classic and Polite Literature*. This was a relatively new digest, established in 1818 by the London publisher John Arliss to capitalise on the magazine boom inaugurated by the runaway success of *Blackwood's*. William Blackwood and his editors would likely have sniffed out juvenilia immediately, but Arliss was trying to make his mark and was desperate for copy, the best of which was going to *Blackwood's* and its rivals the *London Magazine* and the *Edinburgh Review*.

Ainsworth's first submission, under the name of 'T. Hall', was *The Rivals: a Serio-Comic Tragedy*, which may well have been a revised version of his first play from the subterranean theatre, *The Brothers*. (Thomas Hall was one of his dramatic collaborators from the Free Grammar School, who had played the King in *Giotto*.) *The Rivals* is a jaunty two-page skit in which Janvan, King of Bedoea, and his prime minister, Stephens Antesblan, both court the affections of Billingtonia, a fishmonger's daughter. This triangle alludes to the queen consort and the antipathy between George IV and his long-suffering prime minister, Lord Liverpool, then a common subject of satire. The humour is schoolboy – the principals mostly insult one another, with Shakespearean pastiche gleefully degenerating into modern slang:

> STEPHENS: Usurper off! what are you doing there!
> JANVAN: Traitor begone! what shall Bedoea's prince
>   Yield aught to thee, or in his project wince?
>   Quickly begone, or in a porter vat
>   Drowned shalt thou be, I swear it, and that's flat.[10]

They fight, killing each other, and the distraught Billingtonia drinks poisoned gin and also expires. It was good enough for Arliss, and Ainsworth saw print for the first time in 1821 at the age of sixteen. This is a moment of momentous and intoxicating proportion for any aspiring author. From that point on, your heart belongs to the black print. As James Baldwin later reflected on the inevitability of the calling, 'The terrible thing about being a writer is that you don't decide to become one, you discover that you are one.'[11]

And Ainsworth was no dilettante. While Crossley was an ambitious clerk who dabbled in writing, Ainsworth was already an enthusiastic and prolific quill driver. Enthralled and emboldened, he sent more material under multiple names, mostly revised juvenilia written at school or for the family theatre. The purpose of the 'T. Hall' pseudonym was revealed with the next piece Arliss published, in which the disguised author becomes a framing narrator for his own work, now presented as that of an obscure Jacobean playwright:

> Of all the dramatic writers, one who has met with the least attention and perhaps deserved the most, is William Aynesworthe ... His plays are six in number: *Venice, or the Fall of the Foscaris*; *Ximenez*; *Chosroes*; *The Fathers*; *Elvira*; and *Ghiotto, or Treason Defeated*. And I propose, if it be suitable to the nature of the *Pocket Magazine*, to give specimens of each.[12]

A scene from *Venice* was then quoted, and the article modestly concluded, 'This is poetry, and excellent poetry, or I am much mistaken; indeed the lovers of true drama will find that it has been excelled by few except the writers contemporary with our immortal bard.'[13] He also threw in a comparison to another supposedly forgotten dramatist, 'Richard Clitheroe', a further invention he'd managed to flog to the *New Monthly Magazine* (writing as 'W.W.') published by Henry Colburn, 'condemned to so long a period of oblivion'. (Clitheroe, of course, is a town in the Ribble Valley.) As with the lost works of 'William Aynesworthe', the unidentified scholar claimed that his copy of the plays was the 'only one at present extant'.[14] No one would ever find another, either. The trickster who pranked his schoolmasters was spreading his wings.

But Arliss was cannier than Colburn's rather useless editor, the poet Thomas Campbell, and he caught Ainsworth out on a reference to the Upas, the tropical 'tree of poisons', in *Venice*, not widely known in Europe until the eighteenth century. He printed it anyway, with the playful footnote 'How came Mr. Aynesworthe to be acquainted with the Upas tree? Is not this a little Anachronism? We have no doubt, however, that the plays of Aynesworthe are as ancient as those of Clitheroe.'[15] Mr Hall cheerfully replied that 'I only wanted to give thee an opportunity to catch *The New Monthly* napping, which thou most assuredly didst, and very cleverly.'[16]

Literary hoaxes notwithstanding, Arliss liked Ainsworth and he liked his style, the young author becoming a regular contributor, implying he was older than he was in affected, worldly-wise meditations. Writing as 'T. Hall', 'H.A.' and 'W.A.', he had twenty-nine pieces published in the magazine over the next year, including poetry, dramatic fragments, literary translations, essays and short stories. Aside from the one piece in the *New Monthly* and another in the *European Magazine and London Review*, Ainsworth wrote exclusively for Arliss in that first year, cutting his teeth under the patronage of the Gutter Lane publisher, without ever once meeting him in person.

Chapter 2

Tales of Terror

The Regency publishing landscape was an exciting place to be – dynamic, competitive and ruthless. By the turn of the century, advances in papermaking and printing allowed copy to be produced faster and at a lower cost than its Augustan ancestors, while the growth of the industrial middle classes created the perfect market for a new generation of monthly magazines, with *Blackwood's* setting the new standard and blazing an opportunistic and sensational trail that others soon followed. Literary fiction was a major ingredient of the *Blackwood's* formula, with a notable focus on the mad and the macabre. *Blackwood's* positively celebrated the Gothic, and Walter Scott's review of *Frankenstein*, in which he outlined his influential theory of the genre, first appeared in *Blackwood's*, as did Thomas De Quincey's 'On Murder Considered as One of the Fine Arts'.

Imitations soon sprang up. The *London Magazine* published Wordsworth, Shelley, Clare, and Keats, as well as De Quincey's *Confessions of an English Opium Eater* (although he later defected to *Blackwood's*). The *New Monthly Magazine and Universal Register* began as a hardcore Tory rival to Sir Richard Phillips's Radical *Monthly Magazine*. Its co-founder, Henry Colburn, responding to the success of *Blackwood's*, toned down the politics and recast it as the *New Monthly Magazine and Literary Journal* in 1821, the one Ainsworth hoaxed with 'Richard Clitheroe'. Regular contributors included Charles Lamb, Leigh Hunt, Thomas Noon Talfourd and William Hazlitt.

Blackwood's approach to political and publishing rivals was brutal. Lockhart's vituperative attacks on many of the *London Magazine's* regulars, particularly his persecution of Leigh Hunt, resulted in a duel between the rival publication's editor, John Scott, and Lockhart's London agent, J.H. Christie, when Scott was shot and killed. Christie was acquitted of murder, and *Blackwood's* subsequently described Lockhart as 'wet with the blood of the Cockneys'.[1] A similar gallows style characterised *Blackwood's* tales. Unlike the subtler phantasmagoria of eighteenth-century Gothic fiction, these short, sharp shockers thrived on sensational physical and psychological violence, often in contemporary settings. The characteristic style was one of grotesque and clinical reportage, the narrative conveying exaggerated emotional intensity. The point of view was usually first person, and the observational detail placed the reader behind the horrified eyes of the protagonist. As Poe advised in his satirical homage 'How to Write a Blackwood Article', 'Sensations are the great things after all. Should you ever be drowned or hung, be sure to make a note of your sensations – they will be worth to you ten guineas a sheet.'[2] John Galt's 'The Buried Alive' (1821) sums up the common feature of these tales; as the narrator succumbs to a catatonic stupor and is presumed dead, 'The world was then darkened, but I still could hear, and feel, and suffer.'[3]

Other publishers were quick to jump on the bandwagon, with Henry Colburn's *New Monthly Magazine* in particular running regular tales of terror, most notably 'The Vampyre' by John Polidori, his Byronic antagonist, Lord Ruthven, a notable forerunner of Count Dracula. As Leigh Hunt wrote in 'A Tale for a Chimney Corner', 'A man who does not contribute his quota of grim stories now-a-days seems hardly to be free of the republic of letters. He is bound to wear a death's head, as part of his insignia. If he does not frighten every body, he is no body.'[4]

Shaking off the last of his classical education, Ainsworth was quick to embrace this new trend, and as with his flair for melodrama, he had a natural affinity for the genre. Moving away from his *Horae Dramaticae*, he began experimenting with short horror stories. These are a touch underwritten, indicative of a young writer still learning his craft, but as with the dramatic fragments they offer a fascinating insight into influence, productivity and process, as well as foreshadowing his later work as a mature novelist. And although the magazines in which these stories appeared were relatively minor, they did at least see print.

Ainsworth initially seems to take a lot from Scott's darker supernatural ballads – such as 'Glenfinlas' – and the *Winter Evening Tales* of *Blackwood's* regular James Hogg, the 'Ettrick Shepherd'. Early forays are thus very Scottish, set in wild glens and ruined bothies, and blending folklore with Gothic archetypes. The first of these is 'The Dying Laird', which appeared in the *Pocket Magazine* following the morbid poem 'Sir Albert's Bride', wherein the newlywed of the title is lost during a storm at sea, 'The grey sea-weed her pillow'.[5] In the story, the Reverend Esau Grant, fresh from an evening sermon entitled 'Without faith it is impossible to see God', is called to the deathbed of the local squire, whose agitated state he ascribes to his impeding dissolution. Instead, as the laird takes over the telling from the priest's framing narrative, he hears a terrible confession. Many years before, the laird had murdered his brother by pushing him off a cliff, thus inheriting the estate. Now, his brother, 'horribly disfigured', is waiting for him: 'Wherever I turn his shadowy form flits around me, and beckons me away. Look where he stands! Now, now, he calls me! Save me! Save me!' Despite his plea, 'Have I not repented?', the laird dies laughing hysterically, there being little doubt concerning his soul's final destination. It wasn't God he was seeing.[6]

Ainsworth contributed a more polished ghost story to the *European* in December. 'The Baron's Bridal' is more structurally sophisticated and shows how rapidly the youthful Ainsworth was evolving as a stylist. The story is framed by the first-person narrative of a gentleman hunting in the highlands who is advised to take a circuitous path home by a local to bypass 'a spot which is visited by fearful beings'.[7] The grizzled highlander takes over the narrative, telling the story of the Lord of Glenliscair, whose first wife disappeared during a hunting trip. Six months later, as the Baron was on the brink of a second politically advantageous marriage, the Lady of Glenliscair returned:

> All gazed with horror, on the unexpected and unwelcome messenger; it was the form of a woman swoln and discoloured: her long tresses dripping with water, and her pale and sickly cheeks, seemed the residence of corruption. Her blue and watery eyes were fixed on the Baron, while with a voice that thrilled through every vein she sang, —
> 'The moon-beam glistening on the wave
>   Shines on thy bridal bed;
> Where the tide that is thy true love's grave
>   Shall float above thy head.
> In vain I pray'd, — you plunged me in,
>   Where deep the waters roll;
> But heavily now that deed of sin —
>   Shall sink thy parting soul |
> Then away! away! this night you rest
>   Beneath the darkling tide;
> Thy pillow shall be my mouldering breast,
>   And I will be thy bride!'

The Baron expires on the spot, and since then, the Glen of Strathenwater has been Lady Glenliscair's domain, and 'woe be to him that looks upon such forbidden things'.[8]

Although unsettled by the tale, the hunter takes the short cut. Pausing to rest by the river running through the glen:

> I gazed with horror and astonishment on the figure of which I had heard, swoln, pale, and deathly, rising from the water! — I heard its horrible voice singing the words which it sang at the Baron's wedding

Irresistibly drawn towards the water, he pulls himself away by effort of will, only to come to himself, in total darkness, his dog tugging at his coat. Several hours have passed, and he leaves the glen 'at full speed', on one hand putting the vision down to an 'uneasy slumber' but at the same time cursing the 'foul fiend who had so long delayed me', maintaining an uncanny ambiguity between competing explanations. It might have been a dream; it might have been a real ghost.[9]

'The Baron's Bridal' is often confused with 'The Spectre Bride', published in Arliss's *Pocket Magazine* the following year. This is based on a confusion by Ainsworth's Edwardian biographer, Stewart Marsh Ellis, who conflates the two stories. The title 'The Spectre Bride' suggests the influence of Washington Irving's 'The Specter Bridegroom' (1819), an archetypal comedy, in which the protagonists are destined to be together, but something is keeping them apart, the suitor having to pretend to be a ghost. Ainsworth inverts this lighthearted tale by taking the notionally similar premise of a stranger paying court to a nobleman's daughter, the 'gentle Clotilda', and then really marrying her to a supernatural being. After wooing Clotilda and murdering her father, the stranger arranges to meet the smitten girl at a ruined chapel at midnight. In a mockery of the marriage service, presided over by 'a figure too awful even for the darkest imagination to conceive', her lover is revealed as the ancestor of all Gothic immortals, the 'Wandering Jew'. Having stolen her heart, he takes her soul. 'I saw thee in thine hour of purity', he cries wildly, 'and I marked thee at once for my home ... Look below! And see to what thou art destined', prefacing an extravagant climax, in which the ground gives way and the luckless Clotilda is cast into the lake of fire:

> Her delicate form bounded from rock to rock, over billow, and over foam; as she fell, the ocean lashed itself as it were

in triumph to receive her soul, and as she sunk deep in the burning pit, ten thousand voices reverberated from the bottomless abyss, 'Spirit of evil! Here indeed is an eternity of torments prepared for thee; for here the worm never dies, and the fire is never quenched.'[10]

The language is vivid and biblical – the final line paraphrasing Mark 9:48, 'Where their worm dieth not, and the fire is not quenched' – offering an intense depiction of eternal damnation. The evangelical tone reminds one of James Joyce's adolescent terror of hell in *A Portrait of the Artist as a Young Man*, but there's no sign in Ainsworth's childhood of anything similar. In fact, his dissenting family observed a strict monotheism far removed from the Catholic iconography in play in his story. In this orgiastic depiction of the everlasting fire, it is violence and drama that Ainsworth appears to be taking from religion rather than either fear or faith, the Gothic uncertainty of 'The Baron's Bridal' replaced by the explicitly infernal.

The majority of Ainsworth's juvenile writing was Gothic, absorbing the influences of the practitioners of horror rather than suspense. 'The Spector Bride', for example, recalls the violent, Faustian climaxes of William Beckford's *Vathek*, and *The Monk* by Matthew Lewis, while the device of the damned immortal harvesting souls links it to Charles Maturin's *Melmoth the Wanderer* (1820) and the title character's marriage to the innocent Isidora, which takes place in a remote and crumbling chapel and is performed by a zombie. There is no ambiguity in this story, and the Gothic epiphany results not from the collision of an apparently uncanny event with a series of possible explanations but from the shock of the final image. The supernatural and the destruction of innocence were to be recurrent themes in Ainsworth's later work, making 'The Spectre Bride', like *Ghiotto*, a significant early work.

'The Spectre Bride' was followed by 'An Adventure in the South Seas'. In the story, the only passenger on the merchantman *Alceste* lives through a mutiny, being left for dead by the escaping seamen. Following the *Blackwood's* model of exaggerated sensation, the horror of the story is in the narrator's sense of isolation, first listening to the violence above deck, then regaining consciousness to discover he's entirely alone on the ship, and finally taking to an open boat. The premise is good, but like previous stories, the execution is underdeveloped, and the narrative voice almost entirely passive.

'The Cut Finger: A Tragedy in One Act' was more interesting, though a slightly backwards step into comic drama. The story concerns the trials of the sexton Boreall, who moonlights as a bodysnatcher, a very real concern at time of writing. Before flogging the recently deceased Mrs Botherem to a surgeon, Boreall cuts off one of her fingers to steal a ring. The shock revives her, and she runs shrieking from the churchyard, Boreall giving chase. Mrs Botherem eludes capture and makes her way home, only to discover her husband already in the arms of another woman. She attacks the lovers just as the sexton arrives on the scene and nobody survives the ensuing carnage.

Written six years before the Burke and Hare murders, 'The Cut Finger' is one of several contemporary and Gothic responses to the Georgian epidemic of bodysnatching – Samuel Warren, for example, wrote about it in *Blackwood's* in 'Grave Doings', while *Frankenstein* was barely four years old. What separates Ainsworth's entry from the rest is the gallows humour, Boreall seeing himself as an entrepreneur. His name is also a joke, suggesting 'boreal' (from the Greek god Βορέας), meaning 'of the north', indicating that the famously curmudgeonly wit of Mancunians like Dr John Cooper Clarke and Mark E. Smith was already proudly established in the regional psyche, a century and a half before Les Dawson started working the clubs around Deansgate.

By far the most realised of Ainsworth's modern horror stories appeared very quietly in the *Manchester Iris* in September 1822. 'The Half-Hangit' is an atmospheric and immediate account of trial and execution. It is especially horrible as the protagonist is an innocent man. This story represents a much more developed application of the *Blackwood's* technique, with the horror internalised in a first-person narrative of approximately 4,000 words. Ainsworth maintains the intensity throughout the trial until the inevitable verdict, and the climax of the story is the hanging itself. The description is both vivid and unsettling, matching anything in the pages of *Blackwood's* or the *New Monthly*. The narrator loses control of his limbs as he tries to climb the scaffold and has to be helped. He looks at the sea of eager faces waiting for the show in a daze, and finally goes through the unbearable torture of being given a handkerchief to drop when he is prepared. Unable to stand it any longer, he lets go:

> the handkerchief dropped – the boards fell – ! I felt the dreadful jirk [*sic*] through my whole frame – the blood rushed to my head. I felt the veins distend terribly in my temples – my eyes seemed starting out of their sockets, and there were strong shooting pains in the back of my ears. I tried to breathe – a choking sensation ensured. I became convulsed – my hands felt dreadfully painful. I clutched at the air – the convulsions

increased. I thought the veins would burst in my brow. I felt that
my eyes protruded dreadfully. I heaved for breath again, but the
passage was completely obstructed. I shivered all over – my
pains became less intense – and I was soon insensible.[11]

In order to avoid a point of view paradox, Ainsworth's hero is cut down
at the last minute when one of the real murderers confesses, but his
fiancée, Helen, is dead and the language suggests suicide as 'she died
in the hope of reuniting with me'. The story ends with the emotionally
empty man yearning for the death that was once so fearful.

The horror and suspense of the condemned man's expectation of his
own terrible end foreshadows Dickens's later explorations of the same
subject in 'A Visit to Newgate' in *Sketches by Boz*, and 'Fagin's last night
alive' in *Oliver Twist*. But Dickens, like Thackeray in his article 'Going
to See a Man Hanged', stopped short of describing the actual execution,
whereas in Ainsworth's story the agony of expectation is matched by the
physical trauma of death by strangulation. Similarly, while the sadistic
tortures devised by the *Blackwood's* stable bordered always on the fantastic,
or at least the highly improbable, Ainsworth was writing about a sentence
carried out routinely under English law dozens of times every year.

When the *Blackwood's* version of this story, 'Le Revenant', by the
mysterious Henry Thompson, was published in the magazine it caused a
huge public stir. Thomas Hood told William Blackwood that 'Le Revenant'
was 'talked of by every body I know', and it had a profound influence
on both Poe and Dickens.[12] 'The Half-Hangit' predates Thompson's
story by five years. Unfortunately, Ainsworth's finest contribution to the
Blackwood's style of writing appeared in the wrong place, albeit at the
right time. The 'Richard Clitheroe' hoax also appears to have disqualified
him from the pages of *Blackwood's* principal competitor, the *New Monthly*.
It is also possible that his previous publication in the *European Magazine*
(considered seditious by many for its declared sympathy with Catholic
emancipation) would not have pleased outspoken Tories like William
Blackwood, despite Crossley's recommendation. Nevertheless, Ainsworth
visited Edinburgh in August 1822 to present himself to the formidable
publisher, recording their one and only meeting in a letter to his friend:

In the middle of the second chamber, I saw a man advancing
to meet me – 'his face was deathly pale, but his nose was
beaming bright' – this man of the inexpressible visage – for

never before saw I such a one, with those funny teeth of his, that queer one eyebrow up and the other down, with grey streaming locks, – it certainly looked very astonishing. This, you will suppose, was Blackwood.[13]

The subsequent meeting with this apparition was obviously rather strained, although Ainsworth did meet and befriend Walter Scott's son-in-law, J.G. Lockhart. The letter concludes with a brief account of a much more satisfactory meeting with Blackwood's leading business and political rival Archibald Constable, who published the Whig *Edinburgh Magazine and Literary Miscellany*.

Ainsworth had made contact with Constable the previous year in a similar piece of literary precognisance to 'The Half-Hangit'. 'William Aynesworthe's' *Venice, or The Fall of the Foscaris* was originally an early contribution to Arliss's *Pocket Magazine* loosely based on the abdication and death of Francesco Foscari, Doge of Venice, in 1457. When it was announced by the publisher John Murray that Byron was working on a tragedy based on the same subject, Ainsworth took advantage of the press and sent a revised copy of his play to Constable.

He modestly opened his letter 'I consider myself very much like Lord Byron', playing on a physical resemblance that the family often noted, although his subsequent claim that 'I have been several times mistaken for his lordship, and have once even been horse-whipped for him' was probably pushing it.[14] Both pale, with curly dark hair and sharp, intelligent eyes, portraits of Byron and Ainsworth as young men do show a remarkable similarity, and this was picked up by the press again when the latter achieved literary recognition in the 1830s. The *Edinburgh Magazine* saw a chance to get a jump on Byron and Murray, and they followed Ainsworth's jaunty letter with a six-page extract of his tragedy and a very favourable review, which continued Ainsworth's own comparison with the greatest living English poet: 'We cannot say what kind of production will issue from the pen of Lord Byron; but if he excels the one of which we have given here a few specimens, we will allow that he has done wonders.' The review concludes with 'a favourable impression of the talents of the author'.[15] But regardless of talent, the young author's precocity was certainly the equal of the exiled Lord, as well as his eye for the ladies.

Chapter 3

Learning by Doing

Ainsworth left school in 1822 and commenced his legal training. Specialising in conveyancing, he was placed as an articled clerk at the offices of Alexander Kay in Manchester. He detested the work and Kay – a future mayor – and his father despaired of his lack of application, attributing it to idleness rather than a profound misapplication of the young man's interests and talents. In periods set aside to study law, therefore, Ainsworth was still reading the Romantics, spending as much time as possible in his beloved Chetham's Library. There he continued to write, working in the splendid Jacobean Reading Room at a table reputed to have been favoured by Sir Walter Raleigh and a long way from the baleful gaze of his increasingly exasperated father.

He also began to put himself about town, his family connections, good looks and easy charm a passport to the fashionable parties of Manchester Society. And when not revelling in the attentions of the fair daughters of the elite, Ainsworth, Crossley and several old school friends would hang out at the Unicorn Inn at Smithy Door (an ancient street, now long gone, in the shadow of the Collegiate Church) and talk girls, horses and literature. These nocturnal activities were beautifully captured in a rambling piece published in the *Edinburgh Magazine*, in which Ainsworth once more adopted the voice of a third party talking about himself. Artfully entitled 'What shall I write?', the article explores just that, the desire for publication without a subject, before becoming a long anecdote about a night in the Unicorn. Set after dinner, the piece offers a vivid portrait of Ainsworth ('Will Scarlett') and Crossley shooting the breeze over a bottle of port:

> C— is such a man as one would wish to call a friend. Warm hearted and cool headed, the impetuosities of his genius are held in due subjection by the clearness of his judgement.

Though somewhat reserved in company, it is only needful to overcome his backwardness, to be delighted and surprised by his conversation … His writings are the conclusions of frequent examination and deep research, and everywhere show the masterly and delicate hand of a scholar and a gentleman …

Will Scarlett is a different, not opposite, character. Younger than C—, and without so great a command over himself, his inclinations not seldom get the upper hand of his discretion. More formed for society, he possesses far more general attraction than his friend. Naturally gay, he brings mirth and cheerfulness with him, and is therefore every where a welcome visitor. But this is merely the outward ornament that covers the nobler stuff within; for his intellectual powers make him no less admired among his studious associates, than his handsome person (of which, by the way, I imagine Will is by no means insensible), and conversational talents among the ladies and his lighter acquaintances.[1]

Ainsworth's choice of *nom de plume* here indicates that his dandy proclivities were already well established, a feature of his personality that attracted admiration and satire in roughly equal measure when he became an author of note. But beyond the youthful bravado, the respect for Crossley is palpable, as is the nature of the friendship. Each was following the other, Ainsworth's confident charm attracting the shy, bookish Crossley, his knowledge attracting Ainsworth.

Despite his poor showing as a trainee solicitor, Ainsworth the writer raised the bar in 1822 by getting a short story published in the *London Magazine*. 'The Falls of Ohiopyle' is an idealised hymn to the American frontier and what would soon come to be known as 'manifest destiny', suggesting the influence of Crèvecoeur, but the significance of this story is not its subject but the contacts it forged for its author. Notable contributors to the *London Magazine* included Wordsworth, Shelley, Keats, De Quincey, John Clare, Thomas Hood, William Hazlitt, Charles Lamb and Thomas Griffiths Wainewright, art critic and serial killer.[2] Spanning both generations of British Romanticism alongside the writers working under the banners of Constable and Blackwood in Edinburgh, the *London Magazine* represented the Regency literary elite – a dynamic scene to which all young writers aspired.

Charles Lamb – a clerk with the East India Company – had begun publishing the work for which he was to become best known, the *Essays of Elia*, in the *London Magazine* in 1820. These chatty, personal essays, by turns bitter-sweet and extremely funny, were immensely popular and Ainsworth adored them. Under the pretext of being a fellow *London Magazine* contributor, Ainsworth contacted Lamb and the two struck up a correspondence about literature, even lending each other obscure books while Ainsworth toyed with the idea of editing the plays of the Jacobean dramatist Cyril Tourneur. A terrible name-dropper, Ainsworth cites Lamb as a personal friend in his essay 'The Theatre', while Lamb extended an open invitation to his 'friend unseen' to visit him in London, in part to gently deflect a request that he come to Manchester. 'Will your occasions or inclination bring you to London!' he wrote. 'It will give me great pleasure to show you everything that Islington can boast.'[3] (Ainsworth, who rarely saved letters, kept Lamb's correspondence carefully stored for the rest of his life.)

Ainsworth felt emboldened enough by Lamb's kindly indulgence to send him the manuscript of a collection of poems for his appraisal. The feedback was generally positive, and Lamb annotated the manuscript, suggesting cuts where he felt the language became 'a little careless'. This was to be Ainsworth's first book, a slim volume of sixty-two pages entitled simply *Poems* published under the pseudonym of 'Cheviot Ticheburn' by Arliss in August 1822, an interesting nod to the English Catholic poet Chidiock Tichborne, who was hanged, drawn and quartered for his part in a plot to assassinate Elizabeth I. (Ainsworth would later use Tichborne's haunting poem of farewell, 'My prime of youth is but a frost of cares', as an epigraph to his short story 'Mary Stukeley'.) The book comprised two metrical tales, 'The Maid's Revenge' and 'A Summer Evening's Tale', supplemented by three shorter poems. The long poems were still steeped in schoolboy classicism, with allusions including Leda, Narcissus and Arethuse, and imagery so purple that it led one reviewer to remark that 'We could carp, if so inclined, at some of this poet's lines; as, for instance, when he talks of – "First love's indissoluble *tether*", were it not that we have arrived at the end of our own.' He does, however, concede that 'they afford some promise of better things', but (echoing Lamb's more gentle feedback), 'while they are not devoid of poetic spirit or expression, they are wanting in simplicity'.[4] The *Literary Chronicle* similarly saw potential through the obvious inexperience, writing that 'His poems appear to be the effort of a young and undisciplined mind, but possessing some genius which due cultivation may render capable of much higher achievements.'[5] This review concludes that the short poems, or 'songs', were better. The book is dedicated 'To my friend CHARLES LAMB. As a slight mark of gratitude for his kindness and admiration of his character, these poems are inscribed.'

Crossley was in London during this period, completing his own legal training while lodging with his older brother, Henry, and the two friends struck up a lively correspondence, which, as it turned out, would continue for the rest of their lives. These early letters show that Crossley had hawked Ainsworth's manuscript around several London publishers, including Charles and James Ollier, who published Percy Shelley, without success while Ainsworth mithered in Manchester, until he finally admitted defeat and gave the collection to Arliss. Nonetheless, this was a symbolically significant move forward for the young author, who now had a physical book, published in London, under his belt, even if no one much was buying it. He therefore set about throwing the next one together, collecting several short stories and articles that had previously appeared in Arliss's *Pocket Magazine*, the *Edinburgh Magazine*, the *European*, and the *London Magazine*, although oddly not 'The Spectre Bride' or 'The Half-Hangit', which were undoubtedly his strongest pieces at that point. He also wrote a new story for inclusion, 'Mary Stukeley'. This time he found a larger London publisher, not massive but respectable, George and William Budd Whittaker of Ave Maria Lane, who had just published the second edition of *Frankenstein*.

Like the poetry collection, *December Tales* is most impressive in that it existed at all, as the legitimately published second book of a provincial author with no more than eighteen summers on him. Also like the poems, its overall tone is florid and affected, and the narrative voice moves easily into Gothic fantasy and morbid introspection. 'Death is your only sure balance in which to weigh the real worth and importance of individuals' muses the youthful author in the essay 'The Church-Yard', adopting the persona of an old man as he wanders through a forest of headstones reminiscing about childhood.[6] Indicative of an author still learning his trade, this is also a classic exercise in setting for the student of creative writing, strolling around a familiar area (in this case the village of Rostherne in Cheshire, where Ainsworth's mother was born), making topographical observations, recording sensory details, historical facts and listening to memories, before recreating the walk as a short piece of descriptive prose. This Gothic sensibility is developed in the essay 'Recollections' (an updated *Horæ Seniles* from the *Edinburgh Magazine*), with an admittance of the obvious influence of eighteenth-century 'romances of horrors', and a guarded affinity with Catholicism that would also pervade his later work, not because of faith so much as style. The third essay was a rehash of 'What Shall I Write?' retitled 'The Theatre', and this muddle of fiction and journalistic life writing – indicative of the author building a book out of available juvenilia – means that *December Tales* is conceptually neither fish nor fowl.

That said, the new story that opens the little anthology is a notably stronger composition than those written the year or so before. Ainsworth was learning by doing and beginning to find his voice. 'Mary Stukeley' is a tale of desire and betrayal, and a remarkably honest depiction of youthful male sexuality. On the eve of his marriage to the innocent and virtuous Mary Stukeley, an unnamed young man tells of how his passions were aroused through a chance meeting with the mysterious and sexually magnetic Eliza. As events escalate, he ends up bigamously marrying Eliza and Mary and then loses them both. At the conclusion he's an outcast in an irredeemable agony of despair, and relating his story achieves no release. 'Mary Stukely' was by far the young author's most sophisticated story to date in terms of style, narrative structure and content. Freed of the constraints of magazine word limits (and the scythe of deadline), it has considerably more room to breathe. His already accomplished flair for description is enhanced by symbolism and feels much more integrated with plot. Narration is active rather than passive, there's more character development and dialogue, with narrative pace moving neatly between action and reflection. There's a definite structure leading to climax and denouement. The story does not run out of steam or end abruptly, as do many of his earlier attempts.

Otherwise, 'An Adventure in the South Seas' reappears as 'The Mutiny', as does 'The Falls of Ohiopyle'. Another sea story,

'The Englisher's Story' was the original 'December Tale', appearing under that title in the *European* magazine in 1822. This one follows the trend for nautical melodrama that was currently popular on the stage, such as *Black Ralph* and *The Red Rover*. The story is told to the framing narrator by a beggar who once left his love to go to sea, only to discover too late that his best friend on board was in fact the girl he left behind in disguise:

> The barbarian lifted his sword to strike me; when my friend, whom I had not seen during the action, sprang between us, and received the stroke which was meant for me. I caught him as he fell; but that dying shriek – that last expiring glance – that soft pressure – told me all: – it was Eleanor![7]

'The Test of Affection', meanwhile (also published in the *European* the previous year), is darkly comic, recalling the gallows humour of 'The Cut Finger'. A Scottish laird counterfeits his own demise in order to test the fidelity of his prospective beneficiaries, and when they inevitably fail, he scares them off his property by pretending to be his own ghost. The most overtly Gothic tale is 'The Wanderings of an Immortal' (formerly 'The Imperishable One', another *European* story), the confession of a man who sold his soul for eternal life to revenge himself upon his enemies, and now has an eternity to repent. In a particularly lurid passage, the narrator experiences the agony of drowning without dying. Written about a year before 'The Half-Hangit', this description was partly recycled in the graphic hanging scene. There are some strong ideas here, but the rich concept of immortality is chronically underdeveloped – Ainsworth's immortal just doesn't wander enough. The final story of the collection is the strongest of the sea pieces. 'The Sea Spirit' (the last of Ainsworth's contributions to Arliss's *Pocket Magazine*, originally entitled 'The Lady Sprite') is another traveller's tale about shipwrecked mariners who see a ghost from their captain's past.

Reviewers, such as there were, were not impressed, the professional readers sniffing out an amateur disguising his inexperience with schoolboy verbiage. 'What is original is not good', said the *Monthly Review*, 'and what is good is not original', continuing, 'The tales possess little incident and less interest, and this fault is not compensated by the sentiment, which is rarely simple and real.' The reviewer lampoon's

Ainsworth's 'great affectation of knowledge', concluding, 'It is certainly to be regretted that so profound and accomplished a scholar has thrown away any of his labour, and time, on such a perishable production as that which is now before us.'[8]

December Tales was never reprinted. The juvenilia, however, offers an important insight into Ainsworth's influences and early potential. Collectively, this work represents his literary apprenticeship, and he would not have subsequently arrived at the gates of Rookwood Place and the Bloody Tower without first acquainting himself fully with the techniques of the Gothic, the melodrama and the sensational magazine story.[9]

Chapter 4

Our Sir John

Crossley returned to Manchester in the winter of 1823, becoming a partner in the Ainsworth family legal firm. Unlike his friend, his career was now certain. For Ainsworth, on the other hand, the spring of 1824 saw the commencement of another ambitious publishing project, the young writer as ever attempting to run before he could walk. This time, it was a weekly magazine conceived and written with his Manchester Free Grammar School contemporary John Partingdon Aston, who had become a close friend while Crossley was training in London. The son of a Manchester wine merchant, Aston had begun clerking for Thomas Ainsworth after leaving school, but, like Ainsworth, he at that point harboured literary aspirations, recklessly believing writing to be a way to make money.

Needless to say, the *Bœotian* did not make its editors rich. The name playfully alludes to a line from Horace's Epistles that the magazine took as its motto, *Bœotum crasso jurares aëre natum* – 'born in the gross air of the Bœotians' – originally a joke at the expense of Alexander the Great's critical faculties, which refers to the cultural life of Manchester in opposition to London. They actually found a publisher for it, too, the bookseller Thomas Sowler, whose mother just happened to be an Ainsworth. Launched on 20 March 1824, it was not a successful venture, the sixth and final issue appearing on 24 April. Apparently, this was not Ainsworth's first foray into magazine publishing either. In a letter written to Crossley in 1876 concerning the King Street plays, he alludes to 'a little weekly theatrical Journal which I brought out about 1822', which doesn't sound like the *Bœotian*. 'Do you recollect it?' he continues. 'It was the speculation of a printer named, I think, John Lee [another Manchester bookseller] and was published by B. Wheeler, in St. Ann's Square, but naturally failed, as it was sure to do, since I never saw the performances which I pretended to criticise.'[1]

Nevertheless, this youthful collaboration would ultimately lead to the production of a novel that would one day catch the eye of Sir Walter Scott himself.

Shortly after the *Bœotian* came and went, Ainsworth's easy life of minimal legal study, literary dalliance and growing dandyism came to an abrupt end with the sudden and unexpected death of his father of heart failure in June 1824. The eldest son of Thomas Ainsworth suddenly found himself the senior partner at Ainsworth, Crossley and Sudlow, Solicitors, a role for which he was totally unprepared, unqualified and generally unsuited. Despite having always been appalled by the prospect of a career in law, Ainsworth rose to the challenge as the new head of the family business and belatedly applied himself to the study of law, moving to London at the end of the year to complete his training. He took with him the incomplete manuscript of a historical romance, written in collaboration with Aston, called *Sir John Chiverton*.

Having already corresponded at length with Charles Lamb, Ainsworth was now able to meet him face to face. Through his friendship with Lamb, Ainsworth was introduced to the literary society of London, finally meeting his hero Leigh Hunt. 'When we were at school reading the *Indicator*', he later admitted, 'we used to think that if we could ever write essays or verses like Leigh Hunt, we should have reached the utmost height of our ambition.'[2] (The short-lived *Bœotian* was modelled on the *Indicator* and Ainsworth presented Hunt with a bound edition of all six issues.) 'Little Charles Lamb sends me constant invitations,' he wrote to Crossley in March 1825. 'I met Mrs. Shelley at his house the other evening.' Undaunted by this formidable literary widow, the 20-year-old novice asked the author of *Frankenstein* for a date. 'She is very handsome,' he told Crossley. 'I am going to the theatre with her some evening.'[3]

He was also able to develop the friendship with Scott's son-in-law, Lockhart, tentatively begun in Edinburgh a couple of years previously. As Crossley's family also lived in London, Ainsworth politely shared his free time between their home in West Ham and the gatherings at Colebrooke Cottage, the house Lamb shared with his sister in Islington. Crossley's father had moved to London after the death of his wife, where his eldest son Henry was already a successful lawyer. Ainsworth's letters home to Crossley indicate that his relatives attempted to moderate his renewed enthusiasm for the literary lifestyle by constantly reminding him of his professional responsibilities. They didn't have much hope against Elia and his friends and were rather suspicious of Ainsworth after he attempted to seduce one of their housemaids. In a series of letters written to Crossley around Christmas 1824, Ainsworth, reading *Harriette Wilson's Memoirs* after meeting the famous authoress herself, describes his affection for this 'Cockney Aphrodite':

> A lovely girl, short, plump, taper-waisted, and dark-eyed – i' faith a very goodly appearance. You know dark eyes have always been my bane, and these were truly beautiful for a girl 'in her line' – bright, large, and laughing, and so full of kindness that, as Elkington says, it were cruel to disappoint them. Well, on Sunday last I slipped out of the room when your father and some more of his old cronies were at their wine, and got hold of this little girl. She promised to meet me the following evening, and kept her word – but now comes the serious part of the joke. In addition to the little frisky one before mentioned, your father has a cursed superannuated old cook, who being too old for any enjoyment herself, has determined to destroy that of others. This damned old bitch by some means got to hear of it, and communicated the pleasing intelligence to your father and Master George, with whom I am presently at issue.[4]

Ainsworth did somehow manage to pass the bar in February 1826, however, just before his twenty-first birthday.

The newly qualified Ainsworth was not happy, writing to Crossley, 'You ask me whether we have any characters in Chambers. I answer none. They are all dull, dreary, plodding, unintellectual fellows.'[5] As an antidote to the tedium of this unwished-for career, he indulged his pleasure for the opera. This pursuit brought him into the company of the flamboyant lessee of the King's Theatre, John Ebers, a manager notable for his promotion of Italian opera in the 1820s. (Still active, the now rechristened Her Majesty's Theatre has been running *The Phantom of the Opera* since 1986.) He was also an Old Bond Street publisher and bookseller, having inherited a successful bookshop and circulating library, and the widowed father of two charming daughters.

A descendant of Hanoverian stock, Ebers was a handsome and extremely charismatic man. As the young lawyer was such a frequent patron, the two men became friends and Ainsworth was soon writing for Eber's magazine the *Literary Souvenir*, as well as contributing a political pamphlet to his catalogue entitled *Considerations on the best means of affording Immediate Relief to the Operative Classes in the Manufacturing Districts* dedicated to Robert Peel and calling for the repeal of the Corn Laws. As with his juvenile reviews of plays he had not seen, one suspects he didn't have that much of a grasp of the issues and was rather just taking any publishing opportunity that presented itself, as ambitious young writers are wont to do – another example being his *Monody on the death of John Philip Kemble* (the Georgian actor), which was written after *December Tales* at the request of a Mancunian theatre owner and published by John Leigh in 1823. At any rate, he published no more political pamphlets, and as Kemble retired from the London stage in 1817 and moved to Switzerland, it is unlikely that Ainsworth saw any of his plays either.[6]

Ebers was also interested in the manuscript of *Sir John Chiverton*, and he began advertising it in the *Literary Souvenir* while Ainsworth was still revising the incomplete first draft. As his letters to Crossley show, Ainsworth was at that time completely taken in by the silver-tongued and entrepreneurial Ebers, who talked a big game but was in reality increasingly struggling financially under the burden of his lease on the theatre. Ainsworth was also rather keen on Ebers' younger daughter, Anne Frances ('Fanny'), considered by London Society to be a great beauty, so any excuse to visit the Ebers' family home in Regent's Park worked for him. Ebers, like John Arliss, was also desperate for cheap copy, so his gushing enthusiasm for Ainsworth's writing may have been less than sincere. As the senior partner of a successful legal firm, Ebers might have also seen the young man as a good match for Fanny and a possible source of additional and much-needed revenue. The Ebers certainly had him hooked and landed soon enough.

Ainsworth's surviving correspondence with Aston at the time reveal that the manuscript was far from ready for publication. There are several references to 'Our Sir John', and vague plans to complete it at some point and try to get it published, Ainsworth concluding that 'Nobody will buy him in his present state and he would want a great deal of amendment.'[7] Several of these letters nag Aston for promised content for the *Souvenir* and a proposed new miscellany provisionally titled the *Aurora*, for example, 'Did you not promise with a most reliable appearance of truth that you would write with the work agreed upon weekly ... If you will not write, the duty naturally devolves upon me.'[8] Aston's literary aspirations were fading. Like Crossley, and unlike Ainsworth, he was already consolidating his legal career in Manchester and, by his standards, putting aside childish things.

Sir John Chiverton was published by Ebers in July 1826, garnering a couple of very positive reviews. While noting that 'in the denouement of this volume there are faults incident to youthful writings', the *Literary Gazette* concludes a long and fundamentally favourable write-up, 'it is also one of the early works of talent and genius which makes us hope to see many more from the same source'.[9] Colburn's *New Monthly* was even more enthusiastic, another long review beginning:

> This work is destined, or we mistake greatly, to become a permanent favourite with lovers of fiction. If a romantic and affecting story, characters vigorously drawn, and scenes and incidents described with almost the force of reality, constitute an attractive book, then will this tale be probably found in nearly every library from which fiction is not excluded. The admirers of Mrs. Radcliffe, and of the author of Waverley, will find that they may extend their affection yet a little further, and, in 'Sir John Chiverton,' be moved again to tears, or merriment, or awe, at the will of the unknown author and his 'so potent art'.[10]

Like his opposite number in the *Gazette*, this reviewer notes that the story rather falls apart at the end, while 'It is too theatrical'. Nonetheless, he looks forward to more from this young author:

> 'Sir John Chiverton' is evidently the work of a very young man, who is hardly aware of his own powers, and still less of the way in which they may most effectively be employed. The youth of the author is abundantly proved by the exuberant style in which he writes. We hope soon to see another and a longer work from the same pen.[11]

It's also notable that the connection is immediately made between the historical romance and the Gothic – Walter Scott and Mrs Radcliffe. Ainsworth and Aston are blending both genres.

Sir John Chiverton is set just after the Third Crusade. Essentially a Prince John figure, the corrupt and profligate nobleman Sir John Chiverton exploits the absence of better men fighting in the Holy Lands to advance his interests. He has taken possession of the family seat at Chiverton Hall in Lancashire by falsely declaring the rightful owner by inheritance, his sister Ellice, to be insane. Like Ghiotto, he has two henchmen to do his dirty work, the slippery physician Dr Walter Scymel and a huge and silent Moor bodyguard named Mahmood Bali. To repair his ailing fortunes, Sir John plans to marry Isabel, the daughter of the powerful knight Sir Gamelyn de Vancouver. Only Ellice's former suitor, Reginald Prestwyche, lately returned from the Crusades, knows the truth and can thwart Sir John and save Ellice and Isabel. Disguised as a peasant, Reginald contacts Ellice and they attempt to warn Sir Gamelyn that his future son-in-law is not all he seems. Sir John and Scymel allay Sir Gamelyn's misgivings and Reginald is imprisoned in the dungeons of Chiverton Hall. Ellice frees Reginald on the night of the wedding feast but is accidentally killed in a fall while fleeing her brother. Unaware that Ellice is already dead, Reginald gatecrashes the banquet disguised as a minstrel and singing a cryptic song that indicates to the groom that the jig is up. But before either can draw his sword, Sir John succumbs to poison administered by Mahmood Bali for no adequately explored reason. Scymel realises that he has also been poisoned by the slave and dies with a sardonic smile on his contorted lips. Mahmood Bali escapes and the novel bleakly concludes with the sounds of merriment from the celebrations in the courtyard still ringing ironically in the ears of the horrified guests at the bridal, followed by a brief historical denouement on the decline of Chiverton Hall and the 'strange rumours' that 'prevented any one from becoming its tenant'.[12]

There are, of course, shades of the climax of 'The Baron's Bridal' here, while the luckless Ellice is another 'Spectre Bride', falling to her death as melodrama suddenly becomes tragedy. Also in common with several of his earlier short stories is the obviously hasty resolution, as noted by reviewers, which was almost certainly written by Ainsworth in order to meet the deadline imposed by Ebers' advertisements. The First and Second Acts therefore generate a lot of conflict, atmosphere and suspense, but the authors then fail to deliver on what writers often call the 'promise' to the reader implicit in the narrative, when the forces they have marshalled and made vivid must collide at the climax to this story. After an auspicious build-up, *Sir John Chiverton* just stops. Only Isabel has been saved. Ellice has died by accident, Reginald has lost his love, who he could neither save or avenge, Sir John and Scymel are instead dead at the hands of an apparent confederate, the Moor, who then escapes with a mad laugh after Reginald takes a shot at him and misses. As the reviewers acknowledged, there's a lot of potential here, but much of it unrealised, either in a rush to publish or because of a lack of understanding of basic narrative structure. In a couple more drafts, this could have been quite a tidy little Gothic novel.

There has been some dispute over the authorship of *Sir John Chiverton*. When it was published, anonymously, as was the convention at the time, literary journalists assumed it was by Ainsworth, given Ebers' advanced notices in the *Literary Souvenir*, stating that 'A young gentleman of Manchester, and a contributor to our pages, is about to favour the world with a Romance entitled *Sir John Chiverton*.' The *Literary Magnet*, for example, responded:

> To read Mr. Ebers's announcement of *Sir John*, one would suppose the author was a 'pocket unknown', or, as Mr. Colburn calls young D'Israeli in his puffs of *Vivian Grey*, a 'new unknown' ... This tale, written, as we have already stated, by a young gentleman of Manchester, of the name of Ainsworth, reflects great credit upon its author.[13]

As is apparent from Ainsworth's surviving correspondence with Aston, forever chasing him for promised copy before finally giving up and writing it himself, Ebers was going to push his regular contributor and daughter's beau over the absentee collaborator. Ainsworth sent Aston two copies of the first edition, and they continued to amicably share work and discuss reviews by post until they drifted apart in 1828, Ainsworth by then married with children and Aston a prominent Manchester solicitor who never wrote another word of fiction. Ainsworth always credited the novel as a joint production, until finally omitting it from his professional profile altogether, along with the *Poems* and *December Tales*.

In later years, however, Aston claimed sole authorship in private. In a canny attempt to get to the bottom of this without offending anyone, Crossley sent Ainsworth an entry to proof on *Sir John Chiverton* for the *Manchester School Register* in 1871. This was returned with a note saying, 'I have added a line to the memoir of Aston, which will set the matter right. The interlineation is simply – written in collaboration with W. Harrison Ainsworth – as is the fact.'[14] When a similar list of publications of regional note appeared a few years later, however, Aston sent the following letter to its compiler, C.W. Sutton:

> I had the opportunity last evening, for the first time, of seeing your interesting *List of Lancashire Authors*, in which I met with my name mentioned as 'collaborateur with Mr. W. Harrison Ainsworth in the romance of *Sir John Chiverton*'. I have no wish to be held out as an author at all, but if I must be, I desire that it may be done correctly. Mr. Ainsworth never wrote a line of *Sir John Chiverton*, for which I am solely responsible. I am neither anxious to participate in Mr. Ainsworth's celebrity, nor wishful to throw upon him the credit, or discredit, of my juvenile performances, and if any further 'Additions and Corrections' to your *List* be printed, I trust that the correction I now bring under your notice may be attended to. In the meantime, I should be glad to have it notified to the very respectable club under whose auspices the *List* appears.[15]

As a result of this claim, Crossley made a scrupulous handwritten note in the flyleaf of the Chetham's Library's edition of the by then very rare novel, acknowledging the dispute.[16] Ainsworth's reply to him on the matter was, 'I shall not trouble myself about Aston.'[17] As an internationally renowned author, why should he care? – although in 1826 he was an unknown and the publication credit certainly didn't hurt his reputation. He was also given sole ownership of the work in Lockhart's biography of Scott (and the reference in the journal was very newsworthy at the time, Ainsworth then being at the height of his fame as a novelist), and in the 'Memoir of William Harrison Ainsworth' by Samuel Laman Blanchard, published in the *Mirror* in 1842 and often used to preface later editions of *Rookwood*. If Aston was aware of these citations, there's no record that he ever challenged them.

Only after Ainsworth died did Aston make his claims public, writing to the editor of *The Times* in response to Ainsworth's obituary:

> I shall be obliged by the insertion in *The Times* of the following reference to the obituary article on the above gentleman in your issue of the 4th inst., in which it said:– 'While in his teens he wrote and published his romance of "Sir John Cheverton"' (Chiverton), &c. Ainsworth did not write this book, of which I am the author, nor does his name appear on the title-page as the author. In what is described as the second edition (though, in fact, a mere re-issue) his name appears as publisher and only so; nor does 'Sir John Chiverton' appear in the chronological list of Ainsworth's works, printed on the beautifully illustrated card pamphlet, presented to the guests at the dinner given in September last to Ainsworth by the Mayor of Manchester.
>
> My acquaintance with Ainsworth commenced at the Manchester Free Grammar School, and our intimacy increased when he became a fellow clerk with me in the office Mr. Alexander Kay, the solicitor, to whom he was articled.[18] We were both fond of literary pursuits, or what we considered such, and our conversation generally turned on literary subjects. Hulme-hall, an ancient mansion on the late Duke of Bridgewater's estate, was a locality in which we took much interest, and I think it was Ainsworth who suggested to me the writing of a romance in connexion with it. This I did, and hence the production of the work in question, in which the name 'Chiverton Hall' was substituted for 'Hulme-hall'. I communicated the manuscript as the work progressed to Ainsworth, and he attended to its publication. It was originally published by Ebers, but what purports to be the second edition bears Ainsworth's name as publisher in Old Bond-Street, 1827. He had, however, no part in the composition nor do I know that he ever claimed it, and the celebrity he afterwards attained must have rendered the question (had any such existed) of its authorship of very little importance to him.
>
> Our intimacy declined when he established himself in the literary world of London, and I became absorbed in my professional pursuits.[19]

This raised enough eyebrows for the Manchester journalist John Evans – who knew Ainsworth and Crossley – to write a piece for *Notes and Queries* (published on 13 March) relating the story of the *Manchester School Register.* Aston passed away two months later, and this was quoted in the *Manchester Courier* on 13 May, the same day that the *Manchester Guardian* concluded Aston's obituary:

> In early professional life Mr. Aston was not unknown as an anonymous contributor to the popular annuals and periodicals, both in prose and verse. One work, a romance, entitled 'Sir John Chiverton', deserves special mention, being referred to by Sir Walter Scott (as stated in his Life by Lockhart), as one of those literary productions which the great enchanter himself had called into birth.[20]

This in turn led Henry Harwood, a friend of Aston, to write to the editor of the *Manchester Guardian* to confirm that the deceased's letter to *The Times* was 'a statement which Mr. Aston only a few weeks ago verbally confirmed by stating that "Mr. Ainsworth did not write a word of it"'.[21]

The matter was finally closed when Ainsworth's executor, C.H. Hinde, found the following letter to Ainsworth among his papers and sent a copy to the editor of the *Manchester Guardian*:

> October 14th 1841.
>
> Sir,–
>
> In the years 1823, 1824, and 1825 I had the privileged honour to be engrossing clerk at Mr. Alexander Kay's at Manchester, and of being at that time useful to you as amanuensis in copying and collecting material for your celebrated novel of 'Sir John Chiverton'. When you left Manchester you were kind enough to say that you would do what you could for me in case I should come to London. I shall feel very much obliged by your exerting your powerful interests with any gentleman in the profession on my behalf.

Hinde concluded his own letter with, 'I leave the letter to speak for itself without any further comment.'[22] Ainsworth had worked for Kay, Aston for his father.

Literary collaborations are tricky things, as are the memories of elderly men. It seems highly unlikely, however, that Ainsworth did not play a significant part in the writing, apparent from his surviving correspondence with Aston and the style and content of the novel itself. There is much in the text that fits Ainsworth's later writings – the use of a historic building for setting, the descriptive detail applied to architecture and costume, the Gothic sensibility, the melodramatic inheritance plot, the similarity to his early short stories, and sudden and graphic violence. Equally, there are sections that do not suit his method at all, such as a theological dialogue between Scymel and a priest in the fourth chapter, which is probably attributable to Aston. When Lady Jane defends her religious convictions in the debate with the Catholic bishop Gardiner in *The Tower of London* by Ainsworth, for example, her argument is entirely rhetorical; the sceptical arguments of Scymel in *Sir John Chiverton* are much more sophisticated, and indeed radical. Scymel is also an atheist, while Ainsworth's fiction is always concerned with the tension between Protestant and Catholic, or even heaven and hell, and his characters never question basic Christian belief, even though he sometimes did. *Sir John Chiverton* therefore reads like a genuinely collaborative work that was at the very least substantially revised, and probably finished, by Ainsworth, who had considerably more experience and drive than Aston.

Whether written all, in part or even not at all by Ainsworth, the publication of *Sir John Chiverton* did bring the young author to the attention of Sir Walter Scott, who was shown the novel by Lockhart. Scott wrote on *Sir John Chiverton* in his journal and, largely as a result of these private comments (which Lockhart reproduced in his *Life of Sir Walter Scott* in 1838), many critical comparisons between the works of these two very different authors have been made ever since, Ainsworth generally coming off worse. As Ainsworth was a writer ultimately known for his historical fiction, such comparisons have been unavoidable, in addition to the obvious fact that all early nineteenth-century novelists wrote under the shadow of the so-called 'Enchanter of the North'. The commonly held critical belief regarding Ainsworth's first novel is that it is a simple attempt to copy Scott, without any real understanding of the techniques of historical fiction supposedly created by the author of *Waverley*. This intelligence is based not so much on a reading of the actual novel (which, like its two predecessors, went out of print almost immediately), but on the oft-quoted reference to it in Scott's journal. Ainsworth was well liked by Lockhart, who had moved to London at the end of 1825 to take up the editorship of the *Quarterly Review*, and it appears that he was impressed enough by *Sir John Chiverton* to pass a copy on to his father-in-law. Ainsworth was subsequently presented to Scott at the Lockharts' home at Pall Mall. Two concurrent entries in Scott's journal, however, leave no doubt as to his true feelings towards the young novelist, and to his rising generation as a whole:

> *October 17.* Read over *Sir John Chiverton* and *Brambletye House* − novels in what I may surely claim as the stile
> 'Which I was born to introduce −
> Refined it first, and showd its use.'[23]
> They are both clever books; one in imitation of the days of chivalry; the other dated in the time of the Civil Wars, and introducing historical characters. I read both with great interest during the journey.
> I am something like Captain Bobadil who trained up a hundred gentlemen to fight very nearly, if not altogether, as well as myself.[24] And so far I am convinced of this, that I believe were I to publish *Canongate Chronicles* without my name (*nomme de guerre*, I mean) the event would be a corollary to the fable of the peasant who made the real pig squeak against the imitator, while the sapient audience hissed the poor grunter as if inferior to the biped in his own language. The peasant could, indeed, confute the long-eared multitude by showing piggy; but were I to fail as a knight with a white and maiden shield, and then vindicate my claim to attention by putting 'By the Author of *Waverley*' in the title, my good friend *Publicum* would defend itself by stating I had tilted so ill, that my course had not the least resemblance to my former doings, when indisputably I bore away the garland. Therefore I am as firmly and resolutely determined that I will tilt under my own cognizance. The hazard, indeed, remains of being beaten. But there is a prejudice (not an undue one neither) in favour of original patentee; and Joe Manton's name has borne out many a sorry gun-barrel. More of this to-morrow.[25]

This is an elaborate piece of self-irony, in which Scott himself becomes a potential victim because of his disguised authorship of the *Waverley* novels, which he did not publicly acknowledge until the following year. This is also a somewhat sweeping set of assertions, taking us down the route that concludes, as Sir John Marriot wrote, for example, 'The historical novels written before 1814 may be regarded as preparing the way for the advent of Scott. Those that have been written since look back to him with filial piety.'[26]

Scott did not invent the historical novel; he rather continued to develop a mode of fiction already well established in literary tradition. What Scott brought to the model left by writers such as Thomas Nashe, John Leland and, most significantly, Daniel Defoe was a greater balance of fictional narrative and antiquarian detail even if, despite many claims to the contrary by critics, his historical accuracy was often no more genuine than the sporran of Rob Roy proudly on display at Abbotsford. One cannot dispute that Scott's influence on the English novel is enormous, but he was no more the sole Logos than was Dickens, despite his attempts to assimilate every other branch of literature to his own. S.M. Ellis, George J. Worth and Andrew Sanders endorse Scott's belief that *Sir John Chiverton* was very derivative of his own work. S.M. Ellis characteristically interprets this as a compliment while Sanders reads the journal entries as a statement that 'Scott was generally depressed by the poor quality of the work of those who attempted to imitate him'.[27] But this is not the whole story. Scott tended to have an adversarial approach to all his contemporaries. In his introduction to *St Ronan's Well*, for example, he refers to Jane Austen as one of his 'formidable competitors' and seems, with regard to his first obvious followers, Ainsworth and Smith, to be taking a certain amount of pleasure from the palpable hero worship and finding reassurance in the fact that the standard hardly matches his own. Despite this, his concluding remarks betray the fact that he feels slightly threatened. Because of his financial problems, he cannot afford to be overtaken in the marketplace he created by writers he believes to be stealing his ideas, hence the reference to Manton, who died a bankrupt despite his original patent for the breech-loading canon shell (powder behind the shot in a disposable cartridge being the basis of all modern bullet design).

Apparently still preoccupied with these concerns, Scott returns to his 'imitators' the following day:

October 18. – I take up again my remarks on imitations. I am sure I mean the gentlemen no wrong by calling them so, and heartily wish they had followd [*sic*] a better model; but it serves to show me *veluti in speculo* my own errors, or, if you will, those of the *style*.[28] One advantage, I think, I still have over all of them. They may do their fooling with better grace; but I, like Sir Andrew Aguecheek, do it more natural.[29] They have read old books and consult antiquarian collections to get their information; I write because I have long since read such works, and possess, thanks to a strong memory, the information which they have to seek for. This leads to a dragging-in historical details by head and shoulders, so that the interest of the main piece is lost in minute descriptions of events which do not effect its progress. Perhaps I have sind [*sic*] in this way myself – indeed, I am but too conscious of having considered the plot only as what Bayes calls the means of bringing in fine things ... All this I may have done, but I have repented of it; and in my better efforts, while I conducted my story through the agency of historical personages and by connecting it with historical incidents, I have endeavoured to weave them pretty closely together, and in future I will study this more. Must not let the background eclipse the principal figures – the frame overpower the picture.

Another thing in my favour is, that my contemporaries steal too openly. Mr. Smith has inserted in *Brambletye House* whole pages from Defoe's *Fire and Plague of London*.

'Steal! Foh! A fico for the phrase –
Convey, the wise it call!'[30]

When *I convey* an incident or so, I am [at] as much pains to avoid detection as if the offence could be indicated in literal fact at the Old Bailey.

But leaving this, hard pressed as I am by these imitators, who must put the thing out of fashion at last, I consider, like a fox at his last shifts, whether there be a way to dodge them, some new device to throw them off, and have a mile or two of free ground, while I have legs and wind left to use

it. There is one way to give novelty: to depend for success
on the interest of a well-contrived story. But woe's me!
That requires thought, consideration, − the writing out
a regular plan or plot − above all the adhering to [one] −
which I can never do, for the ideas arise as I write, and bear
such a disproportioned extent to that which each occupied
at the first concoction, that (cocksnowns!) I shall never be
able to take the trouble; and yet to make the world stare, and
gain a new march ahead of them all!!! Well, something we
still will do.

'Liberty's in every blow;
Let us do or die!'[31]

The author of *Waverley* is definitely worried, and this entire entry is
an attempt at personal reassurance by undermining the opposition.
The private insecurities reflected in the brittle yet witty comparison
between himself and Jonson's Captain Bobadil and Shakespeare's
Sir Andrew Aguecheek are suddenly replaced by an appeal to the
great Scottish hero Robert the Bruce, the warrior king who drove
Edward II from the field at Bannockburn. Scott concludes his
'remarks' with this morale-building reminder of the Bruce's address
to the troops before battle, a martial prayer to the defeat of the new
wave of English pretenders to his throne of letters. What is therefore
often taken uncritically as an essay on the historical novel is rather
an exercise in the restoration of the great man's own self-confidence.
We forget that iconic writers like Scott and, indeed, Dickens, are still
just human beings in the end, not gods.

Nonetheless, after Lockhart published all the extracts from Scott's
journal concerning *Sir John Chiverton*, Ainsworth − Lockhart made no
mention of a second author − was forever remembered as an 'imitator'
of Scott, to such an extent that even his obituary in *The Times* referred
to Scott's journal entries on *Sir John Chiverton*. Yet in his choice of
setting only, was Ainsworth purely a historical novelist? As his early
stories and plays clearly show, Ainsworth's primary influences were
Gothic. To unproblematically accept that his work mimics Scott is to
necessarily accept that the Gothic romance was nothing more than, as
Scott himself believed, a primitive form of the historical novel. Although

somewhat basic in construction, *Sir John Chiverton* is therefore very possibly the first example in nineteenth-century literature of the struggle to establish a new form of English Gothic, which could escape the established European, medieval and Catholic clichés of the eighteenth-century genre while also taking it back from the model of the historical novel left by Scott. *Sir John Chiverton* was a Gothic novel *set in England*, not Italy, Germany or Spain. This might not sound like a lot, but in the 1820s, the shift in setting was potentially seismic. Even *Melmoth the Wanderer* had got no closer than Ireland.

Chapter 5

The Back Parlour of Literature

Things were getting serious with Fanny. The 'Dedicatory Stanzas To ——.' that preface *Sir John Chiverton* are undoubtedly addressed to her, also suggesting a commitment to lay aside the pen for love's sake and to get a proper job:

I

When last we parted, Lady 'twas in tears,
Thy cheek was dimmed with sorrow's trickling dew,
And from my heart the grief of many years,
Hoarded 'till nigh forgotten, burst anew,
Sad offerings to love and memory true;
Shall ever memory faint, or love be cold?
Ah, no! that cheek may lose its breathing hue,
And those dear eyes their living beams with hold,
But love shall still endure, with faith unknown, untold.

II

Accept the tribute that to thee I bring,
(It is the first, and it will be the last,)
The leisure fruit of fancy's wandering:
But fancy rules no more – her sway is past,
And into other paths my course is cast;
Me now no more shall fiction's dreams beguile;
Their hues like fading rainbows vanish fast;
My feet shall tread in ways of drearier toil,
And fiction hide her wreath, and posey her smile.

III

Yet, if to me a loftier lyre were given,
And round my harp were twined a brighter wreath;

40

If I could snatch immortal verse from heaven,
And pour its melody to souls beneath,
It may be that I would not cease to breathe,
Thy name in accents love should make divine,
And round thy beauteous brows a band enwreath,
A garland bright, whose flowers should brightly shine,
More lovely, and more bright, when sunned by smiles
  of thine.

IV

My Lady Love! am I not far from thee?–
Far, far away – but soon again we meet;
Ye moments swift, oh, yet more swiftly flee,
Ye slower hours, away on winged feet;
Waft me, oh, waft me upon pinions fleet,
Give me again my vows of love to tell,
Steal fond approval from her blushes sweet,
Adore her glowing cheek and bosom's swell,
And win the silent thoughts, that in that bosom dwell.[1]

But already there was trouble in Paradise. Madly in love, the young couple were desperate to marry, but the 21-year-old Ainsworth had little capital to set up a home and, as was the convention, was looking to his prospective father-in-law for a dowry. For the upper and middle classes, dowries were hugely important and viewed as an early payment of the daughter's inheritance. The dowry was conventionally paid in cash, the size of the payment expected to be in direct proportion to the social status of the groom.

Friends and family were concerned at such a hastily planned match, and more than a little sceptical of Ebers' financial stability, to the extent that Ainsworth's mother visited him in London in the summer. Ebers had appointed the famed castrato Giovanni Velluti musical director of the theatre, but his 1826 season was a disaster, despite engaging the popular Italian soprano Giuditta Pasta, the Maria Callas of her day, at a fee of £2,300 for three and a half months. Then Velluti, who was still the theatre's main draw, began to have throat problems, while Ebers' decision to revive Rossini's *Aureliano in Palmira* was another failure. Velluti, who was a terrible diva, was a much better singer than he was a director, and, as Ebers later wrote, he 'became involved in legal turmoils' over a written promise to pay the male singers in his chorus a bonus if they performed well. Seeking parity, the ladies took the matter to the Sherriff's Court and won. Velluti left the theatre and the season came to an abrupt end in August, several performances outstanding and with a deficit of £7,537.[2]

Despite overwhelming evidence to the contrary, Ainsworth believed he could still get a decent dowry, writing to Crossley that:

> I do wish a very advantageous settlement will be made upon me before my marriage takes place. If this is not done and done so as to place it beyond a doubt you may rely upon it no marriage will take place. I do not however have any doubt that this will be affected. In order however that you may form some idea of my intention I may inform you that I shall *expect* at least £5000 in hard cash to be paid down.[3]

In need of rest after seeing the novel to print, and perhaps more than a little overwhelmed by the intensity of life in London, Ainsworth returned home to Manchester for an extended visit. But unable to settle there either, he began shuttling between north and south – then a gruelling coach journey – in order to continue to pay court to Fanny.

His reassurances to his people in Manchester notwithstanding, a surviving letter fragment from Ainsworth to Ebers communicates his anxiety at the increasingly convoluted marriage negotiations (involving some sort of business partnership to offset the dowry), and Ebers' problems with the theatre, the owner having increased the rent from £10,000 to £15,000 on the renewal of the lease.[4] It is undated, but the chronology of events suggests sometime in August after the premature end of the King's Theatre season. It was obviously written hurriedly and in some agitation, having little or no punctuation:

> PRIVATE.
>
> My Dear Sir
>
> I take advantage of a package to Bond Street to enter into a few particulars affecting our proposed engagement which from their nature shall probably render this beyond the limits of an ordinary letter.
>
> You must have perceived the great disadvantage insulting to myself from the visits which I paid every fortnight to

London and how greatly they are incompatible with the intention to marry, and how much they are disapproved of by my friends. You are also aware that it is to my new circumstances and the countenance of these friends that I am to look for support and advancement in life. It therefore becomes abundantly necessary for my work that these frequent and periodical visits to London be discontinued.

This brings us to the point. What arrangement can be made for us to meet the wishes of your daughter without absolutely interfering with my own interests? The proposal submitted to you, recommended as a proposition of your own now struck me as being most feasible.

To this however there are some objections. Namely whether or not the management when completed is not liable to be defeated by the winding up of the affair. I do not wish to say anything that may give offence to your feelings but it is impossible when one's whole prospects in life are at stake to be silent though I feel certain of further difficulty – it would be the height of folly to be so. The tremendous hopes which have been motioned by every particular of the offer and the sum that it has intimated in many of them are sufficient to make me feel some alarm.

The arrangement proposed between us can only be affected by your Bankruptcy and you ought to be aware whether your affairs are in such a state as to make such a situation probable. Should (which God forbid) such a thing take place it might be the means of rendering both your daughter and myself completely wretched, and I should certainly consider myself bound in conscience, although the property might be legally safe, to give it up to the Creditor.

The object I have in saying that which I do from feelings of the inexpressible unhappiness which this event would occasion to Fanny and myself is as follows.

My own business due is trifling at present to be sure, but it is certain, and increasing – and a few years would enable me solely to maintain Fanny myself. I do not wish therefore to tie you down to the performance of your agreement to advance her a certain portion but will at such time as I have a sufficient income to maintain her in the way she has been brought up, gladly fulfil my part of the engagement. But at the same time this must be done without subjecting me to the rigours of coming up to London as frequently. As for myself, the objections to that plan are then being deferred as long. Your proposal promises me an income much greater than the above but subjects me to so many ties in themselves so dreadful that their mere contemplation alarms me …

[The next paragraph is obliterated due to the decay of the paper.]

But suppose for a moment that the marriage had taken place. And year after year I found myself getting behind hand in the world with a wife and family to maintain – Would it not with certainty produce domestic discord and unhappiness and render us both utterly wretched. You as a parent must feel whether if there be any such disgraces you are justified in exploring your daughters [*sic*] token. And if there are whether or not you would not be acting a wise and sane fatherly role to put up with a little initial inconvenience rather than render her miserable.

You know my attachment and devotion to your daughter and I know my own self so well that I am confident …[5]

The rest of the letter is missing. You can sense the internal conflict. He's young – young enough to put in writing that he'd consider himself liable for Ebers' debts if they were related – and he's in love. And despite his legal training, he's hopelessly outclassed by a player like Ebers. This is a plea for reassurance rather than a threat. If S.M. Ellis was aware of this letter, he omitted it from Ainsworth's biography, which does tend to sugarcoat anything unpleasant or omit it entirely. Like Forster's *Life of Dickens*, he only tells half the story.

A further letter to Crossley written around the same time indicated that the marriage was on hold until Ebers sorted out the theatre, and therefore his own finances:

The following arrangement has been made and concluded upon. The match has been deferred for a year or such time as will enable Mr. Ebers to manage his affairs so as to settle an income of at least £300 upon his daughter and myself and in order to give me full time to establish myself in my profession.[6]

It must have therefore come as quite a surprise to Crossley to shortly receive the following two letters:

October 10, 1826.

My Dear Crossley,

You will be surprised to learn that my marriage with Fanny Ebers is about to take place on Wednesday morning next at Marylebone Church. You will perhaps blame me for not disclosing this to you earlier but I had so much unhappiness on a former occasion that I made a decision which I have kept not to divulge it to a soul till the very moment of its celebration.

The settlement is a little altered from the draft drawn in Manchester.

October 11, 1826.

My Dear Crossley,

To you my oldest and dearest friend the intelligence that I just married must be interesting. About an hour ago I was united to Fanny Ebers.

Whether by accident, in frustration or for the sake of propriety, the rest of the second letter has been torn away.

In September, Ebers had travelled to Paris to engage performers for the next season, taking his daughters and Ainsworth with him. This was Ainsworth's first trip abroad and he was enchanted. The city of romance had cast its spell, and a hasty marriage was proposed and agreed. Only Crossley and Ainsworth's mother were told in advance, but not in time to attend, so only Fanny's relatives were there. The bride and groom were both twenty-one when they signed the register at the same vestry table at the newly built Marylebone Parish Church where, twenty years later, Robert Browning and Elizabeth Barrett would do the same after a similarly hasty and private marriage. The couple honeymooned in Bath, Ainsworth still finding the time and energy to write to Crossley.

Back in London, the newlyweds had a suite of rooms at Ebers' house at No. 8, Sussex Place, moving to No. 4 in the beautiful Regency crescent the following year. Now part of the family, Ainsworth was closely connected with the affairs of the King's Theatre. This was the era of the Green Room, where the *beau monde* met to drink, make contacts, and be presented to the beautiful artistes. Pierce Egan's Tom and Jerry hang around the 'Greeny' at Drury Lane in his *Life in London*, which is by far the best description of the adventures of young bloods and old bucks written during this period. Like country cousin Jerry Hawthorn's friendship with the rakish Corinthian Tom, Ainsworth's exposure to the company surrounding his flamboyant father-in-law facilitated the seamless entry of the young Mancunian into fashionable London Society, a process already begun by Lamb and Lockhart. As Egan described the Regency social network:

> 'SEEING LIFE', was their object. To keep all sorts of company – to admire an accomplished mind, whenever they found it – to respect and follow notions of real gentility – and to select the most sensible and agreeable persons in society as their companions.[7]

Whatever its troubles, the theatre was a glittering palace under Ebers' extravagant regime and Ainsworth made some very useful contacts, his only real business sense manifest in the creation of 'deadheads', social influencers who received complimentary tickets and perks in return for favourable notices and reviews. (Ebers had probably worked similar contacts to 'puff up' *Sir John Chiverton*.)

On the advice of Ebers, Ainsworth abandoned his legal career and set up shop as a publisher and bookseller, raising capital by selling his share in the lucrative Manchester law firm – which would have provided a comfortable income for life – confident, apparently, in the commercial acumen of his father-in-law. 'My shop is nearly ready,' he enthusiastically wrote to Crossley in November. 'I have been introduced to some local bibliophiles, the advice they gave me amounted to the ludicrous especially in the instance of Henry Colburn who warn'd me against publications. All of them however think my chances of success very fair.'[8] Ebers' circulating library at No. 27, Old Bond Street was partitioned, and Ainsworth began trading. For a while the business was moderately successful, and it allowed the proprietor to continue mixing with many famous writers of the day, which he enjoyed enormously. 'I am quite in the back parlour of literature,' Ainsworth wrote to Crossley in the New Year:

> not a day passes but I have half a dozen MSS. submitted to me, and were I disposed, could publish for half the people of Letters. You will see I announce a couple of volumes of Tales by Hood. Colburn has a variety of works in the press – he has near thirty 'Tales of Fashionable Life' in preparation. My Cookery Book is in active preparation.

Thomas Hood, whose name is nowadays probably most associated with his powerful poem on the plight of Victorian seamstresses, 'The Song of the Shirt', was a good score. The poet, author and humourist had become a subeditor of the *London Magazine* after John Scott's death, and counted among his friends and colleagues Lamb, Talfourd, the poets 'Barry Cornwall' (Bryan Procter) and John Clare, De Quincey, and the poet, critic and playwright John Hamilton Reynolds, a close friend of Keats. The cookbook – which Ainsworth cheekily asks Crossley to plug in *Blackwood's* – was *The French Cook; A System of Fashionable, Practical, and Economical Cookery, Adapted to The Use of English Families* by Louis Eustache Ude, newly appointed to run the kitchen at the fashionable St James's gambling club Crockford's, and the most famous French chef in London before Alexis Soyer's tenure at the Reform Club a generation later. Ude's *French Cook* was first published in 1813 and was regularly updated and reprinted. Ebers had been publishing it since 1822. There were also plans for a new literary annual:

> Heath, the engraver, and I are going to produce in September the most magnificent Annual ever dreamed about. It is to cost a guinea, and contain twenty plates; the literary matter will be first rate. Amongst other things which will please you, are some lively sketches, in the best *Indicator* style, by Leigh Hunt. The name is execrable – Heath baptises it *The Keepsake*, which to my thinking savours a gift from Tunbridge Wells. Can you not supply me with something better? – at all events, let me have a second title to correct the

first; give me something relating to Fashion, for I intend to enrol all the *littérateurs* of the *Beau Monde* under my banner.

The engraver, illustrator and publisher Charles Theodosius Heath – the illegitimate son of James Heath, Engraver to the King – was another great contact. One of Walter Scott's principle illustrators, Heath was an early adaptor to the new fashion for illustrated annuals and gift-books, working as art editor and chief contributor to the *Forget Me Not*, the *Literary Souvenir*, and the *Amulet*. A kindred spirit, in many ways, to Ainsworth and Ebers, Heath was an energetic and visionary entrepreneur who was often dogged by financial worries. Sensing opportunity in the new market, Heath wanted to become his own proprietor, dealing with publishers on his own terms, holding copyrights (a major bone of contention for him as a commercial artist), and running his own printing house. The *Keepsake* was thus more his own than Ainsworth admits in his letter, and he was never going to change the name. Heath had originally asked Walter Scott to edit the project, knowing he had his own financial problems. In the winter of 1825, Ballantyne and Co and Archibald Constable and Co had insufficient funds to meet a countrywide banking crisis, leaving Scott with a personal liability of £130,000, which he had resolved to pay off with his pen rather than declare bankruptcy. Scott admired the annual but politely declined to edit it, though he did sell Heath three stories originally intended for the *Chronicles of the Canongate* but rejected by his publisher – 'My Aunt Margaret's Mirror', 'Death of the Laird's Jock', and the ghost story 'The Tapestried Chamber'. Indicating his growing stature in London publishing, Heath's next choice for editor was Ainsworth. 'My business certainly improves', he told Crossley, 'and I conceive myself quite established.'

In the same letter, there are signs that publisher Ainsworth is already thinking about writing another novel. His remarks also foreshadow his future reliance on Crossley for raw material:

By the by, I must beg a favour of you. I could at any time make £500, if I could write one of the fashionable novels before mentioned, for which I have lots of incidental material, but lack a continuous plot. Pray turn over your old fancies and suggest one relative to society – give me a few characters, and a good *dénouement*, and you shall see what I will make of it.

He concludes with one of his many attempts to lure Crossley to London: 'Pray, are we never to see you in town? My wife would be delighted to see you, and I have so much to talk about.'[9] As ever, Crossley remained in Manchester while Ainsworth continued to embed himself in literary London, writing in March that:

> My literary acquaintances are become very extensive. Leigh Hunt and I are great friends. As a set-off to him I patronize Dr. Maginn, who is useful in the puffing department. Ollier, is another of my cronies … Croly and I are hand in glove … Lockhart and I are great friends. I am his publisher elect if he writes again.[10]

William Maginn was a *Blackwood's* man and one of the best periodical writers of his generation; Charles Ollier published Percy Bysshe Shelley, Keats and Hunt, the 'Cockney' poets; and George Croly, rector of St Stephen Walbrook in the City of London, was an Irish poet, novelist and historian. All would have their names added to the free list at the opera.

The summer of 1827 saw the birth of the Ainsworths' first child, Fanny, and the bankruptcy of her grandfather, whose extravagant 1827 season had again ended prematurely with a loss of just under £3,000. Ebers blamed his landlord's agents rather than his own management style, which always put the production ahead of prudence, but either way, the family fortune was gone. This was also a disaster for Ainsworth, as he had lent Ebers several thousand pounds.

As a publisher, Ainsworth had intended his business to be of service to literature, cultivating a catalogue of authors whom he respected and whose work may have been rejected in other quarters as not fashionable enough to warrant publication. He ran the enterprise according to the principles of a gentleman, which was always going to be a recipe for disaster. *The French Cook* kept the family afloat, but there were other bestsellers on his list, beginning with a popular annual entitled *Mayfair*, which went to a second edition almost immediately in 1827, a second edition of *Sir John Chiverton*, a reprint of Coleridge's *Wallenstein*, *An Autumn in Greece* by Henry Lytton Bulwer (Edward's elder brother), *Lyric Offerings* by Samuel Laman Blanchard, and *Seven Years of the King's Theatre*. The latter was supposedly written by Ebers, but Ellis believed it to be largely ghostwritten by Aston – who was in London at the time to enter himself as an attorney – while Ainsworth's entry in *The Dictionary of National Biography* suggests that he wrote it. Probably another joint effort, it is a charming, if one-sided, memoir, packed with interesting anecdotes and focusing on the artistes and productions over the problems. It offers an insight into Ebers' genuine passion for opera and his infectious personality, and is a significant document in the history of the rise of Italian opera in Regency London.

Ainsworth also launched the literary career of the Society hostess and social reformer Caroline Norton, whose visits to Old Bond Street became so regular that scandal was rumoured. Norton was known to be unhappily married and was writing to achieve financial independence. Ainsworth arranged the publication of her first collection of poetry, *The Sorrows of Rosalie* (1829), but it was actually published by Ebers, who had by that time taken over the business. Ainsworth edited the first edition of the *Keepsake* in 1828, and published his own annual, the *Christmas Box*, in the same year, which contained an original poem by Walter Scott, 'Bonnie Dundee', written in honour of John Graham, 7th Laird of Claverhouse and 1st Viscount of Dundee, who was killed leading a Jacobite rising in 1689. As a good friend of Lockhart (who was married to Scott's eldest daughter, Sophia), Ainsworth had been bold enough to ask the great man for a contribution to his planned annual when he was introduced. When Scott next visited London in 1828, the Lockharts and the Ainsworths were near neighbours at Sussex Place, so the young publisher was able to thank Scott in person and take the opportunity to pay his agreed rate of 20 guineas, although Scott's usual fee for a periodical contribution was somewhere in the region of £500. Scott found the gesture hilarious and gave the money to his granddaughter, Charlotte, who was playing in the room at the time.

By the beginning of 1829, Ainsworth was already thoroughly sick of running a business. As Ellis wrote, 'This second edition of deserting his profession may appear to indicate instability of character, but the truth was his artistic temperament wholly unfitted him for a commercial career.'[11] Once more impetuous, or just downright careless, Ainsworth quickly offloaded the business on his father-in-law without any real thought for his own legal protection. (From his letters to Crossley in his capacity as Ainsworth's solicitor, it would appear that Ebers owed £12,000 by 1831 in unpaid dowry, personal loans and the sale of the business, none of which was ever repaid.) A second daughter, Emily Mary, was born that year and, despite toying with the idea of a literary project to raise some much-needed capital, Ainsworth resumed his legal practice in 1830, taking chambers at No. 12, Grafton Street. Professionally unfocused as ever, the first embryonic sign of the novel that was to become *Rookwood* appears at this point, in a letter to Crossley where Ainsworth asks, 'Where shall I find a good account of funeral orations? – I don't mean ancient ones, but authentic middle-age speeches delivered over the dead. Do you know where there are any stories of Gipseys [*sic*]?'[12] A third child, Anne Blanche, was also born that year. The Bohemian lifestyle appeared to be over.

Well, almost…

The year 1830 also saw the inauguration of *Fraser's Magazine for Town and Country*, the brainchild of William Maginn and Hugh Fraser. With Maginn as the original editor, and Lockhart and Barry Cornwall immediately on board, their young friend from the days of the Old Bond Street bookshop was naturally invited to attend the literary club that formed itself around the premises at No. 215, Regent Street, being part council of war (against *Blackwood's*), part editorial committee and part bacchanal. Thomas Carlyle, Thomas Medwin, James Hogg, William Mudford, David Brewster, Robert Southey, John Stuart Mill and Coleridge were also early members of the group. How much copy Ainsworth actually contributed to *Fraser's* is a matter of some doubt. Because much of the material is unsigned, Ainsworth's only verifiable pieces are the short story 'La Guglielmina of Milan', and three poems, 'The Wind and the Wave', 'St Augustine and the Boy', and 'One Foot in the Stirrup', but then Count D'Orsay was a 'Fraserian' as well, and he never wrote anything. As the historian Ellen Moers has explained, although many 'Fraserians' were not actively involved in determining the development of the magazine, 'all contributed something to its spirit'.[13] And this spirit flowed both ways. By 1831, Ainsworth was writing *Rookwood*.

Chapter 6

The Design of Romance

In April 1834, *Rookwood: A Romance* was published in three volumes by Richard Bentley, bearing a long dedication by the author to his mother. For Ainsworth and his family, life would never be the same again.

In a preface added to later editions, Ainsworth describes the construction of his famous romance, omitting only the break in work between the winter of 1831 and the summer of 1833, when his life was effectively taken over by legal and financial problems largely engendered by his previous connection with John Ebers & Co. Like *Sir John Chiverton*, the inspiration for the novel came initially from the Gothic charge that the author associated with an ancient building:

> During a visit to Chesterfield, in the autumn of the year 1831, I first conceived the notion of writing this story. Wishing to describe, somewhat minutely, the trim gardens, the picturesque domains, the rook-haunted groves, the gloomy chambers, and gloomier galleries, of an ancient Hall with which I was acquainted, I resolved to attempt a story in the bygone style of Mrs. Radcliffe (which had always inexpressible charms for me), substituting an old English squire, an old English manorial residence, and an old English highwayman, for the Italian marchese, the castle, and the brigand of the great mistress of Romance.[1]

Here, he witnessed the opening of a vault while walking in a cemetery. This exhumation played upon his imagination, inspiring the Gothic opening chapters, which were written before he left Chesterfield. The 'ancient Hall' was Cuckfield Place, Sussex (once described by Shelley as looking 'like bits of Mrs. Radcliffe'), the home of the Reverend William Sergison, a client from the Grafton Street law practice who had become a close friend. (In renaming it in reference to Gunpowder Plotter Ambrose

Rookwood, Ainsworth signals that his House of Rookwood is one of England's old Catholic families.) Chesterfield was the home of the widow of Ainsworth's second cousin James, the formidable Mrs Eliza Touchet. (The Manchester merchant James Touchet had died of a fever in 1821 at the age of thirty-seven.) His exact relationship with Mrs Touchet is not clear, although she does share her Christian name with the mysterious lover from 'Mary Stukeley'. Ellis wrote of her that she was 'a talented woman, of brilliant conversational powers, and although fifteen years older than Ainsworth, had very considerable influence over him to the end of his life'.[2] Ainsworth's own references to Eliza during this period are cryptic. Having arranged to visit Crossley in Manchester from the beginning of August 1831, Ainsworth got no further than Chesterfield, writing to his friend by way of apology:

> You must excuse me a day or two longer. I meant to have been with you on Tuesday, but I fear it will be the latter end of the week. I will not fix a day, therefore don't expect me till you receive a positive letter to say so. You are a man of feeling – a man of philanthropy, and will overlook my errors, I am sure. Chesterfield has charms for me; *that* you know, and therefore I throw myself on your mercy.[3]

Ellis also read this letter and suggests that what attracted Ainsworth to Chesterfield was a peaceful environment in which to write, offering an escape from the constant problems with Ebers and an increasingly troubled marriage, but as Clare Harman has recently suggested, 'it seems highly likely that their relationship was somewhat more than cousinly'.[4] When Ainsworth and Fanny separated in 1835, Ainsworth left to share Kensal Lodge on the Harrow Road with Eliza and her unmarried sister, Anne Buckley. As the Kensal Lodge period saw Ainsworth's famous literary dinners, there are some references to Eliza in the letters and journals of many of his distinguished guests, from which can be gleaned a portrait of a handsome and highly intelligent woman who was fond of sarcasm and not shy of expressing her opinions. Dickens and Forster, for example, seemed quite in awe of her. She had been a famous horsewoman in her youth and loved to tease the men about their less-than-polished 'Cockney' riding styles. Because of Ainsworth's bachelor status, she acted as his hostess. In 2009, a first edition of *A Christmas Carol* inscribed by Dickens to Eliza sold at auction at Christie's in New York for $290,500.

The *Rookwood* preface is Ainsworth's formal statement of what he terms 'the design of romance'. He makes the Gothic transition from medieval Europe to England implicit in his opening paragraph, explains the cultural significance of Dick Turpin and the poetic possibilities of 'flash' underworld slang, and admits that he had 'an eye rather to the reader's amusement than his edification'. Most importantly:

> The chief object I had in view in making the present essay, was to see how the infusion of a warmer and more genial current into the veins of old Romance would succeed in reviving her fluttering and feeble pulse.[5]

Rookwood, then, was to be a Gothic revival.

According to legend, whenever a branch falls from an ancient lime tree in the grounds of Rookwood Place, a death in the family is sure to follow. Under such ominous circumstances, Sir Piers Rookwood dies suddenly, leaving his wife and two sons, one legitimate and one not, to battle over the inheritance against a backdrop of plots, counterplots, supernatural events, ill omens and ancient prophecy. The story begins in the family vault. By the coffin of his mother, Susan, Luke Bradley is told by his grandfather, the sexton Peter Bradley, that he is in fact the son and heir of Sir Piers. Peter hints that Susan did not die of natural causes and at that moment her coffin falls from its shelf, exposing her corpse. In a fit of grief, Luke takes the hand of his dead mother, revealing a wedding ring. He realises he is not illegitimate and resolves to claim his inheritance as Luke Rookwood, eldest son of Sir Piers, unaware that this entire episode has been orchestrated by Bradley for his own mysterious ends. Luke's rival is his half-brother Ranulph, whose mother, Lady Maud Rookwood, is as scheming and manipulative as the sexton.

Another ancient prophecy disclosed to Luke by Bradley foretells that two distant branches of the family will unite and control everything. (In the original text, the font is changed to an 'Old English' style for Gothic resonance):

> When the stray Rook shall perch on the topmost bough,
> There shall be clamour and screaming, I trow;
> But of right, and of rule, of the ancient nest,
> The Rook that with Rook mates shall hold him possest.[6]

The key to this appears to be the beautiful Eleanor Mowbray, Ranulph's cousin and the heir of his grandfather, Sir Reginald Rookwood. Eleanor loves Ranulph, but Luke becomes obsessed with her, as Peter Bradley hoped. He rejects his gypsy lover, Sybil Lovel, in order to pursue Eleanor, whom he intends to force into marriage to fulfil the prophecy. With the help of the highwayman Dick Turpin, Luke almost succeeds but is tricked into marrying Sybil instead of Eleanor, who has been drugged and spirited away to a gypsy encampment. Sybil frees Eleanor and commits suicide, and Luke is killed by Sybil's grandmother, who sends him a poisoned lock of Sybil's hair via the oblivious Turpin. Peter Bradley, now revealed as the estranged brother of Sir Reginald, Alan Rookwood and Lady Rookwood finally confront each other in the vault but 'some secret machinery' entombs them alive as they fight. Ranulph and Eleanor survive and are married in brief denouement, while a L'envoi relates the conclusion to Dick Turpin's career, presenting his hanging at York as a noble and glorious death.

The influence of revenge tragedy and the Gothic novel abound, alongside those of Scott. The Cain and Abel motif, disputed inheritance, manipulative and disguised older relatives and forced marriage to gain property are all present in Scott's minor novel *St Ronan's Well*, published in 1824. The heroines also share the same family name, Mowbray – Scott's character is called Clara – although *St Ronan's Well* was an Austenesque comedy of manners wrapped around a family plot, rather than a Gothic extravaganza. Because of its contemporary setting and surprisingly downbeat ending, *St Ronan's Well* was not, by its author's own admission, particularly popular with readers or reviewers. The same could not be said of *Rookwood*.

Scott, who towered over popular English fiction for a generation, had died in 1832, leaving no obvious heir. For a reading public still mourning his passing and weary of 'silver fork' tales of fashionable life, *Rookwood* was a revelation – a wild ride that combined claustrophobic, charnel-house horror with the romance and adventure of the outlaw and the open road. The novel was further enlivened by a band of gypsy outlaws, and thirty original flash songs and morbid ballads, many of which celebrated illegal behaviour, rendering edgy underworld argot once more fashionable, as Piers Egan had done in *Life in London* during the Regency. As Ainsworth further explained in his preface:

It is somewhat curious, with a dialect so racy, idiomatic, and plastic as our own cant, that its metrical capabilities should have been so little essayed. The French have numerous *chansons d'argot* ... We, on the contrary, have scarcely any slang songs of merit. With a race of deprecators so melodious and convivial as our highwaymen, this is the more to be wondered at. Had they no bards amongst their bands? ... The barrenness, I have shown, is not attributable to the poverty of the soil, but to the want of due cultivation.[7]

Ainsworth was especially proud of 'Jerry Juniper's Chant', which was 'a purely flash song, of which the great and peculiar merit consists in its being utterly incomprehensible to the uninformed understanding'.[8] This particular ditty began...

> In a box of the stone jug I was born,
> Of a hempen widow the kid forlorn,
> *Fake away.*
> And my father, as I've heard say,
> *Fake away.*
> Was a merchant of capers gay,
> Who cut his last fling with great applause,
> *Nix my doll pals, fake away.*[9]

...which means:

> I was born in a prison cell,
> The neglected child of a hanged man's widow,
> *Carry on stealing.*
> And my father, as I've been told,
> *Carry on stealing.*
> Was an excellent dancer,
> Whose last dance was bravely done from the end of a rope,
> *Never mind, my friends, carry on stealing.*

Unlike Egan, however, Ainsworth's connection to the language of the nineteenth-century underworld was strictly academic. In an interview given to the *World* magazine in 1878, he answered the question

'Did you interview thieves and Gypsies to gain authentic knowledge of "flash patter"?' by admitting:

> Not at all. Never had anything to do with the scoundrels in my life. I got my slang in a much easier way. I picked up the Memoirs of James Hardy Vaux — a returned transport. The book was full of adventures, and had at the end a kind of slang dictionary. Out of this I got all my 'patter'.[10]

Vaux had appended a detailed 'Vocabulary of the Flash Language' to his 1819 autobiography to render it comprehensible. (Egan had also edited a new edition of Francis Grose's *Classical Dictionary of the Vulgar Tongue* in 1823, which no doubt came in handy.) Egan was a social explorer, Ainsworth a researcher.

Rookwood was, without a doubt, the publishing event of the decade, and a craze ensued not seen since the days of Tom and Jerry. As an enthusiastic review in *Fraser's Magazine* began:

> The best and most conclusive thing that can be said about this work is, that it has 'created a sensation'. There is a period in the life of literature, as well as in the life of an individual man, when a 'new sensation' is a sort of wonder, or God-send, or at least something to be thankful for; and in this belief we affirm that a very large class of readers have reason to be grateful to the author of *Rookwood*.[11]

And within a couple of weeks of publication, Ainsworth wrote to Crossley that:

> The book is doing famously well here – making, in fact, quite a *sensation*. It has been praised in quarters of which you can have no idea – for instance, by Sir James Scarlett and Lord Durham.[12] I have also received a most flattering letter from Bulwer-Lytton, and it has been the means of introducing me to Lady Blessington and her *soirées*. In fact, as Byron says, I went to bed unknown, arose, and found myself famous. Bentley has already begun to speak of a second edition – he

wants to advertise in all the papers … 'The English Victor
Hugo' has already appeared as a paragraph.[13]

'The English Victor Hugo' – a connection made by the *Monthly Magazine*
(formerly the *European*) – is an indication of the vacuum left by Scott,
a situation that Bentley understood and exploited. Dickens was still
just a court reporter, otherwise unpublished and far from famous, while
the Radical Whig MP and popular novelist Edward Bulwer-Lytton had
already made a lot of enemies. This very handy sound bite, taken up by
literary journalists in London, in fact originated from Crossley himself.
Reviewing *Rookwood* in the *Manchester Herald* in April, in a very
balanced piece (noting, for example, that the plot at times suffered from
hasty composition), he had still concluded that his friend's work would
'eventually establish him as the English Victor Hugo'.[14] In the same letter,
Ainsworth thanks him for sending this – 'A thousand thanks for your
excellent notice of *Rookwood* in the *Herald*. It has done me right good.'

Fraser's therefore took the opportunity to support their man while
also using the review to attack Lytton, who was politically at odds with
the magazine. Several Fraserians – especially the young Thackeray –
also disliked what they considered to be Lytton's pompous and over-
ornamental style, while Maginn simply hated him. 'With Mr. Ainsworth
all is natural, free, and joyous: with Mr. Bulwer all is forced, constrained
and cold,' wrote the anonymous reviewer, who Ainsworth identified to
Crossley as John 'Jack' Churchill. 'Ainsworth is always thinking of –
or rather with his hero: Bulwer is always thinking of himself.'[15] Scenes
from the novel were quoted at length, as were Ainsworth's songs, which
were hailed as the book's 'most original feature', towering in standard
over the efforts of Lytton in his highwayman novel *Paul Clifford*,
which predated *Rookwood* by four years, because 'The humorous is
not Mr. Bulwer's *forte*; and without the relish for humour, no man can
produce a flash song'.[16]

Lytton's recent work was an obvious correlative, and he and Ainsworth
were conceptually linked from the first through the development of what
came to be known as the 'Newgate novel'. The heroes of these novels
were criminals, often lifted from the pages of 'Newgate Calendars',
lurid chapbook accounts of crimes, trials and executions named after
the infamous prison. Like Ainsworth, Lytton as a bestselling nineteenth-
century novelist sits chronologically in the cultural space between the death

of Scott and the rise of Dickens, much more Romantic than Victorian. He was adept at a variety of popular genres, including historical and Gothic romance, and in 1830 published a highly political and redemptive tale of a fictional Georgian highwayman, *Paul Clifford*. The title character was something of an amalgam of several real Newgate Calendar villains and the brooding Romantic hero of Friedrich Schiller's 1781 play *The Robbers*, Karl von Moor. Clifford is imprisoned as a boy for an offence he did not commit. He emerges into the world apprenticed in crime and ready to use these skills to survive, later explaining that 'I come into the world friendless and poor – I find a body of laws hostile to the friendless and the poor! To those laws hostile to me, then, I acknowledge hostility in my turn. Between us are the conditions of war.'[17]

Through his mouthpiece, despite a footnote stating that these sentiments are those of character not author, Lytton is craftily paraphrasing the political philosopher William Godwin, who had written that 'The superiority of the rich, being thus unmercifully exercised, must inevitably expose them to reprisals; and the poor man will be induced to regard the state of society as a state of war.'[18] In a preface to the 1840 edition, Lytton confessed that his novel was 'a loud cry to society to mend the circumstance – to redeem the victim. It is an appeal from Humanity to Law.'[19] A powerful novel in its own day, *Paul Clifford* is now only remembered, if it is remembered at all, for it's opening line, which begins 'It was a dark and stormy night', but in moving beyond the picaresque tradition into recent English history and political allegory, spiced up with a bit of melodrama and adventure, Lytton had essentially created a new genre.

Lytton followed *Paul Clifford* with another exploration of guilt and the moral conflict between violence and visionary ideals, *Eugene Aram* (1832), this time based on a real eighteenth-century murderer. The original Eugene Aram was a Yorkshire schoolmaster of humble origins with a gift for languages who killed his wife's lover. Aram's duality as a brilliant scholar and homicidal cuckold was a rich source for writers, and in addition to appearing in numerous Newgate Calendars he had been the subject of Thomas Hood's popular ballad *The Dream of Eugene Aram* in 1829. The opportunistic Lytton was quick to capitalise, turning a real-life killer into a broadly sympathetic protagonist, portraying Aram as a Faustian seeker after knowledge laid low by poverty, foreshadowing Dostoevsky's Raskolnikov. As with *Paul Clifford*, Lytton used footnotes to distance himself from his hero, but whether by accident or design, his narrative voice can be read as once more siding with a criminal.

Although *Eugene Aram* garnered a massive readership, critical opinion was more divided. Regency icons like Harriette Wilson and Pierce Egan loved it, while the *Athenaeum* hailed the book as a work of genius that probably should not have been written, and the *Spectator* reminded its readers that Bulwer's novel should be read like Byron's *Manfred* and not a Newgate Calendar. William Maginn, who Lytton had caricatured in *Paul Clifford* as the drunken intellectual charlatan 'MacGrawler', unsurprisingly took the most strident view among the voices of disapproval, writing in *Fraser's* that 'We dislike altogether this awakening sympathy with interesting criminals, and wasting sensibilities on the scaffold and the gaol. It is a modern, a depraved, a corrupting taste.' He further suggests, citing copycat murders for profit supposedly inspired by Burke and Hare, that a criminal romance like *Eugene Aram* may similarly incite violence, because the author 'little dreams of the lurking demons he may thus arouse'.[20]

In comparison to Lytton, however, whom Ainsworth greatly admired, what makes *Rookwood's* inclusion of the Georgian highwayman Dick Turpin as a point-of-view character so innovative is the representation of him as a hero, described by his author as 'an English Adventurer', rather than a tortured penitent. Because of the childhood fascination with Turpin, Ainsworth made explicit what Lytton had been accused of in both *Paul Clifford* and *Eugene Aram*, and positively romanticised criminality.

Although following *Eugene Aram* by two years, Ainsworth was too much of an early career novelist to have yet got on the wrong side of the critics, while *Rookwood* was just so much *fun*. The reviews speak for themselves. 'This is one of the most spirited and romantic of "the season's" productions,' began the 'Critical Notice' (which may have been written by Lytton) in the *New Monthly Magazine*:

> Full of life and fire, it excites the reader and carries him onward – much as the true heroine of the tale, the Mare Black Bess, does the true hero of it, the robber Turpin – with mingled sensations of terror and delight. It is a wild story, told with exceeding skill, and wrought up to the highest pitch of which so singular and rare a subject is capable. Moreover, many of the characters are drawn with a master-hand,

and it is evident that the writer has read deeply the character of human kind. The interest of the work is kept thrillingly alive from the outset to the end – there is no time to pause until the volumes are finished – and then, when the mind is in a mood to criticise, the author may well be satisfied with the verdict which the reader cannot fail to pronounce – the book is an excellent one, and the author may take a high station among the romance writers of our time.[21]

Admittedly expressing reservations about the use of slang in the novel, the *Quarterly Review* similarly praised the exhilarating pace of *Rookwood*, concluding that 'We expect much from this writer ... He evidently possesses, in no common degree, the materials of success: a fresh and stirring fancy, and a style which, like the fancy, wants nothing but the bridle. His story, as it is, is one that never flags.'[22] The *Spectator*, meanwhile, described the novel as 'Written with great vigour and wonderful variety – not only of images but of character', while the *Atlas* looked back to the glory days of eighteenth-century Gothic romance and Scott's early novels, gushing that 'It is long since such a work as this has been produced; the author exhibits ability of no ordinary kind.'

As the *New Monthly* review noted, the real hero of the novel as far as the readers were concerned was Dick Turpin. He was the 'X Factor', the unique selling point. 'Commend us to the Ride to York!' said the *Literary Gazette*, 'It is one of the boldest and most effective sketches that we know of in any modern novel,' while *Wheeler's History of Manchester* celebrated 'That portion of *Rookwood*, which is dedicated to Turpin's ride from London to York' as 'certainly the most graphic and life-like delineation in the language'.[23] And as an avid and accomplished horseman, Ainsworth must have loved 'Dick Turpin's Ride' in the *New Sporting Magazine*, which focused on his famous mount Black Bess, explaining that:

Novels and Romances do not often offer subjects for notice, or furnish extracts, coming within the legitimate scope of our publication. The recently published romance of 'Rookwood' is, however, a splendid exception to this remark; and in the wild and wondrous exploits of Dick Turpin and his mare Black Bess, presents us with descriptions and delineations drawn to the life, and with a graphic force and fidelity that cannot fail to delight sportsmen and interest and amuse readers of every class.[24]

The article then extracts from the 'Ride to York' episode at length, taking it to be a true story rather than Ainsworth's invention.

The protean Dick Turpin, 'a sort of hero', enters *Rookwood* in disguise. Set two years before the original outlaw's death, *Rookwood* introduces 'Jack Palmer' in a chapter entitled 'An English Adventurer' with an epigraph from *The Beggar's Opera*, 'Sure the captain's the finest gentleman on the road', thus ensuring that Palmer's true identity is the worst kept secret in the novel.[25] Turpin in disguise is a guest at Rookwood Hall. A drunken discussion promptly ensues between him and the attorney Codicil Coates as to the noble disposition of the highwayman, Turpin arguing that 'It is as necessary for a man to be a gentleman before he can turn highwayman', continuing in a long monologue:

> What are the distinguishing characteristics of a fine gentleman?—perfect knowledge of the world—perfect independence of character—notoriety—command of cash—and inordinate success with the women ... As to money, he wins a purse of a hundred guineas as easily as you would the same sum from the faro table. And wherein lies the difference? only in the name of the game. Who so little need of a banker as he? all he has to apprehend is a check—all he has to draw is a trigger. As to the women, they dote upon him: not even your red-coat is so successful. Look at a highwayman mounted on his flying steed, with his pistols in his holsters, and his mask upon his face. What can be a more gallant sight? The clatter of his horse's heels is like music to his ear—he is in full quest—he shouts to the fugitive horseman to stay—the other flies all the faster— what chase can be half so exciting as that?

'England, sir,' he concludes, 'has reason to be proud of her highwaymen.'[26] The 'English Adventurer' then entertains the company with a celebratory flash song called 'A Chapter of Highwaymen', the fun of the recitation increased by Turpin including himself in the lyric and betting Coates that he can capture himself. This is the first of many jaunty songs about highwaymen, Turpin continuing to praise their rank and exploits in terms of modern chivalry, often seconded by Ainsworth's prominent authorial voice. He even compares the highwayman to the hero of Trafalgar: 'Rash daring was the main feature of Turpin's character. Like our great Nelson, he knew fear only by name.'[27]

There were of course many versions of the life and legend of Dick Turpin already in place in English culture by the time of *Rookwood*, ranging from the official record of his trial and execution to Newgate Calendars and a positive legion of folk songs and tall stories, like the ones Ainsworth grew up with. If a fraction of the contemporary reports of Turpin's behaviour are true, then the original was a nasty piece of work – drunken, profligate, self-serving and sadistically violent. Yet such men, and later the outlaws of the American West, were more often than not portrayed as folk heroes. As the historian Eric Hobsbawm wrote, 'Banditry is freedom, but in peasant society few can be free.'[28] So strong was this perception of the heroic 'gentleman of the road' that it completely overwrote the brutal reality, a myth that has now endured for centuries and can still be seen in popular culture, for example James Mason's brooding antihero 'Jackson' in *The Wicked Lady* (1945), the LWT *Dick Turpin* TV series of the late 1970s, which portrayed Turpin as a handsome Robin Hood figure, and Jake Scott's underrated British film *Plunkett and Macleane* (1999), which combined the bawdy humour of *Carry on Dick* with *Butch Cassidy and the Sundance Kid*.[29] And who could forget 'Stand and Deliver' by Adam and the Ants? (Turpin was also often played by cowboy stars in Golden Age Hollywood, including Matheson Lang, Tom Mix and Victor McLaglen.) Although there hasn't been a highwayman revival lately, Johnny Depp's Captain Jack Sparrow is just Dick Turpin reimagined.

But all of these modern portrayals of Turpin ultimately lead back to *Rookwood*, which in turn goes back to Ainsworth's childhood. 'One of Turpin's adventures in particular, the ride to Hough Green,' he wrote, 'took deep hold of my fancy':

> And then there was the Bollin, with its shelvy banks, which Turpin cleared at a bound; the broad meadows over which he winged his flight; the pleasant bowling-green of the pleasant old inn at Hough, where he produced his watch to the Cheshire squires, with whom he was upon terms of

intimacy; all brought something of the gallant robber to mind. No wonder, in after years, in selecting a highwayman for a character in a tale, I should choose my old favourite, Dick Turpin.[30]

In separating fact from fiction, the best original biographical source is a chapbook entitled *The Genuine HISTORY of the LIFE of RICHARD TURPIN, The noted Highwayman, Who was Executed at York for Horse-stealing, under the Name of John Palmer, on Saturday April, 7, 1739*, told by Richard Bayes and recorded by one J. Cole in conversation at The Green Man in Epping Forest the year Turpin died. Not that such 'histories', written to capitalise on newsworthy trials and executions, are exactly accurate, but this one was at least based on testimony from his original community, and an account of the trial is also appended.[31] This is certainly the wellspring for all the subsequent chapbooks, but despite no doubt already containing many tall tales and conjecture, a distinct criminal portrait clearly emerges that is far from the romanticised version of legend.

According to Bayes and Cole, Turpin was born in Hempstead in Essex in 1705. He was taught to read and write by a tutor called James Smith, then apprenticed to a butcher in Whitechapel, where he married and acquired a reputation for being a bit of a wrong'un. The couple set up in business in Sutton, but the meat trade was no longer guilded and unregulated competition was fierce. Turpin took to stealing livestock from his neighbours until some servants saw him and a warrant was drawn up. Evading capture, Turpin tried his hand at smuggling before he fell in with a band of deer poachers known as 'Gregory's Gang' after its leaders, the brothers Samuel, Jeremiah and Jaspar Gregory, who needed a butcher to help dispose of stolen meat. As Turpin became more active and influential in the gang, they diversified into housebreaking around Essex, Middlesex, Surrey and Kent, with a reputation for demanding valuables with menaces, sexually assaulting maidservants, and stealing horses, their brutality escalating with every raid, as one contemporary newspaper account shows:

On Saturday night last, about seven o'clock, five rogues entered the house of the Widow Shelley at Loughton in Essex, having pistols &c. and threatened to murder the old lady, if she would not tell them where her money lay, which she obstinately refusing for some time, they threatened to lay her across the fire, if she did not instantly tell them, which she would not do.[32]

Beatings, scaldings and severe burns were favourite forms of persuasion, until, pursued by dragoons with a £100 reward on each of their heads, several of the gang were cornered at a pub in Westminster. The youngest, the teenager John Wheeler, turned King's evidence to avoid the gallows; his compatriots were hanged in chains. Descriptions were quickly circulated, including: 'Richard Turpin, a Butcher by Trade, is a tall fresh colour'd Man, very much mark'd with the Small Pox, about 26 Years of Age, about Five Feet Nine Inches high, lived some Time ago at White-chappel and did lately Lodge somewhere about Millbank, Westminster, wears a Blew Grey Coat and a natural Wig.'[33]

On the run, Turpin encountered a well-dressed gentleman on the London to Cambridge road and decided he was worth holding up, much to the delight of the victim, who turned out to be the highwayman Tom King. The pair rode together for three years, keeping a hideout in a cave deep in Epping Forest, until the lair was discovered by a bounty hunting servant who Turpin shot and killed. On the run again, Turpin stole a horse near The Green Man, at which point Richard Bayes became directly involved in the story he was telling, tracking Tom King to The Red Lyon in Whitechapel. He accosted King trying to get to his horse and managed to detain him after the highwayman's pistol flashed in the pan. At this point, Turpin appeared, and King cried out to him to shoot Bayes. Turpin missed and hit King instead, before escaping. King lived for another week, during which he sang like a canary and cursed Turpin for a coward. Using this information, Bayes was able to locate the cave, but Turpin was long gone.

Becoming 'John Palmer' (his wife's maiden name), Turpin had relocated to Yorkshire as a horse trader, although he was in reality riding into Lincolnshire and stealing them. (The nearest we get to 'Black Bess' is a black mare and foal stolen from Thomas Creasy of York during this period.) His disguise well in place, he often joined local gentlemen on shooting parties, and was initially nicked after returning from a hunt a bit worse for the drink and shooting one of his landlord's cockerels in the street. His neighbour, Mr Hall, witnessed the event and admonished him. 'You have done wrong, Mr Palmer', said he, 'in shooting your landlord's cock,' to which Turpin replied that if he stood still while he reloaded, he would shoot him too.[34] Hall told their landlord and Turpin was arrested. Being relatively new to the area, Turpin could not provide any character witnesses, and although he claimed to be a butcher from Long Sutton, something about his vague backstory did not sit well with the examining magistrate. He was detained while further enquiries were made in Lincolnshire, revealing that 'John Palmer' had been suspected of horse theft. He was thus moved to a cell at York Castle while further investigations were conducted. Because Georgian prisoners had to pay for board and lodgings, Turpin was fast running out of money. He decided to write to his wife's brother in Essex for help. Unfortunately, his brother-in-law refused to pay postage on the letter, which was instead held at the Saffron Walden post office. By bizarre coincidence, Turpin's old tutor, Smith, was now the postmaster there and he recognised the handwriting. The authorities were informed, and Turpin was indicted for stealing the black mare, and then identified in court as the notorious highwayman by his old tutor.

On Saturday, 7 April 1739, Turpin was hanged at Micklegate Bar in York, alongside a horse thief called John Stead, at the age of thirty-three. Contemporary accounts agree that he died with style, having bought a new frock coat and shoes for the occasion and hired five mourners. In *Rookwood's* L'envoy, Ainsworth reproduces the essence of Bayes and Cole's account: 'His firmness deserted him not at the last. When he mounted the fatal tree his left leg trembled; he stamped it impatiently down, and, after a brief chat with the hangman, threw himself suddenly and resolutely from the ladder. His sufferings would appear to have been slight.'[35] As Georgian hangings had a short drop, the victim went through the hideous process of strangling under his own body weight. Apparently, Turpin took about five minutes. Bayes and Cole further describe Turpin's corpse being rescued from bodysnatchers and borne through the streets like a martyred saint, before it was buried in lime to render it useless for surgical dissection. He supposedly lies in the graveyard of St George's Church, Fishergate, although the headstone that now graces the spot was not there when Ainsworth looked for it in 1833.

Georgian highwaymen had principally operated on the main roads out of London, taking advantage of long, lonely stretches through commons, heath and woodland. Hounslow Heath, covering the roads to Bath and Exeter, was a particularly dangerous place, as was Shooter's Hill on the Great Dover Road and Finchley Common on the Great North Road.

But as the eighteenth century progressed, more turnpikes, traceable banknotes and expanding cities encroaching into traditional haunts combined to make highwaymen a thing of the past. The country had become a lot smaller, with fewer places to hide, and in 1805, Richard Ford's newly founded Bow Street Horse Patrol largely wiped the mounted outlaws out. 'Turpin was the *ultimus Romanorum*, the last of a race,' wrote Ainsworth in *Rookwood*, 'which (we were almost about to say we regret) is now altogether extinct.'[36] For his generation, highwaymen belonged to a vanished world, and as Lytton had demonstrated, they were therefore ripe for a romantic resurrection.

Turpin was notionally intended as a secondary character. He has an affinity for the roguish Luke and the 'canting crew' at Sybil's gypsy encampment – who provide a lot of comic relief and most of the best songs – and comes into possession of a marriage certificate proving Luke's claim to the estate is legitimate. His plot function is to support the Rookwood Pretender, first for profit but later out of friendship. But he is ultimately the unwitting agent of his demise, passing on a poisoned lock of the now dead Sybil's hair at the behest of her grandmother. He also teases Codicil Coates something rotten, until the lawyer uncovers his identity and he is forced to flee. Ainsworth casts the pursuing Coates in the role of Richard Bayes at the inn where Turpin accidently kills Tom King, initiating the epic chase that is the fourth book of *Rookwood*, entitled 'The Ride to York', the heart of the novel while having nothing whatsoever to do with the main plotline.

'The Ride to York' is an exhilarating narrative, written by a man who knew his horses as well as his history. Ainsworth was completely possessed by his subject, later writing that 'The Ride to York was completed in one day and one night':

> Well do I remember the fever into which I was thrown during the time of composition. My pen literally scoured over the pages. So thoroughly did I identify myself with the flying highwayman, that, once started, I found it impossible to halt. Animated by kindred enthusiasm, I cleared every obstacle in my path with as much facility as Turpin disposed of the impediments that beset his flight. In his company, I mounted the hill-side, dashed through the bustling village, swept over the desolate heath, threaded the silent street,

plunged into the eddying stream, and kept an onward course, without pause, without hindrance, without fatigue. With him I shouted, sang, laughed, exulted, wept. Nor did I retire to rest till, in imagination, I heard the bell of York Minster toll forth the knell of poor Black Bess.[37]

He based the episode on the ride to Hough Green, another apocryphal story in which Turpin rode so quickly from a robbery at Dunham Massey (then in Cheshire) to Hough Green (then in Lancashire) that he was able to establish an alibi.[38] 'The Ride to York', on the other hand, attributed to Turpin since *Rookwood*, often as a historical fact, comes from a legend about the seventeenth-century highwayman John Nevison, or 'Swift Nick', which goes back to an account by Daniel Defoe in his 1727 work *A tour thro' the whole island of Great Britain*. Either way, as the contemporary reviews and sales demonstrate, Ainsworth's enthusiasm was infectious, to the point where unlicensed theatrical adaptations and penny dreadful knock-offs of *Rookwood* frequently excised the Gothic plot about the rival brothers entirely and just did the Dick Turpin bits, perhaps indicating a longing for a lost cultural innocence in a rapidly changing world. The moonlit heaths were forever shrinking now and becoming less magical by the year.

The sincerest form of flattery followed, as Turpin was rehabilitated as a national treasure, inspiring a run of highwayman penny dreadfuls that flourished well into the 1860s. W.S. Sutter's play *The Adventures of Dick Turpin and Tom King* and H.D. Milner's *Turpin's Ride to York* packed them in at the penny theatres; *Rookwood* Book IV was republished twice (unacknowledged) as *Turpin's Ride to York*, and *Dick Turpin's Celebrated Ride to York*, and Henry Downes Miles's picaresque *Dick Turpin, The Highwayman* was a popular novel, going through four editions. The only real voice of critical dissent came from the notoriously contrarian John Forster, who wrote in an *Examiner* review:

Turpin, whom the writer is pleased with loving familiarity to call Dick, is the hero of the tale. Doubtless we shall soon see Thurtell presented in sublime guise, and the drive to Gad's Hill described with all pomp and circumstance. There are people who may like this sort of thing, but we are not of that number ... The author has, we suspect, been misled by the example and success of 'Paul Clifford', but in 'Paul Clifford' the thieves and their dialect serve for illustration, while in 'Rookwood' the highwayman and his slang are presented as if in themselves they had some claim to admiration.[39] [John Thurtell had murdered the professional gambler William Weare in 1823 and had received a huge amount of press.]

He did, however, hedge at the end, which was unusual for a man known for his abrasive directness, but he and Ainsworth were friends, as were many other of the novel's supporters. Forster therefore concluded that another reading was possible, as the book had admirers 'among people of good judgement'.

Forster, like Ainsworth, is another towering figure in nineteenth-century letters who is largely remembered now only as Dickens's first biographer. In his own day, as Lytton once said of him, 'more than any living critic, he has served to establish reputations'.[40] *Fraser's* had given the *Examiner* short shrift in their glowing review, anyway, as well as giving the *Athenaeum* a kick for gently taking the mickey out of *Rookwood's* style with 'its villains are most villainously villanous [*sic*], and its terrors are most terribly terrible'.[41] But while finding the Gothic excess of the novel so over the top as to become ludicrous, the *Athenaeum* reviewer had still praised the portrayal of Black Bess and Turpin's ride to York.

In any event, for Ainsworth that year, there was no such thing as bad publicity. As his friend Samuel Laman Blanchard later wrote, 'the effect of this publication was to place Mr. Ainsworth in the first rank of writers of romantic fiction.'[42] And as for the largely forgotten highwayman, his fame was also now assured. Almost everything we think we know about Dick Turpin in national myth in fact comes from the pages of *Rookwood.*

Chapter 7

The Novelist of the Season

In the July number following *Fraser's* extravagant review of *Rookwood*, Ainsworth's portrait (the first of many by Daniel Maclise) appeared in the magazine's 'Gallery of Literary Characters', the subject splendidly vain in the *outré* attire of the dandy, clutching a riding crop and flanked by images of highwaymen. The accompanying caption, written by Maginn himself, was packed with innuendo, comparing Ainsworth's good looks to those of Byron and D'Orsay:

> We have not the pleasure of being acquainted with Mrs. Ainsworth, but we are sincerely sorry for her – we deeply commiserate her case. You see what a pretty fellow THE young Novelist of the Season is; how exactly, in fact, he resembles one of the most classically handsome and brilliant of the established lady-killers – the only darling of the day … We may, without a swagger, apply to Ainsworth what Theodore Hook has sung of D'Orsay *le beau*:
> 'See him, gallant and gay,
> With the chest of Apollo, the waist of a gnat;'
> – But then comes the rub for Mrs. A.; as well as the rhyme for 'gay:'
> 'The delight of the ball, the assembly, the play!'
> Alas! it were well if 'balls, assemblies, and plays' were all; there are also such things, not undreamt-of in the philosophy of the Mayfair fair ones, as *boudoirs* and *tête-à-têtes*; and the best we can say for this Turpin of the cabriolet, whose prance will never masticate a beef-steak, is, that if he escapes scot-free during the first month of the blaze of his romance, he is a lucky as well as a well-grown lad. Of this all concerned may be only too sure, that many a dove as well as a crow will, on the present occasion,

'Make wing to the Rooky-wood.'

Well, Heaven send him a good deliverance! But when we see how even whey-faced, spindle-shanked, mask-smelling baboons, get on occasionally among feathers and furbelows, when once they have attached any thing like a rag of notoriety to their names, we own we regard with fear and trepidation the fiery furnace of flattering sighs, through which this strapping A-Bed-Nego must endeavour to bring his jolly whiskers unsinged.[1]

This was rather closer to the mark than even Maginn probably intended. Fanny did not participate at all in the social whirl that now surrounded her celebrity husband, keeping quietly in the background, running the house and raising the girls, and struggling to keep the peace between Ainsworth and her father. Years of gentile poverty, with Ainsworth writing around his law practice and often escaping to Chesterfield on the quiet on his way to Manchester, had taken its toll. Now *Rookwood* was finally bringing money and prestige, strain on the marriage was increasing for exactly the reasons Maginn was hinting, whether real or imagined. Increasingly stressed and exhausted, and never fully recovered from the successive births of her three children, Fanny's health began to suffer.

Worse, at least from Fanny's point of view, as Ainsworth had written to Crossley, an introduction from Lytton had gained him entrance to the inner circle of one of the most colourful women of the Regency, Marguerite Gardiner, Countess of Blessington, an intimate of Byron's whose fashionable *soirées* at her house in Seamore Place, Park Lane were a hub for the London intelligentsia. This was the acknowledged centre of all that was considered brilliant in art and literature. Because anyone who was anyone attended these salons, it was here that Ainsworth met many of his closest friends, most notably Lytton, Talfourd, the Liberal politician Lord Albert Conyngham, Benjamin Disraeli and John Forster. He was also able to deepen ties with Thackeray, whom he already knew through *Fraser's*.

Ainsworth, with his dark, curly hair and youthful features, strongly resembled Lady Blessington's constant companion, the flamboyantly bisexual Count Alfred D'Orsay (her son-in-law by her stepdaughter, now separated, and, it was rumoured, her lover, as well as that of her late husband). *Miladi* adored him, once famously placing herself on a

71

hearthrug between D'Orsay and Ainsworth and declaring that she was supported by the 'two handsomest men in London'.[2] And Ainsworth adored her back, as did everyone else, at least all the men. Like Eliza Touchet, Lady Marguerite was another intelligent, independent and sexually magnetic older woman; she and Ainsworth met just before her forty-fifth birthday. As she was then editing an annual called the *Book of Beauty*, she tapped Ainsworth for a story, sending him an engraving of a beautiful woman around which it might be written. 'A Night's Adventure in Rome' was the result, a tidy revenge tragedy with a neat twist, very much in the style of *Rookwood*.

Ainsworth was also invited to Holland House, the home of the Whig politician Henry Vassall-Fox, 3rd Baron Holland, and his brilliant wife, Elizabeth Vassall Fox, the political hostess whose salon included Henry Brougham, 1st Baron Brougham and Vaux and then Lord Chancellor, the historian Thomas Babington Macaulay, the poets Tom Moore and Samuel Rogers, the colourful writers Theodore Hook, Sydney Smith and Washington Irving, and two prime ministers (one serving) – Lord John Russell and Earl Grey.

Like D'Orsay, Ainsworth, then twenty-nine, was a colourful dandy, and he was as good-looking as Maginn had joked. In *Mervyn Clitheroe*, he described himself in the 1830s:

> Though I had entered upon man's estate, I still possessed a very youthful appearance, and I have seen the upper lip of many a bewitching Andalusian dame more darkly feathered than mine was at the period in question. Some people told me I was handsome, and my tailor (excellent authority, it must be admitted) extolled the symmetry of my figure, and urged me to go into the Life Guards ... I was a hard rider, fond of shooting, and of all field sports, and had stalked deer in the Highlands, and speared the wild-boar in the woods of Germany ... To complete my personal description, I may refer to the passport which I obtained on going abroad, and where I find the following items in my signalment: – 'Hair, dark brown, and worn long; eyebrows, arched; eyes, blue; forehead, open; nose, straight; mouth, small; chin, round; visage, oval; complexion, rosy; beard, none; height, five feet eleven inches.' As these particulars were meant to convey

some idea of me to foreign authorities, they may possibly serve the same purpose to the reader.[3]

From numerous Society reports, as well as Daniel Maclise's equally numerous sketches and portraits, the above can be read as a fair description rather than the mere vanity of middle age. In his bespoke high-collared coats, brightly patterned waistcoats and tight trousers, and positively chandelier with bejewelled pins and gold rings, Ainsworth, like his fictional counterpart, had always cut quite a dash.

But Ainsworth's newfound fame as a bestselling novelist, the fulfilment of an ambition for which he had sweated since his teens, laboriously building up publication credits, making connections and refining his craft, only served to alienate his wife from him further. Humiliated by her husband's public flirtations with Lady Blessington and others, Fanny left to return to her family home in 1835, taking the girls with her. Ainsworth moved into Kensal Lodge with Eliza.

Ainsworth did not seem particularly distraught at the separation, although he did miss his children, whom Ebers made it very difficult to see. In fact, he appeared quite liberated, gathering around him an ever-increasing circle of distinguished friends, commencing his own literary salon, and starting the next novel. Always a convivial and generous host, Ainsworth, now notionally the head of the household, kept open house at Kensal Lodge – which was not a particularly large dwelling – and if calling, one might be swept into a crowded double drawing room and presented to men such as the artists George Cruikshank, Daniel Maclise and future Pre-Raphaelite William Dyce; Lytton, Thackeray, Forster, Disraeli, D'Orsay, Laman Blanchard and the publisher John Macrone. One of the people he invited was the young Charles Dickens.

In 1835, although already possessed of considerable talent and ambition, the 23-year-old Dickens was just another freelance journalist in the Darwinian world of London publishing. As a court reporter, he covered debates in the Commons as well as following election campaigns around the country and reporting on them for the *Morning Chronicle*. These travels became the bases for a series of 'sketches' of everyday life that he flogged to the *Morning* and *Evening Chronicle*, the *Monthly Magazine*, the *Carlton Chronicle* and *Bell's Life in London*. These had put him on Ainsworth's radar, but he was still largely unknown and professionally unconnected. Dickens admired Ainsworth greatly. He was *the* literary celebrity to emulate – a rising genius, a bestseller, and a charming and handsome bachelor with a legion of adoring fans. In order to fit in with the Ainsworth/D'Orsay set, Dickens spent more on clothes than he could comfortably afford, and in Frederic Kitton's *Charles Dickens by Pen and Pencil; Anecdotes and Reminiscences Collected from his Friends and Contemporaries*, the portrait of Dickens in the early 1830s that emerges is of another dandy, in 'a swallowtail coat with a very high velvet collar; a voluminous satin stock with a double breast-pin; a crimson velvet waistcoat over which meandered a lengthy gold chain'.[4]

It was through Ainsworth's often impromptu social gatherings at Kensal Lodge that Dickens first met John Forster, who would thereafter stick to him with the loyalty of a guard dog, as well as Lytton, Talfourd (to whom *The Pickwick Papers* is dedicated), and Maclise (to whom we owe the striking 1839 portrait of Dickens at his desk presently on display at the National Portrait Gallery). Ainsworth also introduced him to Macrone, the man who would go on to publish *Sketches by Boz*, and Cruikshank, who would illustrate it. Dickens met Macrone before Forster, as chronicled in the latter's *Life of Dickens*:

> The opening of 1836 found him collecting into two volumes the first series of *Sketches by Boz*, of which he had sold the copyright for a conditional payment of (I think) a hundred and fifty pounds to a young publisher named Macrone, whose acquaintance he had made through Mr. Ainsworth a few weeks before.[5]

Ainsworth loved the original *Sketches* and had strongly advised Dickens to release them in book form, which is why he introduced him to Macrone, an innovative and independent young publisher based in St James's Square who was handling the third edition of *Rookwood*. Macrone also published the fourth edition, to which was added a series of vivid illustrations by Cruikshank, thus beginning a long and productive partnership between the artist and Ainsworth as well as Dickens. He died tragically young of influenza in 1837. By the time the *Sketches* saw print, Dickens had also befriended Forster:

> The first letter I had from him was at the close of 1836 from Furnival's Inn, when he sent me the book of his opera of the

Village Coquettes, which had been published by Mr. Bentley; and this was followed, two months later, by his collected *Sketches*, both first and second series; which he desired me to receive 'as a very small testimony of the donor's regard and obligations, as well as of his desire to cultivate and avail himself of a friendship which has been so pleasantly thrown in his way' ... I had met him in the interval at the house of our common friend Mr. Ainsworth, and I remember vividly the impression then made upon me.[6]

Sketches by Boz of course gathered considerable popular and critical acclaim, its success and promise leading Chapman and Hall to approach Dickens to provide the text for a serial about a gentlemen's sporting club called the 'Nimrod Club' based around Robert Seymour's humorous illustrations. Seymour, down on his luck and in need of a hit, had in mind a monthly illustrated serial specifically modelled on *Life in London*, which still remained the benchmark for such writing. Dickens and Seymour did not see eye to eye on the direction of the project, which became *The Pickwick Papers*, and the sensitive, near-bankrupt artist committed suicide with a fowling piece after revising the illustrations for the second issue. Dickens had rejected the originals, and Seymour's wife always blamed him for her husband's suicide. Although a bit of a slow burner, once the cheery Cockney problem-solver Sam Weller appeared in Part Four, its success was assured, the final instalment selling 400,000 copies. When *The Pickwick Papers* was published as a luxuriously leather-bound novel, Dickens gave his complimentary copies to the three most important people in his life, writing to Forster: 'Chapman and Hall have just sent me, with a copy of our deed, three "extra-super" bound copies of *Pickwick*, as per specimen inclosed. The first I forward to you, the second I have presented to our good friend Ainsworth, and the third Kate has retained for herself.'[7] ('Kate' was Catherine Hogarth, who Dickens had married on 2 April 1836.) By November 1836, he had assumed the editorship of Bentley's new *Miscellany* and began serialising *Oliver Twist*, ditching an agreement with Macrone for a novel, his stock now raised considerably by the sales of *Pickwick*, and leaving Ainsworth rather awkwardly in the middle of the dispute, as his letters to Macrone indicate.[8]

Although Ainsworth was seven years Dickens's senior, their friendship made perfect sense. These equally mercurial personalities had much in common – both had a passion for theatre, loved riding and taking absurdly long walks in the countryside. They were also both workaholics, while remaining incredibly convivial, celebrating every professional achievement with a huge dinner. In these respects, they were very much of the same generation. As Peter Ackroyd observes in his biography of Dickens, both were 'part of that eminently social, gregarious, energetic, vivacious group which we have come to call "Early Victorians"'.[9]

Forster, meanwhile, was a natural networker. Born in Newcastle in 1812 of good family but poor parents, he was educated under the patronage of a benevolent uncle and, like Dickens, had fought his way into the literary establishment on his talents, his work ethic and an almost ruthless intelligence. Having his way to make, with no money or influence behind him, Forster pursued useful friends, not in a parasitic way but on the principle of mutual advantage. He would introduce friends to other friends and encourage them to help each other, thus placing all parties under obligation to him. As Ainsworth once said of him, 'I cannot explain the secret of his influence over people. He had a knack of making people do as he liked, whether they liked it or not,' adding, with reference to Forster's famously abrasive and arrogant personality, 'It was difficult at all times to put up with the bluster of the "arbitrary one".'[10]

An interesting example of Forster's technique can be seen in the following letter from Ainsworth to Macrone in the summer of 1836:

> Forster, whom I saw yesterday, tells me that Colburn is anxious to publish Browning's new poem Sordello. I hope you will not let this work, which will, at all events, do you credit as a publisher, slip through your hands without due consideration. It is impossible to foretell in such a case as the present whether the work will pay or not. My own opinion, from all I hear and know of Mr. Browning, is that it will do so. But at all events, it will do what I am so desirous you should do for yourself — contribute to fan your character as a publisher of taste and discrimination; and viewed only in this light is a very desirable undertaking for you. You should see Forster as soon as you can, and come to some positive understanding on this point.

The poet Robert Browning was still a relative unknown at this point. *Sordello* is a complex poem, and Ainsworth's appreciation of its value does him credit as a literary critic. The following month, he reports having now met the young poet in another letter to Macrone:

> I had yesterday, as I anticipated, the pleasure of making your new Poet's acquaintance, and from what I saw of him — and from what I heard and saw — I am induced to form a very high opinion of him. He is full of genius ... Sordello complete, he is to write a Tragedy for Macready — and I feel quite sure that he has great dramatic genius.[11] As, moreover, his Tragedy is to be written for and produced next season, you will have no reason to regret your immediate under-taking.[12]

Because of Macrone's untimely death, he never did publish *Sordello*, which Browning continued to rework until it finally saw print in 1840.

While Dickens was consolidating his career, Ainsworth was equally hard at work on the next novel. As critics and readers alike were as one in their celebration of Turpin as the real hero of *Rookwood*, his choice of follow-up was surprising, especially as the preface to the single-volume edition of *Rookwood* concluded with more than a hint that a novel on another outlaw was coming: 'If I should again "take the air upon the heath at eventide", it shall be in the company of the gayest "minion of the moon", the rifler of hearts and purses, the chivalrous CLAUDE DU-VAL.'[13] (Claude Du Vall – or Duval – was a French highwayman active in Restoration England.) *Crichton* – originally dedicated to Lady Blessington – was instead a historical novel charting the adventures of the dashing Scots polymath James ('the Admirable') Crichton at the court of Henri III of France – a real historical figure known for his extraordinary academic accomplishments before his murder at the age of twenty-one in 1582. This was clearly a figure that had always interested Ainsworth, having been cited as the subject of a play by 'Richard Clitheroe' in his youthful *New Monthly* prank. Presumably, he didn't want to repeat himself by just writing another *Rookwood*.

Crichton was to be published by Macrone, but getting it off the ground was a nightmare, publication delays dissipating the momentum built up by *Rookwood*. Ainsworth's correspondence with Macrone shows a lot of technical problems with the printers – Hansard of Paternoster Row – involving typographical errors (there was a lot of Latin) and arguments about typeface. Macrone also took an age deciding with Ainsworth on an artist, initially suggesting Thackeray, who was then in Paris studying art and could thus reproduce authentic locations from the story, although Ainsworth's first choice was Maclise. Ainsworth nevertheless thought very highly of Thackeray, then just another struggling literary journalist, and took every opportunity to promote him, Thackeray writing to Macrone, 'Give Ainsworth a shake of the hand he has praised me so much that I must love him ever after.'[14] And then Macrone died, the project passing to Richard Bentley.

Writing the book was arduous, curtailing many of Ainsworth's social activities. His often-daily correspondence with Crossley also dropped off, establishing a pattern whereby he went quiet when writing a new novel unless in search of research material. Crossley, for example, translated two works by the original Crichton – the *Epicedium* on Cardinal Borromeo and his *Gratulatio* to Gaspar Visconti – from Latin into English so Ainsworth could append them to the novel. These appendixes are symbolic of the project as a whole, which eschews the spontaneity of *Rookwood* for historical accuracy and scholarship, complete with footnotes and passages in Latin, Spanish and old French. Unlike its predecessor, which, like *Sir John Chiverton* was more a Gothic than a historical romance, *Crichton* is *very* historical. Whether or not Scott would have approved or seen more 'dragging in' is open to question, Ainsworth's meticulous detail in setting often getting in the way of the already complicated story, in which Crichton bests the academics of the Sorbonne, enters the intrigue-laden court of Henri III (and the power behind the throne, Catherine de' Medici and her agent, the sinister alchemist Ruggieri), foils a conspiracy against the king and gets the girl, Esclairmonde, the Princess of Condé. The evocation of time, place, personalities and politics is therefore impressive – aside from a rather hasty happy ending – but in a form more suited at times to nonfiction than fiction, despite Ainsworth's flair for brisk narrative pacing.

The first edition of *Crichton* sold out on the day it was published, 1 March 1837, probably in anticipation of another *Rookwood* – but while the reviewers were unanimous in their applause, the character of Crichton himself was too remote, clean-cut, perfect and invulnerable to appeal to fans of Dick Turpin. The novel therefore ultimately failed to achieve the popular appeal of its predecessor, largely by being too clever for its own good.

Ainsworth had been kicking around the idea of a *Pickwickesque* serial provisionally entitled *Lions of London* with Macrone, but this died with the publisher. Instead, because of the ultimately lukewarm public response to *Crichton*, he bowed to public pressure and started thinking about a more obvious follow-up to *Rookwood*, writing to Crossley in May, 1837:

> I think you will be glad to hear that I propose visiting Manchester for a few days next week, when I hope to spend some pleasant hours with you ... I want to consult you about my new romance which is a tale of the reign of George the first – and as that monarch cuts a conspicuous figure in the story, I shall really be thankful if you can lend me any memoirs, or other matter, relating to him, or put me in the way of finding them. My exact year is 1724. I mention this that you may just direct your thoughts to the period. It is my intention to introduce Jack Sheppard. Have you any history of Old Newgate? or any pictures of that prison ... I need to write, or attempt to write, a sort of Hogarthian novel – describing London at the beginning of the eighteenth century. But all this, and a good deal more, we will talk over when we meet.[15]

Until the end of the following year, the new romance is referred to as *Thames Darrell*. 'Thames' was the hero of the tale, an orphan ignorant of his noble birth adopted by a Southwark carpenter and named from the river from which he was rescued as a baby, having been thrown in and presumed drowned by his wicked uncle. But just as Dick Turpin had dominated the author's fancy and divided the text of *Rookwood*, the character of Jack Sheppard – a Georgian thief once famous for his daring prison escapes – completely takes over, overwriting Thames Darrell in both central role and title. The planned historical novel on George I thus became the purest of Ainsworth's Newgate narratives, *Jack Sheppard*.

Chapter 8

Dickens in Manchester

Ainsworth expected 1838 to be another good year, writing to Crossley that:

> I have a tremendous year before me. And though *Thames Darrell* is a heavy mill-stone enough – it is nothing to what is to come. In sober seriousness, I mean to write as hard as I can, and make as much as I can, in every way. I have no lack of employment if I choose to accept it – and, indeed I have already accepted a reasonable years [*sic*] work. I think I told you that Dickens and I are about to illustrate Ancient and modern London in a Pickwick form. He expects much from this.[1] [The letter accompanied the repayment of a £150 loan, with interest, from Crossley, who frequently bailed him out against future profits from the next book.]

The proposed collaboration, which was a resurrection of the *Lions of London* project, with Ainsworth writing the historical sections, Dickens the contemporary, never came to fruition, although they later worked together on *The Pic Nic Papers* 'By various hands', a collection published by Colburn and edited by Dickens to raise money for John Macrone's widow and children.

Ainsworth remained estranged from his own wife and her family, although he was begrudgingly allowed some access to his daughters. While working on the first draft of *Jack Sheppard*, on 6 March 1838, he received the news that Fanny had died at her father's house in Notting Hill, aged just thirty-three. He had just started 'Epoch II', the second act of the novel, which is set twelve years after the first. It was also twelve years since he and Fanny had impetuously married, full of youthful love and hope, and the chapter he wrote that day recorded his emotional state, opening:

Twelve years! How many events have occurred during that long interval! how many changes have taken place! The whole aspect of things is altered. The child has sprung into a youth; the youth has become a man; the man has already begun to feel the advances of age. Beauty has bloomed and faded. Fresh flowers of loveliness have budded, expanded, died. The fashions of the day have become antiquated. New customs have prevailed over the old. Parties, politics, and popular opinions have changed. The crown has passed from the brow of one monarch to that of another. Habits and tastes are no longer the same. We, ourselves, are scarcely the same we were twelve years ago.

Twelve years ago! It is an awful retrospect. Dare we look back upon the darkened vista, and, in imagination, retrace the path we have trod? With how many vain hopes is it shaded! with how many good resolutions, never fulfilled, is it paved! Where are the dreams of ambition in which, twelve years ago, we indulged? Where are the aspirations that fired us — the passions that consumed us then? Has our success in life been commensurate with our own desires — with the anticipations formed of us by others? Or, are we not blighted in heart, as in ambition? Has not the loved one been estranged by doubt, or snatched from us by the cold hand of death? Is not the goal, towards which we pressed, further off than ever — the prospect before us cheerless as the blank behind? — Enough of this. Let us proceed with our tale.[2]

On the same day, he wrote to Crossley: 'My poor wife is no more. She expired yester-morning, after a severe and painful illness at her father's house at Kensington Terrace. It has been a great shock to me – for notwithstanding our differences, I can never forget she was my wife, and the mother of my children.'[3]

He kept writing.

Despite the consistent sales of *Rookwood* (which went to five editions within the first three years of publication), and a modest showing from *Crichton*, Ainsworth's extravagant lifestyle had left his private finances depleted. The death of Fanny also plunged him back into another stressful and expensive legal battle with her family, this time over the custody of his three daughters. 'I am so bothered that I hardly know which way to turn,' Ainsworth later wrote to Crossley. 'She is giving me all the trouble she can.'[4] 'She' was Fanny's sister Emily, who blamed Ainsworth for her sister's untimely death. Emily had taken the children out of school and was denying Ainsworth any access. Forster, the fixer, who belonged to the Inner Temple although he never practised, was helping Ainsworth negotiate informally, backed up by a London lawyer called Loaden. 'I saw Forster respecting the proposed arrangement on behalf of my children,' Ainsworth wrote to Crossley a couple of weeks after Fanny's death, 'And agreed with him, that he should have an interview with Miss Ebers':

> Mr. Loaden advised me in conclusion, to take matters quietly, to see as much as possible of my children; and in every way to engage their affection: and to commit myself to writing. Thus far I have followed his advice ... I must however say that this line of conduct is extremely repugnant to my feeling. It seems to me like a tacit acknowledgement of the weakness of my cause ... Forster thinks the plan suggested by Mr. Loaden is the only safe course. One thing is certainly clear, that if I am to claim the children I am not in a condition to meet any claims the Ebers may charge against me, if they can substantiate them.

Speaking from bitter experience, he concluded the letter, 'I doubt the possibility of my outwitting the Ebers.'[5]

Emily's plan was to adopt the children as her own, and to get them away from Ainsworth by moving to France. Ainsworth fought tooth and nail but did not get his 'little girls' back until autumn 1839, and then only after John Ebers had got £300 out of him for two years of backdated maintenance. He survived financially during this period by borrowing money from Crossley, writing that:

> If needful, I can obtain the advance from Bentley. But it will be attended with bother, and a humiliating sense of obligation, which I would gladly avoid ... I have many other friends to whom I could apply, but you are the only person to whom I choose to be under such an obligation.[6]

These problems dogged Ainsworth throughout the composition of *Jack Sheppard*, although Ellis omits the entire episode from his biography, noting only that Forster 'acted as confidential agent for Ainsworth in a delicate family matter, which it is not within the province of this work to detail'.[7]

Dickens, Ainsworth and Forster remained very tight, Forster later writing of this period:

> A friend now especially welcome, also, was the novelist, Mr. Ainsworth, who shared with us incessantly for the three following years in the companionship which began at his house; with whom we visited, during two of those years, friends of art and letters in his native Manchester, from among whom Dickens brought away his Brothers Cheeryble, and to whose sympathy in tastes and pursuits, accomplishments in literature, open-hearted generous ways, and cordial hospitality, many of the pleasures of later years were due.[8]

This is about as close to gushing as Forster ever gets, although for someone so influential in Dickens's early years – and godfather to one of his children, Henry Fielding Dickens – Ainsworth's name only appears seven times in Forster's *Life of Dickens*.

Dickens visited Manchester twice that year, Forster inevitably in tow, dining with Crossley and several other of Ainsworth's old friends. Dickens was then writing the serial that would become his third novel, *Nicholas Nickleby*, and in private Ainsworth and Crossley weren't that impressed, Ainsworth writing to Crossley in April:

> I met Lockhart the other day looking quite the old man – and very much shaken with rheumatism. He is so much altered that I scarcely knew him. Of course you have read his last volume of the life of Scott. I have been greatly delighted with it … I am sorry to hear what you say about *Nicholas Nickleby*. I feared it was not so well adapted for general popularity as the *Pickwick* – though in reality far better. But the truth is, to write for the mob, you must not write too weak. The newspaper level is the true line to take.

> In proportion as Dickens departs from this, he will decline in popular favour. Of this I am certain. I think, however, he has so much tact that he will yet retrieve himself ... I asked Lockhart what he thought of the *Pickwick*. He said he thought 'it was all very well' – 'but', with one of his usual laughs, 'damned low!'[9]

Ainsworth, it would seem, had learned from *Crichton*, and was adapting his style to suit his market. There's also a trace of professional rivalry creeping in – or wishful thinking – as Dickens's ascendancy after the glory days of *Rookwood* must have been as disconcerting as it was sudden. Because of the Ebers, Ainsworth's own third novel, *Jack Sheppard*, was also falling behind schedule.

Too busy to accompany Dickens, Ainsworth was excited for his friend to see his beloved home town. Determined that he should receive a warm welcome, he provided him with letters of introduction to Crossley and Gilbert Winter, another friend and lawyer:

> I am sure it will give you pleasure to receive this note, handed to you, as it will be, by my friend Mr. Charles Dickens, and I am equally sure that it will give you pleasure to show him any attention in your power during his stay in Manchester. I rather suspect that he is reconnoitring for character; and, perhaps, you may aid his researches; but, at all events, you can help him to the best glass of wine in Manchester, and that will materially assist his judgement in coming to a conclusion of the habits of my townsmen ... I greatly regret that I cannot accompany him. Apropos of accompaniments, I forgot to mention that Mr. Browne, the artist, who illustrates *Nicholas*, will travel with Dickens so that I must beg you to extend your hospitality to him. Pray let them see the Club – and taste its cookery.[10]

The 'Club' was the Unicorn Inn at Smithy Door, where the teenaged Ainsworth and his friends had hung out in the *Pocket Magazine* period. 'Mr. Browne' was Hablot Knight Browne, or 'Phiz', who illustrated several of Lytton's, Dickens's and Ainsworth's books over the years. Forster then joined the party, warranting a further introduction:

It appears you are to have a meeting of literary men in Manchester. I have given Dickens a letter to you, and now I wish to add a special introduction for my friend Forster, who you will know by reputation. This is Dickens's most intimate friend, as well as mine, and he visits Manchester in order to see it in company with Dickens.[11]

The next day, he adds, 'Dickens's object is to see the interior of a Cotton mill – I fancy with reference to some of his publications.'[12]

Dining with Winter and Crossley, Dickens met the calico merchants Daniel and William Grant, brothers from Scotland who had moved to Manchester and caught the wave of commercial growth that had accompanied industrial expansion. Now very rich and affable men, they were immortalised by Dickens and Phiz in *Nicholas Nickleby* as the key secondary characters Charles and Ned Cheeryble, the jovial, generous and wealthy twins who never forgot their humble origins. Everything went very well, Crossley communicating his favourable impressions of the company to his friend, as did they, Ainsworth writing back:

> Dickens and Forster called on me on Sunday to give me an account of their expedition to Manchester and to bring me their two Olivers, Twist and Cromwell – have you read *Oliver Twist*? ... Dickens is an excellent fellow – I am glad you like him – and so is my friend Fury-Fire-the-Faggot [Forster]. The twain expressed themselves highly, most highly, delighted with you and G. Winter's attention.[13]

In private, though, Dickens made fun of his provincial hosts, writing to Forster:

> I guessed Crossley at once, by the 'shibboleth of authorship' and the repetition of the 'no' which is the style of oratory that regaleth the ears of the Borough-reeve. It is a malicious thing to say, but I should better like to see our dear good friend at a dinner of his fellow townsmen (or *by* his fellow townsmen) than any mixed sight of pleasure and comicality that I can imagine.[14]

He was right about the borough-reeve, though (the chief municipal officer in unincorporated towns); Gilbert Winter had been one in the mid-1820s.

Dickens and Forster returned to Manchester early in the new year, this time accompanied by Ainsworth, who arranged that they should stay with his friend, Hugh Beaver, a successful mill owner. 'I don't know whether I ought to test your hospitality so far as I am about to do,' he wrote to Beaver:

> but, at all events, I trust the peculiarity of the case will plead my excuse. I am about to visit Manchester on the 12th of January in company with my friends Mr. Charles Dickens, the author of the *Pickwick Papers*, and Mr. Forster, the author of the *Life of Cromwell*. Now, could it be consistent with your arrangements to receive us from Saturday the 12th to Wednesday the 16th the utmost extent of our stay?

This letter is particularly interesting in that Ainsworth appears to now cheerfully defer to Dickens's superior literary stature, adding that 'You will find both my friends most agreeable, each informed men – and I need not enlarge upon the merits of Mr. Dickens; as, by common consent, he has been installed in the throne of letters, vacated by Scott.'[15] Crossley and Winter organised a dinner in honour of the two literary giants, but no one seems to have dared give one primacy over the other, causing Ainsworth to fret a bit more than somewhat, writing to Crossley:

> It is the wish of all three of us to get the public dinner over as soon as possible; and we should therefore prefer its taking place on Monday the 14th. We dine at 'The Temple' [Beaver's house on Cheetham Hill Road] at 7.30 on Saturday, where you will be invited. We will dine with you on Tuesday, and on Wednesday at Stocks [Gilbert Winter's house]. Now, in respect to the public dinner. Is it to be given to me or Dickens— or to both? Acting upon your former letter, I invited my friends to accompany me, imagining the dinner was to be given in my honour: but I have no feeling whatever in the matter, and only desire to have a distinct understanding about it. If the dinner is given expressly to

Dickens, I think a letter of invitation should be sent him. But you are the best judge of the propriety of this step; and it might be only giving needless trouble, as he is sure to come if the dinner is to be given to me. However, I should be glad to know it as soon as possible, in order to prepare myself for the event, as I should like it to go off with éclat. I shall feel greatly obliged by your giving me an accurate idea of the arrangement of the toasts, etc. I must own I feel rather nervous when I think of it, but I will endeavour to acquit myself with credit.[16]

This was to take place, Ainsworth had told Beaver, 'at the Club on Monday the 14th, with Mr. G. Winter in the chair'. Crossley's biographer, Stephen Collins, notes that oddly there is no report of the dinner in the press, although it undoubtedly took place. The 'Club' is similarly mysterious, though Collins makes an informed guess that it was the Union Club on the corner of Mosley Street and Nicholas Street. But wherever it was, Ainsworth wrote to Crossley about it again, still mithering that 'I am devilish nervous about the speechifying'.[17] This is out of character, and Collins reads this as a clear sign of rivalry between the two writers, which seems likely, as well as a genuine anxiety that the charismatic Dickens could upstage him on his home turf.[18] It seems to have gone well, though, Ainsworth writing to Crossley after the event that 'we had a jolly journey up to town, and are all looking forward to seeing you here to repay your hospitality'.[19] As ever, Crossley did not take up the invitation to London.

February saw Dickens's twenty-seventh birthday, which he celebrated with his closest friends, as can be seen from this surviving invitation to the actor J.P. Harley:

I took it into my head yesterday to get up an impromptu dinner on this auspicious occasion – only my own folks, Leigh Hunt, Ainsworth, and Forster. I know you can't dine here in consequence of the tempestuous weather on the Covent Garden shores, but if you will come in when you have done Trinculizing, you will delight me greatly, and add in no inconsiderable degree to the 'conviviality' of the meeting.[20] [Harley was playing Trinculo in Macready's production of *The Tempest*.]

Of course, Ainsworth was invited, being one of the inner circle. And their professional relationship was similarly close. In January 1839, *Jack Sheppard* had begun its serial run in *Bentley's Miscellany*, edited by Dickens. *Oliver Twist* was at this point coming to a conclusion in the same magazine, and for four months they appeared together, both illustrated by George Cruikshank, and both stories about young boys drawn into the criminal underworld. 'I hope you like "Jack",' Ainsworth wrote to Crossley. 'You will be pleased to hear that it has made a most successful launch. Bentley is in tip-top spirits.'[21]

Things were looking up for Ainsworth, but as often happened in his stories, there was a storm gathering.

Chapter 9

A Sort of Hogarthian Novel

Jack Sheppard was worth the wait. *Oliver Twist* was a hard act to follow, but however difficult the business of life had been during its composition, *Jack Sheppard* showed its author at the top of his game, his craftsmanship honed by the two previous novels and his keen sense of the public taste for outlaws and antiheroes. The scholarship of *Crichton* was still there, in the vivid evocation of Georgian London, but now in balance with a crisply paced and tightly plotted adventure; more realistic and emotionally deep than *Rookwood*, while retaining some sensational gothic flourishes.

Along with a dash of *The Beggar's Opera*, *Jack Sheppard* notionally follows the structure of William Hogarth's series of engravings *Industry and Idleness* (1747), parallel narratives across twelve plates charting the lives of two apprentices who start out at the same point but come to very different ends, one living a life of vice, the other virtue. *Jack Sheppard* is thus the story of two apprentices, the fictional Thames Darrell and the historical Jack Sheppard. The novel is divided into three 'epochs', a three-act dramatic structure that suits Ainsworth's fundamentally theatrical style. Epoch the First, set in 1703, takes place in one night when the protagonists are newly born babies and acts as a prologue. Epoch the Second, 1715, covers a few days in June and shows the adolescent Jack's fall from grace and into the clutches of the evil thief-taker and criminal mastermind Jonathan Wild, and the beds of the prostitutes Edgeworth Bess and Poll Maggot. Thames, meanwhile, falls into the equally nasty hands of his evil uncle, Sir Rowland Trenchard, who is Wild's silent partner. Epoch the Third, 1724, shows the six months leading up to Jack's capture and execution. It opens with Jack at the height of his success as a criminal, and the return of Thames, who escaped his uncle and fled to France where he became a prosperous merchant. Disgusted at a murder that takes place during a robbery arranged by Wild, Jack turns against him and helps Thames restore his family fortune, except when locked up, which allows Ainsworth to recreate the daring prison escapes that had guaranteed the original Jack Sheppard his place in the Newgate Calendars. Wild murders Sir Rowland and traps Jack at his mother's graveside. Jack dies bravely on the gallows, Thames's birthright is established, and he marries his childhood sweetheart, Winifred, his old master's daughter. We are reassured, in one of Ainsworth's characteristic historical closures, that Wild was convicted and hanged 'seven months afterwards, with every ignominy, at the very gibbet to which he had brought his victim'.[1]

In his own day, the original John 'Jack' Sheppard had achieved a certain notoriety, not for his crimes (which were unremarkable acts of burglary around Holborn in the early 1720s), but for his increasingly ingenious and cheeky prison escapes. He even broke out of the condemned hold at Newgate and, when recaptured, was placed in a fortified room in the heart of the gaol known as the 'Castle', chained hand and foot with 300-pound iron fetters and attached to the stone floor with an iron staple, just to be on the safe side. Here he held court like a celebrity in a green room. Hogarth himself was one of the crowds of gentry who paid the turnkeys 1/6 to visit Jack Sheppard in the Castle in 1724, by now famous for his previous escapes as well as his open defiance of the thief-taker Jonathan Wild. Hogarth's father-in-law, Sir James Thornhill, also visited Sheppard and painted a portrait of him that looked more like that of a poet than a housebreaker. Ainsworth cheekily dramatises the scene in his chapter 'How Jack's portrait was painted', placing Thornhill, Hogarth and John Gay together, suggesting, probably correctly, that Jack inspired both *The Beggar's Opera* and *Industry and Idleness*. When Jack became tired of all this attention, he escaped again. Unfortunately, he wasn't very bright, and he was recaptured, dead drunk, in an alehouse on Newgate Street, still within sight of the prison. He was hanged at Tyburn on 23 November 1724, aged twenty-two. He did not die well; being a small man, the drop didn't break his neck and he took a long time to strangle under his own body weight.[2]

Half a dozen or so biographies of Sheppard were in circulation by the day of his execution (as well as numerous broadsheets, ballads and a couple of plays), including two pamphlets often attributed to Defoe, which became, and remain, the principal sources on Sheppard for later writers.[3] His story also seems likely to have inspired *The Beggar's Opera* as Ainsworth conjectured – MacHeath, like Sheppard, having two lovers, while Mr Peachum is undoubtedly modelled on Jonathan Wild, of whom Defoe also wrote a short biography after his execution the following year.[4] The fame of the real Jack Sheppard and Jonathan Wild was an early example of a media-generated fad, however, and they were soon forgotten.

While *Oliver Twist* and *Jack Sheppard* continued their popular runs in *Bentley's* (*Nicholas Nickleby* being serialised at the same time by Chapman and Hall), Dickens was becoming increasingly dissatisfied with his relationship with Richard Bentley, much as he had with John Macrone. Undoubtedly on the rise but not yet on the A-list, when Dickens had signed with Bentley towards the end of 1836, the £20 a month salary to edit the *Miscellany* and £500 each for two serials had seemed perfectly equitable. This had been raised by Bentley the following year to £30 a month and £750 for each serial. Now, his fame and saleability assured by the *Sketches*, *Pickwick*, *Oliver Twist* and *Nicholas Nickleby*, Dickens still felt that he was being exploited, despite being under a mutually agreed contract. He was also finding the strain of his editorial responsibilities and writing two complex serials simultaneously too much. As he had started working on the second serial, *Barnaby Rudge*, after returning from Manchester, his first thought was to withhold it from Bentley. Forster talked him out of this, and an agreement was made with Bentley to delay it for six months, with the proviso that Dickens committed to editing the *Miscellany* for another six months and agreed to take on no other new projects. The fee for *Barnaby Rudge* was also raised to £4,000 and Bentley sold him the copyright to *Oliver Twist*. Negotiations broke down, however, and Dickens's penultimate communication with his employer, the one before his letter of resignation, was bristling with anger. 'If you presume to address me again in the style of offensive impertinence which marks your last communication,' he wrote, 'I will from that moment abandon at once and for ever all conditions and agreements that may exist between us.'[5] Between the low self-esteem of Dickens's poverty-stricken childhood, his resulting and lifelong fears over money, and his need to always be right, Bentley had clearly touched a nerve, and Dickens resigned as editor of the *Miscellany* two days later. Whatever this was remains a mystery, as the days covering these events in Dickens's diary have been torn out. From this point on, Dickens dealt only with Bentley's solicitors.

Probably because he wanted a safe pair of hands to see out the last episodes of *Oliver Twist*, Dickens persuaded Ainsworth to go after the editorship. After some initial trepidation on both sides – Ainsworth wasn't keen on taking up a Dickens cast-off while Bentley later claimed that Ainsworth was 'forced upon' him – he signed with Bentley at a salary of £51 a month, agreeing, as had Dickens, to also provide two serials. Forster, who had been advising Dickens and Ainsworth, thought the additional obligation a bad move, writing to Ainsworth:

> I write to you one hasty but most earnest entreaty not to sign any such agreement as that you described to me last night. I foresee the result if you do: you will be in Bentley's power. I implore you not to do it. You deceive yourself; most men do. But why have men friends if a friend should not, at such a moment, interfere to avert the ill consequence of such self-delusion, so miserably common to all of us. Don't disregard what I now say to you. You can accomplish all you desire with Bentley, without putting on his fetters. Nor is it from him alone you will run the danger of incurring serious annoyance — but from all who are made parties to this agreement — the mass of the public included. As your sincerest friend, let my advice have some influence with you. I could not sleep last night for thinking of the misery you were wilfully incurring. Remember what I told you yesterday — that you are now in a better position than Bentley. You can get all you wish from him, and hold a superiority over him, if you do not wilfully and willingly put yourself beneath his feet.
>
> Your friend as you know me,
> John Forster.[6]

Ainsworth decided not to take this advice, and the brittle Forster immediately took this as a personal slight. Soon, rumours began to spread that Forster was behind Dickens breaking his contract. Further gossip quite mistakenly (or maliciously) put it about that the originator of the first rumour was Ainsworth (the source appears to have been Bentley), leading Dickens to attack on his friends' behalf, writing to Ainsworth:

My dear Ainsworth,

If the subject of this letter, or anything contained in it, should eventually become the occasion of any disagreement between you and me, it would cause me very deep and sincere regret. But with this contingency — even this before me, I feel that I must speak out without reserve, and that every manly, honest, and just consideration impels me to do so.

By some means — by what means in the first instance I scarcely know — the late negotiations between yourself, myself, and Mr. Bentley, have placed a mutual friend of ours in a false position and one in which he has no right to stand; and exposed him to an accusation — very rife and current indeed, just now — equally untrue and undeserved ...

He then outlined his case, at length, concluding:

But however painful it will be to put myself in communication once again with Mr. Bentley and openly appeal to you to confirm what I shall tell him, there is no alternative unless you will frankly and openly, and for the sake of your old friend, as well as my intimate and valued one, avow to Mr. Bentley yourself that he [Forster] is not to blame, that you heard him again and again refuse to interfere although deeply impressed with the hardship of my case — and that you proposed concessions which he, feeling the position in which he stood, could not have suggested. Believe me, Ainsworth, that for your sake, no less than on Forster's account, this should be done ... I do not mean to hurt or offend you by anything I have said, and I should be truly grieved to find I have done so. But I must speak strongly because I feel strongly, and because I have a misgiving that even now I have been silent too long.

My dear Ainsworth, I am
Faithfully yours,
Charles Dickens.[7]

A distinct cooling of the friendship followed, despite Ellis's predictably upbeat conclusion that 'Happily this disagreeable affair did not cause any breach of the intimate friendship existing between Dickens and Ainsworth'.[8] Peter Ackroyd is much closer to the mark, writing:

> Dickens, on this occasion as on so many others [was] being guided principally by his impetuosity in private dealings as well as by his readiness to take offence. Notably, too, in this instance, and again in so many others, is his refusal to believe that he is ever mistaken or ever in the wrong; throughout his life he always needed to be *right*, and any attempt to suggest that he was not wholly without blemish was met at once with irritable aggression.[9]

Ainsworth, who took over from Dickens in March, was a model editor. His payments to contributors were generous and prompt, he personally read all submissions, and was unfailingly courteous to his writers, being particularly keen to support young authors. He never rejected a piece without replying with constructive and kind feedback, and suggestions for alternative routes to publication. In short, he treated his contributors with the same warmth and respect as his friends, and significant work commissioned and published in *Bentley's* under Ainsworth's stewardship included a further series of Barham's *Ingoldsby Legends*, Longfellow's 'The Village Blacksmith', 'The Wreck of the Hesperus' and selected poems from *Voices of the Night*, and Poe's 'The Fall of the House of Usher'.

When Dickens had passed the reins to Ainsworth, he concluded his final editorial:

> In fact, then, my child, you have changed hands. Henceforth I resign you to the guardianship and protection of one of my most intimate and valued friends, MR. AINSWORTH, with whom, and with you, my best wishes and warmest feelings will ever remain. I reap no gain from parting from you, nor will any conveyance of your property be required, for in this respect you have always been literally Bentley's Miscellany and never mine … With hat in hand, I approach side by side with the friend who travelled with me on the old road, and presume to solicit favour and kindness in behalf of him and his new charge, both for their sakes and that of the old coachman, Boz.[10]

J. Hain Friswell later wrote of this handover that 'The new whip, having mounted the box, drove straight to Newgate.'[11] That he did, although it was Dickens and Bentley who had commissioned *Jack Sheppard.*

The serial was a triumph, surpassing even the glory days of *Rookwood.* In October, before its completion in the *Miscellany,* Bentley published *Jack Sheppard* as a triple-decker novel, including twenty-seven engravings by Cruikshank and a portrait of the author by R.J. Lane. The success of the book staggered literary London. Sales were enormous, initially exceeding 3,000 copies a week, eclipsing those of *Oliver Twist,* which Bentley had published the previous year. 'For a time,' recalled the journalist and publisher Henry Vizetelly, 'Dickens's star paled.'[12] As with *Rookwood,* the penny-a-liners paid homage, knocking the book off shamelessly. *The History of Jack Sheppard* by John Williams depicted Jack as a heroic figure who infiltrates the criminal underworld as part of a scheme to restore the rightful inheritance of Edgeworth Bess, a pure and persecuted heroine rather than an aggressive prostitute; *The Eventful Life and Unparalleled Exploits of the Notorious Jack Sheppard* by T. White concentrates on the Jacobite intrigues of secondary character Mr Kneebone, cramming a brief summary of Sheppard's career into the conclusion, and *The Life and Adventures of Jack Sheppard* by G. Purkess simply plagiarises Ainsworth. 'The success of Jack is pretty certain,' Ainsworth wrote to Crossley in the autumn. 'They are bringing him out in half the theatres in London.'[13]

And so they were. By the end of October, there were eight stage versions running concurrently in London. Ainsworth and Cruikshank publicly supported these unlicensed adaptations of their work, whereas Dickens, in general, loathed it when it happened to him; Forster, for example, reporting that 'I was with him at a representation of his *Oliver Twist* ... at the Surrey Theatre, when in the middle of the first scene he laid himself down upon the floor in a corner of the box and never rose from it until the drop-scene fell.'[14]

Ainsworth, on the other hand, endorsed J.T. Haines's version of *Jack Sheppard* at the Royal Surrey Theatre while Cruikshank acted as an adviser to the set designers and builders. The author's letter to the manager, G.B. Davidge, praising the production, was printed on all programmes and daily newspaper advertisements (for which he received a one-off royalty payment of £20, the only money he ever made directly from any of these dramas, although several were still running when he died):

> Sir, – Having, in compliance with your request, witnessed your Rehearsal, and perused the Drama founded on JACK SHEPPARD, in preparation at the Surrey Theatre, I am satisfied it will furnish a complete representation of the Principal Scenes of the Romance; and have, therefore, no hesitation in giving my entire sanction to the performance. The fact of the whole of the Scenery having been superintended by Mr. George Cruikshank, must be a sufficient guarantee to the Public for its excellence and accuracy.[15]

He also furnished W.T. Moncrieff of the Victoria Theatre with an advance copy of the final instalment of the serial for his scriptwriters.

By far the best loved of all these plays was J.B. Buckstone's version at the Adelphi starring the legendary Mrs Keeley (Mary Anne Goward) as Jack Sheppard. What made 'Bucky's' production different was his astute inclusion of many of the flash songs from *Rookwood*. Each performance concluded with a raucous encore of 'Nix My Dolly, Pals' by the full cast and the audience, led by Jack, Blueskin (played by the equally famous Paul Bedford), Poll Maggot and Edgeworth Bess (the very lovely Mrs Nailer and Miss Campbell), which had been set to music by G.H. Rodwell, operatic composer and proprietor of the theatre. As Sir Theodore Martin later wrote of this period:

> 'Nix my dolly, pals, fake away!' travelled everywhere, and made the patter of thieves and burglars 'familiar in our mouths as household words'. It deafened us in the streets, where it was so popular with the organ-grinders and German bands as Sullivan's brightest melodies ever were in later day. It clanged at midday from the steeple of St. Giles, the Edinburgh Cathedral ... it was whistled by every dirty guttersnipe, and chanted in drawing-rooms by fair lips, little knowing the meaning of the words they sang.[16]

As a sign of the beginnings of a cultural shift from Regency to Victorian, however, the critics who had lauded *Rookwood* and *Crichton* a few years before now lined up to tear into *Jack Sheppard*. As 'Bon Gaultier', for example, Martin and collaborator Professor William Aytoun set out to 'open people's eyes to the dangerous and degrading taste of the hour', with Newgate pastiches of Wordsworth:

> Turpin, thou shouldst be living at this hour,
> England hath need of thee …

> Great men have been among us, —Names that lend
> A lustre to our calling; better none;
> Maclaine, Duval, Dick Turpin, Barrington,

> Blueskin and others, who called Sheppard friend …

And Shelley:

> I met a cracksman coming down the Strand,
>   Who said, 'A huge Cathedral, piled of stone,
> Stands in a churchyard, near St Martin's Le Grand,
>   Where keeps Saint Paul his sacerdotal throne.
> A street runs by it to the northward. There
> For cab and bus is writ "No Thoroughfare",
>   The Mayor and Councilmen do so command.
> And in that street a shop, with many a box,
>   Upon whose sign these fateful words I scanned:
> 'My name is Chubb, who makes the Patent Locks;
>   Look on my works, ye burglars, and despair!'
> Here made he pause, like one that sees a blight
>   Mar all his hopes, and sighed with drooping air,
> 'Our game is up, my covies, blow me tight!'[17]

Thackeray similarly used satire to express his disapproval, contributing a serial to *Fraser's* called *Catherine, A Story* four months after *Jack Sheppard* commenced in *Bentley's* under the pseudonym 'Ikey Solomons, Esq., Jr' (Ikey Solomon was an infamous Regency fence lately transported).[18] The story was based on the Newgate Calendar favourite, Catherine Hayes, who had manipulated her son and her lover into murdering her husband in 1726. The story sends up Ainsworth's florid historical style, and Thackeray frequently interrupts the narrative with polemics about the current fashion for criminal romance:

> And here, though we are only in the third chapter of this history, we feel almost sick of the characters that appear in it, and the adventures which they are called on to go through. But how can we help ourselves? The public will hear of nothing but rogues; and the only way in which poor authors, who must live, can act honestly by the public and themselves, is to paint such thieves as they are: not dandy, poetical, rosewater thieves; but real downright scoundrels, leading scroundrelly lives, drunken, profligate, dissolute, low; as scoundrels will be. They don't quote Plato, like Eugene Aram; or live like gentlemen, and sing the pleasantest ballads in the world like Jolly Dick Turpin ... or die white-washed saints, like poor 'Biss Dadsy' in 'Oliver Twist'.[19]

At its conclusion, the serial becomes a literary essay on Dickens and Ainsworth. There's also a companion article – 'William Ainsworth and *Jack Sheppard*' – which suggests that the novel and its manifold theatrical adaptations could turn impressionable boys to a life of crime, echoing Maginn's dire warning in 1834. This was as much about Thackeray's frustration at so far failing to succeed as an author while what he believed to be immoral and badly written books made their creators rich and famous. Generally speaking, nobody got the joke. *Catherine* failed to find popular favour either as a satire or a Newgate narrative (much to the chagrin of its author), and it's notable only as the first full-length novel by the future author of *Vanity Fair.*

But *Catherine* was just the beginning. When *Jack Sheppard* was released as a novel in three volumes, the *Athenaeum* used the occasion to publish a long article on contemporary literature and the condition of England within a review, arguing that a decline in national standards of taste, intellect and morality was distressingly apparent: 'Should an ambassador from some far distant country arrive on our shores for the purpose of overreaching us in a convention, we know not where he could find a better clue to the infirmities of the national character, than in the columns of our book advertisements.' To the *Athenaeum*, the issue was that literature no longer set the standard, but merely reacted to the popular market. 'In the present age,' the review continued, 'writers take their tone from the readers, instead of giving it; and in which more pains are taken to write down to the mediocrity of the purchasing multitude.'[20] This was a response to a relatively recent development in the relationship between arts and commerce, the old system of literary patronage having been largely replaced by subscription and commercial publishing. For writers, this was good and bad. For the lucky ones, writing became a respectable profession, offering, as in Dickens's case, the opportunity for social advancement as well as a decent income. It also made them slaves to the free market, the same as everyone else.

The *Athenaeum* was, however, careful to avoid any personal attacks. *Jack Sheppard*, on the other hand, was given no quarter:

> If we consider Mr. Ainsworth in the usual light of a mere caterer for the public appetite, and as devoting his talents to a popular work either at his own or his publisher's suggestion, we must freely admit his book to be on a level with the usual specimens of the class, and at least as good as the occasion required. It is not his fault that he has fallen upon evil days, and that, like other tradesmen, he must subordinate his own tastes to those of his customers ... *Jack Sheppard*, then, is a bad book, and what is worse, it is a class of bad books, got up for a bad public; and it is on the last account that we select it for observation, as a specimen of one of those literary peculiarities, which we consider to be signs of the times.[21]

The work of Henry Fielding and John Gay is then invoked as an example of the morally and aesthetically appropriate way of using criminal biography, as long as readers have the brains to appreciate it:

> Writings of this class, it is true, will in all ages be above the general level of the public; too superior for vulgar use, and too exalted for general taste ... without a prompt and exercised intelligence in the reader, without a familiarity with the noble and the beautiful, the irony is lost, the spirit is overlooked, the Beggar's Opera becomes a mere Tom and Jerry, and Jonathan Wild another Jack Sheppard.[22]

Dickens's *Oliver Twist* is excepted, but concern is expressed as to whether he might be popular for the wrong reasons, his readers excited by his 'strong flavour' rather than his 'undercurrent of philosophy'. The piece ends with a flash dialogue scene from *Jack Sheppard*, concluding, 'Such is the "elegant and polite literature" which leads authors on their way to fortune and to fame in this the middle of the nineteenth century.'[23]

A couple of days later, the *Standard*, a daily that reviewed plays rather than books, attacked Ainsworth's novel in an otherwise favourable notice for Buckstone's adaptation at the Adelphi:

> Most persons have heard of Captain Ainsworth's *Life and Death of Jack Sheppard*, and many there are who have had sufficient pertinacity of purpose to wade through the almost endless rubbish, balderdash, twaddle, and vulgarity of which it consists.[24]

Sensing blood in the water, and still sulking about the *Bentley's* disagreement and the fact that Ainsworth had outsold his idol, Forster wrote a damning review of *Jack Sheppard* in the *Examiner*:

> We notice this 'romance' with very great reluctance, because we have thought the author capable of better things. It is however in every sense of the word so bad, and has been recommended to circulation by such disreputable means, that the silence we meant to preserve upon the subject would be almost as great a compromise with truth as the morals of the book or the puffs of the bookseller.
>
> Bad as we think the morals, we think the puffs more dangerous. Our silence would never have been broken if the book had been suffered to rest on its own merits. Little danger might then have been anticipated. Poisonous work is done by means of more cunning doses, nor are the ways of licentiousness, for those classes into whose hands such a book was in that case likely to fall, paved with such broad stones.

Even worse, Ainsworth had assisted Moncrieff in his adaptation of the novel at the Surrey, which Forster described as 'the very worst specimen of rank garbage thus stewed up'.[25] Dickens and therefore Forster despised

Moncrieff, who had dramatised both *The Pickwick Papers* and *Nicholas Nickleby* despite objections by the author. To Forster, Ainsworth was colluding with the enemy.

And the fear of the influence of the *Jack Sheppard* plays – over which Ainsworth had no control and from which he received neither fee or royalty – was spreading; not just a fear that working-class boys might take up a life of crime over poverty, factory, field or the army, but that the rebellious nature of their heroes could foster rebellion itself. 'I have been struck', wrote the author and dramatist Mary Russell Mitford to her friend Elizabeth Barrett, 'by the great danger of these times of representing authorities so constantly and fearfully in the wrong, so tyrannous, so devilish as the author has been pleased to portray it in Jack Sheppard.' She concluded:

> Of course Mr Ainsworth had no such design, but such is its effect; and as the millions who see it represented in the minor theatres will not distinguish between now and a hundred years back, all the Chartists in the land are less dangerous than this nightmare of a book.[26]

Although Ainsworth wrote to Crossley that 'Forster's article has been perfectly innocuous, and has done no harm whatever here. In fact, Jack is carrying everything before him,' he must have realised that a moral panic – the so-called 'Newgate Controversy' – was escalating.[27] Even though it initially did his sales more good than harm, his name was increasingly linked to the debate on crime and the attendant fear of the new urban working class. The author of the novel was becoming a convenient scapegoat for its theatrical adaptations, which were increasingly believed to be disseminating moral corruption to the masses and inciting crime, Forster leading the argument by suggesting that there was a potential danger to society 'in the adaptations of the "romance" that are alike rife in the low smoking rooms, the common barbers' shops, the cheap reading places, the private booksellers', and the minor theatres'.[28] Laman Blanchard, a more loyal friend, later wrote of the vituperative critical backlash:

> Critics, who had always a passion for heroes in fetters before, now found out that housebreakers are disreputable characters. They were in raptures with the old-established brigand still, and the freebooter of foreign extraction; they

could hug *Robin Hood* as fondly as ever, and dwell with
unhurt morals on the little peccadilloes of *Rob Roy*; nay,
they had no objection to ride behind *Turpin* to York any day,
and would never feel ashamed of their company; but they
shook their heads at *Sheppard*, because low people began to
run after him at the theatres.[29]

As the sociologist and criminologist Stanley Cohen wrote in his seminal
study *Folk Devils and Moral Panics* (1972), 'Societies appear to be
subject, every now and then, to periods of moral panic.' Cohen defined
this phenomenon as:

A condition, episode, person or group of persons emerges to
become defined as a threat to societal values and interests;
its nature is presented in a stylized and stereotypical fashion
by the mass media; the moral barricades are manned by
editors, bishops, politicians and other right-thinking people;
socially accredited experts pronounce their diagnoses and
solutions; ways of coping are evolved or (more often)
resorted to; the condition then disappears, submerges or
deteriorates and becomes more visible.[30]

In contemporary cultural theory, this process is referred to as a 'deviance
amplification spiral'; those leading the charge are known as 'moral
entrepreneurs'.[31]

This 'effects theory' was considered borne out when, on 5 May 1840,
the former Whig MP for Surrey, the legendarily eccentric Lord William
Russell, had his throat slit by a servant while he slept in his Mayfair home.
The murderer, the Swiss-born valet François Benjamin Courvoisier,
attempted to stage a robbery to misdirect the authorities, but then left all
the loot poorly concealed in his master's house, including a ten pound
note stuffed behind the wainscoting. It was clear to the police that this was
unlikely behaviour for a burglar, and it came out soon after that Russell had
caught his man stealing the plate, and demanded his immediate resignation.
Courvoisier had decided to resolve the matter by permanently silencing
his master, rather than giving up his position without a reference.[32]

The murder caused a sensation. These were scary times for the
ruling classes. The cities were growing at an unprecedented rate, with

London packed with Irish and Jewish immigrants, the homeless, the unemployed, housebreakers, prostitutes and pickpockets, and a new industrial labouring class that had organised into the Chartist movement, calling loudly for electoral reform. At the opening of Parliament that January, Lord Brougham had warned that the country was facing revolution.[33] Had the spirit of the Newport Rising arrived in the capital, Londoners wondered, had Russell's murder been politically motivated? Then reports emerged that Courvoisier had got the idea after reading *Jack Sheppard*…

In the novel, Jack's companion Joseph Blake, or 'Blueskin' – another real Newgate Calendar villain – kills the wife of Jack's old master by cutting her throat during a botched robbery. Although in the name of avarice rather than insurrection, a working-class man had risen up against his master after apparently reading a Newgate novel. After the killer was condemned, Forster returned to his original review in the *Examiner*, which foretold such a disaster, writing a damning editorial that again denounced *Jack Sheppard*:

> In Courvoisier's second confession, which we are more disposed to believe than the first, he ascribes his crimes to the perusal of that detestable book, 'Jack Sheppard'; and certainly it is a publication calculated to familiarize the mind with cruelties and to serve as the cut-throat's manual, or the midnight assassin's *vade-mecum*, in which character we now expect to see it advertised …
>
> If ever there was a publication that deserved to be burnt by the common hangman, it is 'Jack Sheppard'.[34]

The fact that this piece was an editorial also indicated that the matter had now moved out of the literary columns and onto the front pages, which was very bad news for Ainsworth.

You couldn't *buy* publicity like this. The book continued to sell while its author became a pariah, forced to withdraw from candidacy for the Athenaeum Club to avoid the humiliation of rejection, writing to Lady Blessington that:

> After all, your kind exertions on my behalf, in respect to the Athenaeum, were thrown away, — or rather, I was unwilling

to avail myself of them, having been given to understand that I should meet with formidable opposition from a hostile party, whom I must term the Anti-Jack-Sheppardites; and have thought it better to let things take their course, and withdraw.[35]

He was also blackballed at the Trinity Club, the letter informing him of this sent by John Forster, still claiming to be a great friend and signing off 'Always believe me, my dear boy, affecty. Yrs'.

During this period, Ainsworth was engaged with the monumental task of writing two serials for Bentley simultaneously. In consequence, he did not write to Crossley for the better part of the year, and his opinions on the *Jack Sheppard* panic are therefore largely unknown, although he later confided the following to Murdo Young, the editor of the *Sun*, regarding a favourable review of a mid-century reissue of *Jack Sheppard*:

> Permit me to thank you — and to thank you most heartily — for the very gratifying notice of the Cheap Re-issue of my Tales, which you have given in this day's Sun. Your reviewer has done me a great service, and one for which I must ever feel grateful. I allude to his gallant defence of Jack Sheppard. He has spoken the truth, and justified what he advances. The book was run down in certain quarters because it was thought necessary to run down the writer — and a 'cry' was raised. But though this gave an ill reputation to the work in question, the main object of the assailants was unsuccessful. They did not shake my popularity. The attacks, however, gave me considerable annoyance at the time; but I assure you none of them gave me half so much pain as I have just now experienced pleasure in reading the honestly indignant defence which you have been good enough to insert in The Sun.[36]

The young reviewer was Charles Kent, who became the proprietor in 1863, and to whom Ainsworth also wrote on the subject:

> I have just received The Sun of last evening, containing your review of Jack Sheppard. Need I say how much I am indebted to you for that review? It must be gratifying to

me; but it displays great generosity and courage in you to speak out as you have done on the present occasion. I did intend to introduce the republication of this much maligned romance with some prefatory remarks; but I could not have done so without offence to some persons, who, to serve their own purposes, got up a 'cry' against me, but with whom my quarrel is now arranged. It required some forbearance to let the occasion pass, especially as I am sure I could make my case good, for I really believe the romance to be harmless — as harmless at least as Oliver Twist and Paul Clifford. By the bye, I have never compared the last edition of Oliver Twist with the first; but I suspect there are considerable alterations to fit it for the scrupulous reader. This edition of Jack Sheppard has undergone neither revision nor modification. I have left it as I wrote it, with all its sins upon its head. Of this be assured, that in this work, which you have so gallantly and (I believe) so justly defended, I never had the remotest intention of holding up vice to admiration. If I have done so, I believe Hogarth to be equally culpable. Again accept my heartiest thanks, and believe me always

Very sincerely your obliged
W. Harrison Ainsworth.[37]

In an even more candid follow-up, he wrote that 'literature is divided into cliques', and when 'you belong to one party you are run down by another, and if you belong to no party you are run down by all, as I have been'.[38] Without naming any names, it's pretty clear who Ainsworth thought had it in for him, and why.

At the time, only the Courvoisier accusations caused him to publicly break his silence, in a letter to *The Times* that repudiated the confession. 'I have taken means to ascertain the correctness of the report', he wrote, 'and I find it utterly without foundation':

The wretched man declared he had neither read the work in question nor made any such statement. A Collection of Trials of Noted Malefactors (probably 'The Newgate Calendar') had indeed fallen in his way, but the account of

Jack Sheppard contained in this series had not particularly attracted his attention. I am the more anxious to contradict this false and injurious statement because a writer in *The Examiner* of Sunday last, without inquiring into the truth of the matter, has made it the groundwork of a most violent and libellous attack on my romance.

The Times published this letter on 7 July, the day after Courvoisier was hanged outside the debtor's door at Newgate in front of a crowd of nearly 40,000 people. Two days later, *The Times* published a reply from William Evans, the Sherriff of London and Middlesex, contradicting Ainsworth's claim, writing that 'I think it is my duty to state distinctly that Courvoisier did assert to me that the idea of murdering his master was first suggested to him by a perusal of the book called "Jack Sheppard", and that the said book was lent to him by a valet of the Duke of Bedford.'[39] If this is true, it is likely that Courvoisier was trying to offset his own blame by claiming he was a victim of the pernicious literature the newspapers were talking about. Looking at a rope, one will presumably try anything.

Thackeray attended the hanging, as did Dickens, not as a voyeur but a journalist who was opposed to public executions. While expressing his disgust, he also took another shot at Dickens. In a piece for *Fraser's* entitled 'Going to See a Man Hanged', he continued to criticise the unrealistic portrayal of Nancy. 'Boz, who knows life well,' he wrote, 'knows that his Miss Nancy is the most unreal fantastical personage possible; no more like a thief's mistress than one of Gessner's shepherdesses resembles a real country wench.' He then really threw down the gauntlet with 'He dare not tell the truth', concluding that 'not being able to paint the whole portrait, he has no right to present one or two favourable points as characterising the whole, and therefore had better leave the picture alone altogether.'[40]

When the drop fell, Thackeray admitted that he could not look. He developed this argument the following month in *The Times* in a review of a new edition of the works of Henry Fielding:

The world does not tolerate now such satire as that of Hogarth and Fielding, and the world no doubt is right in a great part of its squeamishness ... It is wise that the public modesty should be as prudish as it is; that writers should be forced to chasten their humour, and when it would play with points of life and character which are essentially immoral, that they should be compelled, by the general outcry of incensed public propriety, to be silent altogether.[41]

Ainsworth was again judged and found wanting, because 'Vice is never to be mistaken for virtue in Fielding's honest downright books', whereas, in *Jack Sheppard*, 'Ainsworth dared not paint his hero as the scoundrel he knew him to be; he must keep his brutalities in the background, else the public morals will be outraged, and so he produces a book quite absurd and unreal, and infinitely more immoral than anything Fielding ever wrote. *Jack Sheppard* is immoral actually because it is decorous.'[42] This was an impossible proposition, apparently calling for a literary realism and accurate reportage, while simultaneously cutting any subject that might cause offence to public morals. With Thackeray, you could never win.

What the moral entrepreneurs like Thackeray and Forster were calling for amounted to industry self-censorship. One thing was sure – the Newgate novel was dead, and maybe Ainsworth's career as well.

Chapter 10

Fallout

Dickens, meanwhile, kept his head down and his powder dry. In private, however, he was more inclined to vent, writing to R.H. Horne that 'I am by some jolter-headed enemies most unjustly and untruly charged with having written a book after Mr. Ainsworth's fashion. Unto these jolter-heads and their intensely concentrated humbug, I shall take an early opportunity of temperately replying.'[1]

He also quietly deleted a footnote in *Sketches by Boz* praising *Rookwood* in the 1839 edition. When he did temperately reply, it was in a new preface to *Oliver Twist* added to the 1841 edition. His argument was that of realism over romance, specifically answering Thackeray's challenge that he 'dare not show the truth':

> The greater part of this Tale was originally published in a magazine. When I completed it, and put it forth in its present form, it was objected to on some high moral grounds in some high moral quarters.
>
> It was, it seemed, a coarse and shocking circumstance, that some of the characters in these pages are chosen from the most criminal and degraded in London's population; that Sikes is a thief and Fagin a receiver of stolen goods; that the boys are pickpockets, and the girl is a prostitute ...

However,

> What manner of life is that which is described in these pages, as the everyday existence of a Thief? What charms has it for the young and ill-disposed, what allurements for the most jolter-headed of juveniles? Here are no canterings on moonlit heaths, no merry-makings in the snuggest of

all possible caverns, none of the attractions of dress, no embroidery, no lace, no jackboots, no crimson coats and ruffles, none of the dash and freedom with which 'the road' has been time out of mind invested.[2]

Dickens allowed John Gay his McHeath, Lytton his Paul Clifford, and Daniel Defoe his Newgate biographies. The damning reference to the romanticism of 'the road' is therefore reserved solely for the work of his old friend, Ainsworth. *Oliver Twist*, he argued, was absolutely not a Newgate romance, but instead Dickens's 'humble attempt' to 'dim the false glitter surrounding something which really did exist, by shewing it in its unattractive and repulsive truth'.[3]

Clearly addressing Thackeray, Dickens described Nancy as a 'prostitute' in this preface, although, he admitted, she had to be particularly well-spoken. Flash slang was another Newgate code to be avoided, and a distraction from the real issues of urban poverty and crime that Dickens wanted his audience to confront. And unlike Thackeray, Dickens refused to turn away, and dared his readers to look with him.

'Truth', therefore, was his watchword; capitalised and multiply repeated in the final paragraph, Dickens positively bellowed the word at Thackeray and his critics, frustrated at having to explain what had been so obvious to him his whole life, and hammering his realism home through his justification of the depiction of Nancy:

It is useless to discuss whether the conduct and character of the girl seems natural or unnatural, probable or improbable, right or wrong. IT IS TRUE. Every man who has watched these melancholy shades of life knows it to be so. Suggested to my mind long ago – long before I dealt in fiction – by what I often saw and read of, in actual life around me, I have, for years, tracked it through many profligate and noisome ways, and found it still the same. From the first introduction of that poor wretch, to her laying her bloody head upon the robber's breast, there is not one word exaggerated or overwrought. It is emphatically God's truth, for it is the truth ... It involves the best and worst shades of our common nature; much of its ugliest hues, and something of its most beautiful; it is a contradiction, an anomaly, an apparent impossibility, but it is a truth. I am glad to have had it doubted, for in that circumstance I find a sufficient assurance that it needed to be told.[4]

Thus, Dickens concluded, the Newgate Controversy offered no reason for a literary novelist to abandon the subject of crime and social deprivation, so long as it was never glamourised. And with this powerful statement, he reframed the public debate, placing his own work in a very different camp to Ainsworth's and occupying the moral high ground left by Fielding and Hogarth. So masterful and assured was his defence of *Oliver Twist*, that the moral panic that could have seriously damaged his career in fact affirmed it, and he continued to write about the lot of the poor for the rest of his life. Ainsworth, however, did not, and the promised novel on Claude Duval was never written.

Thackeray, of course, was having none of this, and shortly thereafter expressed his opinion in Mr Punch's 'Literary Recipes':

A STARTLING ROMANCE
Take a small boy, charity, factory, carpenter's apprentice, or otherwise, as occasion may serve – stew him well down in vice – garnish largely with oaths and flash songs – boil him in a cauldron of crime and improbabilities. Season equally with good and bad qualities – infuse petty larceny, affection, benevolence and burglary, honour and housebreaking, amiability and arson – boil all gently. Stew down a mad mother – a gang of robbers – several pistols – a bloody knife. Serve up with a couple of murders – and season with a hanging-match.

N.B. Alter the ingredients to a beadle and a workhouse – the scenes may be the same, but the whole flavour of vice will be lost, and the boy will turn out a perfect pattern – strongly recommended for weak stomachs.[5]

But despite Thackeray's views on the matter – he was as intractable as his rival – Dickens's project was now thoroughly divorced from the 'Newgate School' of romance, heralding half a century of Victorian Realism, before Modernism shifted the paradigm again.

Even though he prudently avoided any more Newgate writing, it is virtually impossible to find any reference to Ainsworth's work written after this episode that does not damn him by association. For example, in a review appearing in *Graham's Magazine* in March 1841, ostensibly on Ainsworth's historical novel *The Tower of London*, Edgar Allan Poe begins, 'The authorship of this work does a little, and but a little, more credit to Mr. Ainsworth than that of "Jack Sheppard". It is in no spirit of cavilling that we say that it is rarely our lot to review a work more utterly destitute of every ingredient requisite to a good romance,' and concludes, 'Such libels on humanity, such provocations to crime, such worthless, inane, disgraceful romances as "Jack Sheppard" and its successors, are a blot on our literature and a curse to our land.'[6] Six months later, he took exactly the same tack with a review of *Guy Fawkes*. Poe also cast Ainsworth as one of the pilots of the hot air balloon *Victoria* attempting to cross the Atlantic in 'The Balloon-Hoax' of 1844, in which Ainsworth, *in propria persona*, is used to parody his own melodramatic prose style in 'Mr. Ainsworth's MS':

> The waters give up no voice to the heavens. The immense flaming ocean writhes and is tortured uncomplainingly. The mountainous surges suggest the idea of innumerable dumb gigantic fiends struggling in impotent agony.[7]

Unlike the satirical attacks of Thackeray, this particular burlesque actually enhanced Ainsworth's reputation as, with all such pranks, quite a lot of readers believed it. As the literary historian Harold Beaver put it, 'who but Ainsworth – romantic visionary on high – contributes that bold, creative stroke: of making a bid for North America?'[8] As Poe attacked nearly everyone who was making more money than he was, his reviews of Ainsworth were hardly unusual; nonetheless, he already had a rich critical bandwagon on which to jump, although Ainsworth had supported his work in *Bentley's Miscellany*.

This shift in the cultural narrative is nowhere more apparent than in R.H. Horne's collection of essays *The New Spirit of the Age*, written in 1844. This project was intended to update William Hazlitt's *The Spirit of the Age: Or, Contemporary Portraits* (1825), a collection of character sketches portraying twenty-five men whom he believed to represent significant trends in the thought, literature and politics of his age. Now, a generation later, wrote Horne, 'a new set of men, several of them animated by a new spirit, have obtained eminent positions in the public mind'.[9]

Richard Henry (later 'Hengist') Horne was a poet, literary critic and adventurer, serving in the Mexican Navy during the war of independence and later joining the Australian gold rush. He had written for the *Athenaeum* and is chiefly remembered for the epic poem *Orion* (1843). A close friend of Dickens, he later became a subeditor on *Household Words*. He also counted among his inner circle Robert and Elizabeth Barrett Browning, both of whom contributed to *A New Spirit of the Age*. As Hazlitt's 'Contemporary Portraits' had characterised the Romantics, Horne's book was intended to identify and establish a new canon for the Victorians.

Dickens, of course, was considered the perfect embodiment of the new age, and his portrait introduced the collection, Horne writing that 'Mr. Dickens is manifestly the product of his age. He is a genuine emanation from its aggregate and entire spirit. He is not an imitator of any.' Making a connection with the grotesque realism of Hogarth, the misconception that Dickens was a Newgate novelist was again explained for anyone that may still be confused or misinformed:

> Mr. Dickens is one of those happily constituted individuals who can 'touch pitch without soiling his fingers'; the peculiarity, in his case, being that he can do so without gloves; and, grasping its clinging blackness with both hands, shall yet retain no soil, no ugly memory. That he is at home in a wood – in green lanes and all sweet pastoral scenes – who can doubt it that has ever dwelt among them? But he has also been through the back slums of many a St. Giles's.[10]

On the matter of any superficial similarity between Dickens the moralist and satirist unsullied in the underworld and the author of a 'flash Newgate Calendar hero', it is patiently explained that:

> The secret was fully understood, and admirably practised by Sir E.L. Bulwer in his novel of 'Paul Clifford'; it was grievously misunderstood, except in the matter of dialect, by Mr. Ainsworth in his 'Jack Sheppard', which was full of

Fig. 1. Ainsworth, aged 12 (leaning against crate on the right) in 1817, at the tuck shop opposite the Manchester Free Grammar School, enthralled by old soldier John Leigh's account of surviving Bunker Hill. From his semi-autobiographical novel *Mervyn Clitheroe*, 1858.

Fig. 2. (*Above left*): 'The Enchanter of the North'. Sir Walter Scott by Henry Raeburn, 1822.

Fig. 3. (*Above right*): Ainsworth aged 21, miniature painted while honeymooning in Bath, 1826.

Fig. 4. Mrs Fanny Ainsworth aged 21, just married, companion miniature.

Fig. 5. 'After much deliberation, it was resolved that we should meet together, and dine…' The Fraserians' New Year dinner; group portrait by Daniel Maclise, 1835.

Fig. 6. The author of *Paul Clifford* and *Eugene Aram.* Edward George Earle Lytton Bulwer-Lytton, 1st Baron Lytton by Henry William Pickersgill, 1831.

Fig. 7. 'I'll let 'em see what I think of 'em!' Dick Turpin outrides his pursuers on the Enfield Highway at the start of his Ride to York. By George Cruikshank for the 4th edition of *Rookwood*, 1836.

Fig. 8. (*Above left*): George Cruikshank by an unknown artist, 1836.

Fig. 9. (*Above right*): Marguerite Gardiner, Countess of Blessington by Sir Thomas Lawrence, 1822.

Fig. 10. 'THE young Novelist of the Season'. Ainsworth, aged 30, by Daniel Maclise, *Fraser's Magazine*, 1834.

Fig. 11. Young Charles Dickens by Daniel Maclise, 1839.

Fig. 12. Chalk and pencil sketch of Jack Sheppard in the Condemned Hold of Newgate Prison, attributed to Sir James Thornhill, 1724.

Fig. 13. Engraving of Ainsworth, aged 34, for first edition of *Jack Sheppard* by Richard James Lane, 1839.

Fig. 14. Part One of *The Tower of London* serial, 1840.

Fig. 15. 'Guy Fawkes laying the train' by Cruikshank, *Guy Fawkes*, 1840.

Fig. 16. 'The Execution of Jane' by Cruikshank, *The Tower of London*.

Fig. 17. 'The Burning of St. Paul's' by John Franklin, *Old St. Paul's*, 1841.

REYNOLDS'S MISCELLANY

Of Romance, General Literature, Science, and Art.

EDITED BY GEORGE W. M. REYNOLDS,

AUTHOR OF "THE MYSTERIES OF LONDON," "FAUST," "PICKWICK ABROAD," &c. &c.

No. 29. Vol. II.   SATURDAY, MAY 22, 1847.   Price 1d.

MR. CHARLES DICKENS, SIR E. BULWER LYTTON, AND MR. WILLIAM HARRISON AINSWORTH.

Fig. 18. (*Above*): 'Herne flying into the burning woods with Mabel' by Cruikshank, *Windsor Castle*, 1842.

Fig. 19. (*Left*) 'The three most popular writers in England' (Dickens, Lytton and Ainsworth) by John Dicks, *Reynolds's Miscellany*, 1847.

Fig. 20. 'Nan Redferne and Mother Chattox' by Sir John Gilbert RA, *The Lancashire Witches*, first illustrated edition, 1854.

Fig. 21. Ainsworth in the Chair for the examination of candidates for the flitch of bacon at Great Dunmow town hall, *Illustrated London News*, 1855.

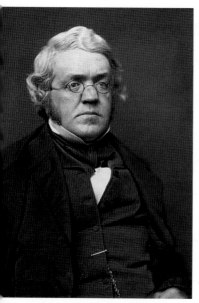 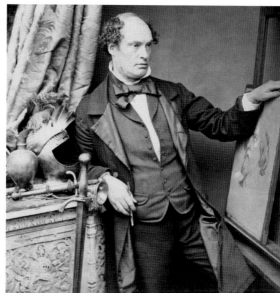

Fig. 22. (*Above left*): Daguerreotype of William Makepeace Thackeray, 1855.

Fig. 23. (*Above right*): Daniel Maclise in 1857, albumen print.

Fig. 24. Ainsworth in the 1860s.

Fig. 25. James Crossley c. 1877.

Fig. 26. John Forster by
Charles Edward Perugini, 1887.

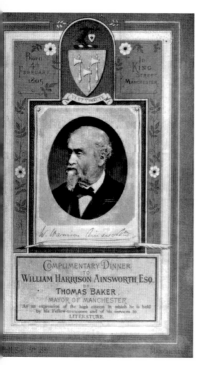

Fig. 27. Souvenir brochure for the mayoral banquet in Manchester, 1881.

Fig. 28. 'To the greatest axe-and-neck-romancer of our time' by Edward Linley Sambourne, *Punch*, 1881.

PUNCH'S FANCY PORTRAITS.—No. 50.

W. HARRISON AINSWORTH.

To the greatest Axe-and-Neck-Romancer of our Time, who is quite at the Head of his Profession, we dedicate this Block. *Ad multos Annos!*

Fig. 29. The Ainsworth family vault in Kensal Green Cemetery, where Ainsworth is buried with his mother and brother.

Fig. 30. Alice Nutter sculptured by David Palmer, for the 400th anniversary of the trial of the Lancashire Witches in 2012, Roughlee, Lancashire.

unredeemed crimes, but being told without any offensive language, did its evil work of popularity, and has now gone to its cradle in the cross-roads of literature, and should be henceforth hushed up by all who have – as so many have – a personal regard for its author.[11]

For Horne, then, like Thackeray, the 'secret' is to show, as unflinchingly as propriety allows, a scene of violence or depravity in the realistic manner of Hogarth. That is, for an illustrative, moral purpose. The only positive nod in the direction of Ainsworth, who is castigated for writing for popular entertainment, is an acknowledgement of his linguistic realism, along with an awkward attempt at a personal compliment, reiterated later in the otherwise vicious chapter devoted to him in the same work, regarding the esteem in which the subject is held socially, presumably as an affable host rather than as an author. The outlaw text, meanwhile, like its namesake, is buried at the crossroads in the traditional manner befitting an executed felon.

Such opening remarks do not bode well for Ainsworth, although, surprisingly, his friends Lytton and the historical novelist G.P.R. James, with whom he shared many stylistic similarities, are treated with considerable respect in their subsequent portraits. The creator of *Paul Clifford* and therefore the father of the contemporary Newgate novel, for example, is presented as 'one of the most prolific authors of our time; and his various accomplishments, habits of research, and extraordinary industry, no less than his genius, will entitle him to the rank he holds as one of the most successful, in that branch of literature in which he eminently excels'.[12] James is introduced with:

Of all historical novelists, Scott justly occupies the first place. If he did not create that kind of composition, he was the first who brought it into general favour ... It is not too much to say that the most successful of those who have trodden the same track in England is G.P.R. James. There is no writer, of his particular class, now living, so familiar to the public at large; not one who has drawn so extensively upon sources not always accessible to the readers of novels; not one who has laboured with such unremitting diligence, and such uniform popularity. If he has never greatly succeeded, we know no instance in which he has greatly failed.[13]

Given Ainsworth's continuing public popularity as a historical novelist, this is a brutal snub.

George Payne Rainsford James was even more prolific than Ainsworth. Because of his mass production of rather monotonous historical romances, we might wonder at Horne's endorsement of his position in the literary hierarchy compared with the complete rejection of Ainsworth's art, especially as James's hundred-strong collected works include such titles as *The Robber*, *The Brigand*, *The Smuggler*, *The Convict*, *The Gypsy* and *The King's Highway*. Again, it is a question of the moral centre of the novel:

> All his works, without distinction, are pervaded by moral feeling. There is a soul of true goodness in them – no maudlin affectation of virtue, but a manly rectitude of aim which they derive direct from the heart of the writer.[14]

James, whose novel *Forest Days* concerns Robin Hood, was, like Lytton, much more interested in portraying the plight of a morally good man driven outside society by tyranny or injustice. He also generally set his tales a safe distance from both England and the nineteenth century.

In *A New Spirit of the Age*, it is significantly apparent that Ainsworth has failed the test of the times. He is immediately separated from Lytton and James in the opening paragraph of his own chapter, although at least he was included as a literary influencer – with his sales, even Horne daren't leave him out:

> From the historical novel and romance, as re-originated in modern times, by Madame de Genlis and Sir Walter Scott, and adopted with such high success by Sir E.L. Bulwer, and with such extensive popularity by Mr. James, there has of late years sprung up a sort of lower or less historical romance, in which the chief part of the history consisted in old dates, old names, old houses, and old clothes.[15]

Ainsworth is merely a 'reviver of old clothes' in this analysis. His novel *Old St Paul's* (1841) is presented as a poor plagiarism of Defoe and is dismissed as 'generally dull, except when it is revolting'. 'The truth must be told,' the unidentified author exclaims, although the 'truth' seems to have more to do with the continued moral crusade against the individual author than a serious consideration of undoubtedly important contemporary fiction (the paradox being that Horne still has to include him).[16] *This* truth is very apparent, as the Newgate scandal is once more regurgitated and again the drop falls on Ainsworth:

> With regard to the Newgate narrative of 'Jack Sheppard' and the extraordinarily extensive notoriety it obtained for the writer, upon the residuum of which he founded his popularity, so much just severity has already been administered from criticism and from the opinion of the intellectual portion of the public, and its position has been so fully settled, that we are glad to pass over it without further animadversion.
>
> The present popularity of Mr. Ainsworth could not have risen out of its own materials. His so-called historical romance of 'Windsor Castle' is not to be regarded as a work of literature open to serious criticism. It is a picture book, and full of very pretty pictures. Also full of catalogues of numberless suits of clothes. Such a passion, indeed, has he for describing clothes, that he frequently gives us two suits with a single body, one being concealed under the other ... As to plot or story it does not pretend to any.[17]

That must have hurt. Like Poe's opportunist and partisan reviews, the commentary on whatever happens to be Ainsworth's most recent novel is always prefaced by *Jack Sheppard*, invading the textual body like a virus. After this, the critic has *carte blanche* to say anything, however spiteful, ill-informed or downright libellous. The quip regarding Ainsworth's penchant for costume detail becomes doubly dreadful here, as the antiquarian authenticity of G.P.R. James has already been lavishly praised. Even more unsettling for the author's career is an endnote explaining that the previous article was a 'joint-production' of four reviewers, each of whom were relieved of the assignment when their highly critical intentions had become apparent to the editor, who, in turn, explains that Ainsworth is 'usually spared in public' because he is 'so much esteemed and regarded in private'.[18] This can hardly have offered much consolation, especially to an author who prided himself, not without foundation, upon his antiquarian knowledge and research skills.

In the broader cultural context, Ainsworth was at the centre of a battle between Regency and Victorian values, and as *Jack Sheppard* showed, he had failed to realise how fast the times had changed. Industry, trade and sobriety were in – outlaws, flash slang, and the lifestyle these things implicitly endorsed, were now absolutely out. And when the new Victorians attacked Ainsworth, he was frequently compared with Regency bestsellers who were now considered immoral and therefore socially dangerous. Both the *Examiner* and the *Athenaeum* had placed his style back in the 'time of Tom and Jerry' (Egan's Georgian rakes), and critics like J. Hain Friswell were still keeping this tradition alive in the 1870s:

> He is, perhaps, not so much to be blamed, poor man, being a person of small attainments and not a very strong intellect, as the times in which he was born. In that yeasty and lively age, in which the results of a long war, deeds of violence at sea and on land, the press gang, cheating lawyers, bad laws, a debauched king and court, a 'frowsy old Floribel', had produced among the people a taste for such literature as the 'Memoirs of Harriette Wilson', accompanied by books less vicious only in degree, and not quite as bad in intention, such as 'Tom and Jerry', 'The Corinthian Club', and the like.[19]

Once again, Ainsworth is stripped of his status as an early Victorian, as the literary elite continue to define themselves in opposition to their immediate ancestors. And once again, the critics still can't ignore him because of his continued commercial success. All they can do is insult him.

By the 1850s, the tenuous link between popular entertainment and working-class depravity had become accepted and repeated as an almost scientific fact, not just by the literary men but the social explorers, Henry Mayhew writing in his seminal study *London Labour and the London Poor*:

> In many of the thoroughfares of London there are shops which have been turned into a kind of temporary theatre (admission one penny), where dancing and singing take place every night … It is impossible to contemplate the

ignorance and immorality of so numerous a class as that of the costermongers, without wishing to discover the cause of their degradation. Let anyone curious on this point visit one of these penny shows, and he will wonder that *any* trace of virtue and honesty should remain among the people. Here the stage, instead of being the means for illustrating a moral precept, is turned into a platform to teach the cruellest debauchery. The audience is usually composed of children so young, that these dens become the school-rooms where the guiding morals of life are picked up.[20]

The following year, in his epic social study, *Memoirs of Extraordinary Popular Delusions and the Madness of Crowds*, the Scottish journalist Charles MacKay echoed Mayhew:

In the penny theatres that abound in the poor and populous districts of London, and which are chiefly frequented by striplings of idle and dissolute habits, tales of thieves and murderers are more admired, and draw more crowded audiences, than any other species of representation. There the footpad, the burglar, and the highwayman are portrayed in their natural colours, and give pleasant lessons in crime to their delighted listeners. There the deepest tragedy and the broadest farce are represented in the career of the murderer and the thief, and are applauded in proportion to their depth and their breadth. There, whenever a crime of unusual atrocity is committed, it is brought out afresh, with all its disgusting incidents copied from the life, for the amusement of those who will one day become its imitators.[21]

He then carefully differentiated high from low culture within the more literary 'adventures of noted rogues', which were, he wrote, 'delightful', so that the outlaw creations of Schiller, Scott and Byron could be spared any charges of the corruption of public morals, just as the original Newgate critics had done with Hogarth and Fielding. Under the new Victorian taboo of representation, Ainsworth, however well his titles continued to sell, was thereafter excluded from the literary canon, an exclusion that persists to this day.

As Ainsworth moved on to his epic histories of the British monarchy, Lytton downgraded Eugene Aram to an accessory rather than the murderer, and Dickens conquered the world, Thackeray finally laid the Newgate novel to rest in a false start to the sixth chapter of *Vanity Fair* called 'The Night Attack', written in the manner of *Jack Sheppard*:

> One, two, three! It is the signal that Black Vizard had agreed on.
> 'Mofy! is that your snum?' said a voice from the area. 'I'll gully the dag and bimbole the clicky in a snuffkin.'
> 'Nuffle your clod, and beladle your glumbanions,' said Vizard, with a dreadful oath. 'This way, men; if they screak, out with your snickers and slick! Look to the pewter room, Blowser. You, Mark, to the old gaff's mobus box! and I,' added he, in a lower but more horrible voice, 'I will look to Amelia!'[22]

When he revised the novel in 1853, this passage was omitted, Thackeray considering it no longer relevant as a contemporary satire. Of course, the Newgate novel had not gone anywhere other than into popular as opposed to literary culture, and dandy highwaymen rode on in penny magazines and cheap theatres, until revived by other means as pirates in Stevenson's *Treasure Island*, suggesting, perhaps, that if only *Jack Sheppard* had been written earlier or later than it was, then none of this would have happened.

Chapter 11

A Dark and Bloody History

Despite the *Jack Sheppard* furore, Ainsworth was now at his creative zenith. January 1840 saw the commencement of two original serials, *Guy Fawkes* and *The Tower of London*, which were to be written and run concurrently throughout the year while he continued to edit *Bentley's Miscellany*, *Guy Fawkes* in the magazine from January to November, *The Tower of London* in separate monthly shilling instalments from January to December. Both projects were illustrated by Cruikshank and published by Bentley.

The Tower of London is an epic with a Protestant protagonist, Lady Jane Grey; *Guy Fawkes* a brooding Gothic tragedy with a Catholic hero. Because *The Tower of London* became such a seminal work – a bestseller in its own day, which British schoolchildren were still being taught in the 1950s – *Guy Fawkes* tends to be overlooked, but it remains, nonetheless, a fascinating and surprisingly subversive piece of creative non-fiction.

After its serial run, *Guy Fawkes: or, The Gunpowder Treason. A Historical Romance* was published as a triple-decker novel in July 1841. The tale begins in the summer of 1605, by which time the gunpowder conspiracy was already well advanced. The story arc covers the attempt to destroy Parliament on 5 November and Robert Catesby's failed insurrection in the north. It ends in the spring of 1606 with the execution of Father Henry Garnet. The narrative is divided into three 'books'. 'The Plot' begins with the graphic execution of two seminary priests in Manchester – under King James's anti-Catholic laws, their very presence on English soil was a capital offence. The execution is interrupted by the ravings of the prophetess Elizabeth Orton, who escapes the pursuivant and his guards by diving into the Irwell. This scene introduces the novel's two protagonists, both of whom attempt to save the half-mad woman. Humphrey Chetham (in real life, the founder of Ainsworth's beloved Chetham's Library) is a Protestant gentleman who argues with the arresting officers, while Guy Fawkes saves Orton from drowning. Orton dies prophesying her rescuer's death on the scaffold.

After this arresting opening, Book the First remains in Lancashire, the action set around the ancestral seat of the Radcliffes, one of many old Catholic families who live in constant fear of government oppression. Sir William Radcliffe broadly supports the conspirators, and his daughter is torn between the love of the innocent Humphrey Chetham (a union divided by faith) and a deep attraction to Guy Fawkes. In a supernatural interlude, Fawkes meets the alchemist Dr John Dee, who raises the spirit of Elizabeth Orton, her ghost once again predicting disaster. Similarly, in a pilgrimage to St Winifred's Well, Fawkes receives a divine vision warning him against the plot. At the end of Book the First, the Radcliffes are discovered to be harbouring the priests Fathers Oldcorne and Garnet, and the conspirators flee to London as Ordsall Hall is sacked by government troops.

Book the Second, 'The Discovery', follows the events immediately leading to the failed bombing attempt on 5 November, diverting only from the historical record to marry Guy Fawkes to Viviana Radcliffe, who does not approve of the plot and urges him to abandon it. Fawkes, like all the conspirators, is however bound by oath. Book the Third, 'The Conspirators', follows the torture and trial of the plotters and Viviana's attempts to move her husband to repentance. This he does, by her deathbed in the Tower of London, going to his own execution both bravely and contentedly. The novel concludes, as it began, with the execution of a Catholic priest, Father Garnet, the principal Jesuit of England. As ever, Ainsworth's historical *mise-en-scène* is a synergy of meticulous antiquarian research and Gothic sensibility, featuring necromancy, ill omens, violent death and ghostly visitants.

Nowadays, the image of Guy Fawkes has become synonymous with anti-establishment protest. This modern symbolism began in the 1980s British comic strip *V for Vendetta*, a dystopian revenge tragedy with an anarchist heart by Alan Moore and David Lloyd. The politically unaligned 'Anonymous' network of hackers and activists have taken as their emblem the 'penny-for-the-guy' mask worn by Moore's protagonist, along with the ethos of the character. History becomes fiction becoming history again; but while the cultural significance of Moore's subversive hero is huge, the connotative seeds of Guy Fawkes as a revolutionary freedom fighter, rather than a terrorist to be burnt in effigy, were in fact sown in Ainsworth's novel.

In choosing the less contentious form of straight historical fiction, it would notionally seem that Ainsworth had once more entered Scott's realm. Scott's prose had an innovative sense of the plight of the individual within complex and threatening times. In his influential study, *The Historical Novel*, the critic and cultural historian Georg Lukács identified the refinement and influence of Scott's technique in the work of Pushkin and Tolstoy:

> What matters in the historical novel is not the re-telling of great historical events, but the poetic awakening of the people who figured in these events. What matters is that we should re-experience the social and human motives which led men to think, feel and act just as they did in historical reality ... Scott thus lets his important figures grow out of the being of the age, he never explains the age from the position of its great representatives, as do the Romantic hero-worshippers. Hence they can never be central figures of the action. For the being of the age can only appear as a broad and many-sided picture if the everyday life of the people, the joys and sorrows, crises and confusions of average human beings are portrayed. The important leading figure, who embodies an historical movement, necessarily does so at a certain level of abstraction.[1]

Lukács called such a protagonist – typified, for example, by Scott's fictional hero Edward Waverley – the 'mediocre hero'.

But Ainsworth's approach to the stories of British history remains very different from Scott's. Ainsworth's historical novels were, as John Moore put it, 'history in gorgeous Technicolour'.[2] Ainsworth's approach to historical fiction therefore endorses Lady Clarinda's assertion in *Crotchet Castle* that 'history is but a tiresome thing in itself; it becomes more agreeable the more romance is mixed up with it'.[3] The Hollywood analogy is a good one. Ainsworth loved melodrama and his work translated effortlessly to the Victorian stage. His central characters were not the average or mediocre heroes so necessary to Scott's historical project but the kings, queens and outlaws of England. The closest correlative today is therefore the costume drama, specifically those in which the protagonists are famous historical figures, often within the monarchy, for example, *The Crown*, *Victoria*, *The Tudors*, and *Gunpowder* (the latter closely following Ainsworth's design by focusing on Robert Catesby's failed revolt in the north after Fawkes's capture). And although immensely popular in television, film and general fiction, this is a genre model that is – according to Lukácsian critics – lightweight and romantic rather than defamiliar and therefore literary.

R.H. Horne had been equally quick to label Ainsworth's fiction in opposition to that of Scott in his remarks about 'lower or less historical romance'. In contrast, he wrote, the significance of the 'great' writer of historical romance was in his ability to:

> throw the soul back into the vitality of the past, to make the imagination dwell with its scenes and walk hand in hand with knowledge; to live with its most eminent men and women, and enter into their feelings and thoughts as well as their abodes, and be sensitive with them of the striking events and ruling influences of the time; to do all this, and to give it a vivid form in words, so as to bring it before the eye, and project it into the sympathies of the modern world, this is to write the truest history no less than the finest historical fiction; this is to be a great historical romancist – something very different from a reviver of old clothes.[4]

In the same year that Horne published his essays, the Russian literary critic V.G. Belinskii similarly wrote that to read a novel by Scott 'is like living in the age he describes, becoming for a moment a contemporary of the characters he portrays, thinking for a moment their thoughts and feeling their emotions'.[5] This again foreshadows Lukács and what he called the 'classical form of the historical novel', having a cultural significance that the historical *romances* did not.

The Lukácsian analytical model remains so pervasive in academic literary study, however, that any work of historical fiction that is not seen to conform is easily rejected as somehow artistically inferior and (particularly if the work was popular) therefore unworthy of anything other than a casual dismissal or a witty remark. Coupled with the curse of Newgate, this is a common and unhelpful approach to Ainsworth, being only partially more accurate than J. Hain Friswell's suggestion in *Modern Men of Letters* that the author was simply not very intelligent. Following Lukács and, indeed, Horne, Andrew Sanders has written of Ainsworth, for example, that:

> His didacticism is of a peculiarly unimaginative kind, however, for he was not so much concerned with moral teaching as with the value of facts and dates ... Many of his important historical characters are presented with a destructive ambiguity simply because he has not thought out the implications of his plots with sufficient thoroughness ... This ambiguity is equally evident in the treatment of ordinary citizens. In his stories, unlike Scott's, the common people are allowed to express the novelist's prejudices without appearing to have evolved any kind of understanding of what is happening to them. They are rarely more than spectators observing events which they have no power to influence.[6]

Thus, *any* historical novel not written in the manner of Scott or Tolstoy, as defined by Lukács's Marxist historicism, is badly written and deserves to be not just ignored but actively *disremembered*.

The comparison with Scott is always misleading. As Ainsworth's histories are concerned with the well-known stories of equally well-known historical figures of title, position and political power, it is actually more useful to compare his work with that of Sophocles or even Shakespeare. Just as theatre audiences know that Oedipus will marry Jocasta and that Richard II will be usurped by Bolingbroke, Ainsworth and his readers accepted that Lady Jane Grey was only a nine-day queen, that Guy Fawkes would never fire the fatal train and that both would be executed. In retelling these stories, Ainsworth overcame historical determinism by using the devices of Tragedy, embracing inevitability and exploring character; in Aristotelean terms showing the protagonist's moral defect (the *hamartia*), his or her recognition of its existence (the *anagnorisis*), and the consequences of its existence (the *peripeteia*).

Guy Fawkes and Lady Jane in *The Tower of London* are both tragic heroes, robbed of individual agency and doomed to act out the fate that history dictates. In the female characters, this disposition is manifested by an almost angelic passivity, in the male, a brooding melancholy. Guy Fawkes and Lady Jane are therefore often forewarned by Cassandra in her many guises, but, like the Trojans, they pay no heed. 'Go not to the Tower. Danger lurks therein,' Jane is told by a mysterious old woman when she enters London in the opening chapter.[7] In *Guy Fawkes*, Elizabeth Orton warns Fawkes of his fate both as she dies and when her spirit is raised by Dr John Dee, astrologer to Elizabeth I and Warden of the Collegiate Church, Manchester:

> 'Spirit of Elizabeth Orton,' cried Fawkes, 'if indeed thou standest before me, and some demon hath not entered thy frame to delude me, – by all that is holy, and by every blessed saint, I adjure thee to tell me whether the scheme on which I am now engaged for the advantage of the Catholic Church will prosper?'
>
> 'Thou art mistaken, Guy Fawkes,' returned the corpse. 'Thy scheme is not for the advantage of the Catholic Church.'
>
> 'I will not pause to inquire wherefore,' continued Fawkes. 'But, grant that the means are violent and wrongful, will the end be successful?'
>
> 'The end will be death,' replied the corpse.
>
> 'To the tyrant – to the oppressors?' demanded Fawkes.
>
> 'To the conspirators,' was the answer …
>
> 'Shall we restore the fallen religion?' demanded Fawkes.
>
> But before the words could be pronounced the light vanished, and a heavy sound was heard, as of the body falling on the frame.
>
> 'It is over,' said Doctor Dee.[8]

Fawkes thus knows his fate throughout the novel. There are numerous other omens, including the vision at Saint Winifred's well telling Fawkes his plot will fail, being '*not* approved by Heaven'.[9]

Although Orton is precise regarding the failure of the plot, she is ambivalent on the possibility of the restoration of the 'Old Religion'. This was an inflammatory issue in 1840 as well, anti-Catholic feeling running high after the repeal of the Test and Corporation Acts in 1828 and Catholic emancipation in 1829. The revival of Bonfire Night as an anti-Catholic protest dates from this period. In this febrile atmosphere, stoked by Tories over Irish immigration, Ainsworth's preface to *Guy Fawkes* is nothing short of astounding:

> The tyrannical measures adopted against the Roman Catholics in the early part of the reign of James the First, when the severe penal enactments against recusants were revived, and with additional rigour, and which led to the remarkable conspiracy about to be related, have been so forcibly and faithfully described by Doctor Lingard, that the following extract from his history will form a fitting introduction to the present work.[10]

He then quotes the historian and Catholic Priest John Lingard at length on James I's persecution of English Catholics, concluding, 'From this deplorable state of things, which is by no means over-coloured in the above description, sprang the Gunpowder Plot.'[11] By suggesting that the Gunpowder Plot was an act of justified desperation rather than Jesuit-funded terrorism, Ainsworth was taking a potentially greater risk than he ever did in *Jack Sheppard*. It is odd, therefore, though not unexpected, that the literary historian Nicholas Rance confidently described Ainsworth as 'patriotic and anti-Catholic'.[12] In his own day, Ainsworth had to field the opposite accusation because of his romantic affection for the Jacobites, leading S.M. Ellis to clarify that 'Probably it was the author's high praise of the Penderals, and other Roman Catholic families who aided Charles II, which originated the prevalent belief that Ainsworth was himself a member of the Old Faith: it may be well to state here that such was not the cause; he lived and died a member of the Church of England.'[13]

Professor Rance's comment, meanwhile, is a characteristic misreading of the companion novel to *Guy Fawkes*, *The Tower of London*, considered in isolation as a condemnation of Mary I rather than as the Protestant half of a balanced pair. Taken together, what Laman Blanchard called the 'twin-born romances' justify the author's further claim in his preface that 'One doctrine I have endeavoured to enforce throughout – TOLERATION'. This plea for tolerance is also linked to the painful experience of the *Jack Sheppard* controversy, and in a passage later removed from subsequent editions, Ainsworth concluded his loaded preface with:

> From those who have wilfully misinterpreted one of my former productions, and have attributed to it a purpose and an aim utterly foreign to my own intentions, I can scarcely expect fairer treatment for the present work. But to that wider and more discriminating class of readers from whom I have experienced so much favour and support, I confidently commit this volume, certain of meeting with leniency and impartiality.[14]

This dedication to his public betrays his increasing isolation from the literary elite and, also, his growing annoyance with them. His confidence in his audience was well founded, however; *Guy Fawkes* proved to be extremely popular and *The Tower of London* the most successful novel of his career.

Rather than being portrayed by Ainsworth as a religious fanatic, Fawkes the tragic hero is a soldier – a brave and pious man who believes in his political actions. His hubris is complicated, because he has sworn a binding oath to the plot, despite his conviction that 'I am well assured it will not be successful'.[15] Knowing he is doomed to failure, torture and violent death (as do we), Fawkes's real battle is not against the State, or Destiny, but with himself. His spiritual dilemma is almost Christ-like, and he struggles internally to reject the worldly (his life and his love Viviana), and accept his fate as a religious martyr.

As his protagonists are doomed, the only positive closure that the author has to offer his audience is the salvation of their souls. Fawkes is in Purgatory because he pursued the plotter's path despite repeated warnings from heaven. Viviana – now his wife – surrenders herself in order to see her husband in the Tower, and to make him repent of his mortal error in an embodiment of nineteenth-century moral design: they are tortured, their faith tested, and they must die before their implicit resurrection to the life eternal. As John Reed argues, 'Victorian readers, accustomed to consider earthly existence as probation for eternity, did not find affirmations of the redemptive effects of suffering unusual in their literature.'[16]

Guy Fawkes, a national pariah, burnt in effigy for centuries, is therefore finally allowed salvation when he repents by Viviana's deathbed. Viviana then expires, while Fawkes prays beside her. To the end, Viviana represents the Catholic majority, who would never countenance violence, whatever the ends. She is the conscience of the text, offering a counter argument to armed insurrection. Fawkes's fate, of course, is to be hanged, drawn and quartered. Because of his repentance, however, 'Guy Fawkes's tranquillity of mind did not desert him to the last. On the contrary, as his term of life drew near its close, he became more cheerful and resigned.'[17] On the scaffold, he sees Viviana in the crowd and knows they will be reunited in heaven.

In *The Tower of London*, Lady Jane Grey assumes a similar spiritual trajectory. She is Fawkes's Protestant double, and the twin texts are therefore in symmetry. 'My lord, I have lived in the Protestant faith, and in that faith I will die,' she tells Bishop Gardiner. 'In these sad times, when the power of your Church is in the ascendant, it is perhaps needful there should be martyrs in ours to prove our sincerity.'[18] As Fawkes is to be a Catholic martyr, Jane is to be a Protestant one. After imprisonment and initial despair, she gains strength through faith and refuses to recant to save herself, and, like Viviana, becomes beautiful and serene through her suffering, supplications and acceptance of her fate. Like Fawkes, she becomes actively cheerful as she finally rejects the worldly altogether and faces her own death. She also sees a vision of her dead spouse waiting for her just beyond the scaffold.

Where these characters differ is in the actual nature of their martyrdom. At the time of writing, the redefinition of a traditional folk devil as a Catholic martyr would have been a very dangerous thing for the author and for the government. Fawkes's political status therefore remains ambiguous. Viviana, the moderate Catholic, saves his soul by persuading him to abandon his conviction that his war was a just one. Ainsworth's historical frame, however, seems to suggest that it was, making Guy Fawkes another romantic outlaw. Lady Jane's Protestant martyrdom is, of course, beyond dispute. Both novels can be read, therefore – beneath the Gothic melodrama, romance and adventure – as English Morality Plays that seek to redistribute moral value in the narrative of history across faiths.

Like its companion piece, *The Tower of London* is also set during a period of enormous political upheaval in England. The story encompasses the political plots and counterplots to gain control of the country after the death of Edward VI, the nine-day reign of Lady Jane Grey, the coronation of Mary I, her marriage to Philip of Spain, the restoration of the Catholic faith in England, and Sir Thomas Wyat's failed insurrection.

Following the king's death without a male heir, the Protestant aristocracy fear that the succession of his Catholic half-sister Mary would jeopardise the English Reformation. The Duke of Northumberland is determined to take power through the coronation of his daughter-in-law, Jane, and consequently to make his son, Lord Guilford Dudley, the king. When this fails and Mary I is crowned while Northumberland goes to the block, Dudley's fanatical obsession to regain his former position leads to a doomed attempt at revolution and, ultimately, the executions of him and his wife. Meanwhile, the Archbishop of Canterbury schemes with the French ambassador to depose Mary and replace her with the Protestant Elizabeth. The arch-plotter is the Spanish ambassador, Simon Renard, who manipulates everybody in order to force the marriage between Mary and Philip of Spain and 'establish the Inquisition in the heart of London within six months'.[19] Some light relief is provided by the lives and loves of the servants and soldiers who actually run the *Gormenghast*-like citadel, particularly the three giants of the Tower, Og, Gog and Magog, and the dwarf Xit, whom they torment something rotten. There is also a subplot involving the lovers Cuthbert Cholmondeley and Mistress Cicely similar to the disastrous romance of Agnes and Raymond in Matthew Lewis's Gothic novel *The Monk*.

Ainsworth begins the novel with Jane's entry to the Tower as queen on 10 July 1553 and ends it with her execution on 12 February the following year. This allows the author the use of two coronations, a royal wedding, several executions and a siege without recourse to undue invention as, he explains in his preface, he was 'Desirous of exhibiting the Tower in its triple light of a palace, a prison, and a fortress'.[20] In a device inspired by *Notre Dame de Paris*, the Tower itself is at the heart of the narrative, a 'character' in its own right, and a controlling metaphor for the nation's history. Like Hugo's Gothic masterpiece, *The Tower of London* is a 'book of stone':

> 'There you behold the Tower of London,' said Winwike, pointing downwards.
> 'And there I read the history of England,' replied Renard.
> 'If it is written in those towers it is a dark and bloody history,' replied the warder.[21]

Ainsworth's preface demonstrates the scope of this unique project:

> It has been, for years, the cherished wish of the writer of the following pages, to make the Tower of London – the

proudest monument of antiquity, considered with reference to its historical associations, which this country, or any other possesses – the groundwork of a romance … to contrive such a series of incidents as should naturally introduce every relic of the old pile – its towers, chapels, halls, chambers, gateways, arches, and draw-bridges – so that no part of it should remain unillustrated.[22]

The minute particulars of the Tower's architecture and history were obsessively researched by both Ainsworth and Cruikshank, who consequently produced their best collaborative work. As the author constructed a parallel narrative of romance and antiquarian detail, the artist produced forty atmospheric engravings and a further fifty-eight woodcuts devoted to purely architectural features.

Fact and fiction are skilfully blended, resulting in a cohesive whole so complete in detail that its reputation as an authority on the history of the Tower endured as late as the 1950s. *The Tower of London* is, for example, quoted as a work of reference in *A Pageant of History: The Reigns of our Kings and Queens, Famous People and Events in our History* (1958), a standard history textbook for every schoolchild in post-war Britain. (The novel is also equipped with a full index.) When Edmund Swifte, Keeper of the Crown Jewels, wrote an account of a ghostly encounter in *Notes and Queries*, a page reference to Ainsworth's description of the Anne Boleyn room and Cruikshank's accompanying illustration is given: 'For an accurate picture of the *locus in quo* my scene is laid.'[23] As A.L. Rowse noted in *The Tower of London in the History of the Nation*, 'It was this work that formed the impression of the Tower in most people's minds throughout the Victorian Age, as it did mine as a schoolboy in remote Cornwall early this century.'[24]

This was both Ainsworth's purpose and achievement. When he began his work, the Tower was an abandoned garrison, closed in most part to the public, mutilated by modern alteration, and dangerously neglected: 'One important object the author would fain hope his labours may achieve. This is the introduction of the public to some parts of the fortress at present closed to them … They are the property of the nation, and should be open to national inspection.'[25]

Sales were enormous and as the serial progressed, thousands of visitors sought out the places depicted by Ainsworth's words and

Cruikshank's pictures. As a result, the Tower was restored as one of the first Victorian museums and a patriotic symbol in the national psyche at the dawning of the new era. The novel was therefore extravagantly dedicated to the queen: 'Finally, beseeching God to bless these realms, and its ever precious jewel, our gracious QUEEN VICTORIA, and the infant princess newly given to us; to save them as the apple of His eye; and to protect them with the target of His power against all ill.'[26]

Forty years later, Ainsworth was still turning national landmarks into Gothic castles populated with fated monarchs, paupers of noble birth, Gothic villains and terrible apparitions in an epic and ongoing process of psycho-geography. *The Tower of London* had set the standard for a very unique history of England.

Chapter 12

The Dance of Death

As soon as *The Tower of London* concluded, Ainsworth threw an enormous celebratory dinner at the Sussex Hotel and promptly began the next serial, *Old St Paul's, A Tale of the Plague and the Fire*, the first instalment of which appeared in *The Sunday Times* on 3 January 1841. Ainsworth received £1,000 for his labours (the equivalent of around £60,000 today), the copyright reverting to him on completion. The hotel in Bouverie Street was close to his printers, Bradbury and Evans, and Ainsworth kept a room there where he would often work through the night to meet a deadline before dashing down with the corrected proofs of his latest instalment. Guests at this dinner included Dickens, Forster, Maclise, Cruikshank, Blanchard, Talfourd, Major Elrington (Governor of the Tower), Edmund Swift (Keeper of the Regalia) and John Blackwood, son of the formidable Edinburgh publisher William. John Blackwood wrote home of this occasion:

> There was a great deal of speechmaking, and 'butter me and I'll butter you' seemed to be the principle on which they all went. Talfourd, in giving Ainsworth's health, touched upon the excellence of the company assembled. In coming to the Booksellers he gave a panegyric upon them, and said they could boast the presence of a Longman and a Fraser. Ainsworth whispered to him, and he said, 'But Scotland hath a thief as good; one who is the representative of one who had Scott for his friend and Wilson for his inspired aid – one who did more than any other for the advancement of literature on the other side of the Tweed.' Ainsworth returned, and then went on to toast almost the whole of the company individually. About the centre he gave me, and begged to introduce me to the company as one who,

he doubted not, would shortly take a leading part in London publishing. He spoke very handsomely about our father ... George Cruikshank was very good. He sang *Lord Bateman* and some others. The claret and champagne were as plenty as could be wished.[1]

Cruikshank, the vice-chair, also stuck Ainsworth with his half of the bill.

Cruikshank did not illustrate the serial although he apparently thought he was going to. (The original serial was unillustrated, but Ainsworth employed John Franklin to produce twenty plates for the three-volume edition later published by Hugh Cunningham.) The reason for this is unclear, although it may have had something to do with Cruikshank putting it about that he had come up with the idea for the new serial – and several others – which Ainsworth had supposedly appropriated and secretly sold. He later published his grievances in a pamphlet entitled *The Artist and the Author. A statement of facts ... Proving that the distinguished author, Mr. W. Harrison Ainsworth, is 'labouring under a singular delusion' with respect to the origin of 'The Miser's Daughter', 'The Tower of London', etc.* in 1872, claiming also the partial authorship of *Oliver Twist*. As his Victorian biographer Blanchard Jerrold noted, Cruikshank quarrelled with everyone he worked with, and in later years such smouldering resentments tended to exaggerate all the imagined wrongs. In 1872, the trigger had been a review in *The Times* of Andrew Halliday's revival of *The Miser's Daughter* at the Adelphi. Cruikshank wrote to the paper that 'as my name is not mentioned in any way in connection with the novel — not even as the illustrator — I shall feel greatly obliged if you will allow me to inform the public through the medium of your columns of the fact (which all my private friends are aware of) that this tale of *The Miser's Daughter* originated from me, and not from Mr. Ainsworth.' He went on to qualify this: 'I do not mean to say that Mr. Ainsworth when writing this novel did not introduce some of his own ideas; but as the first idea and all the principal points and characters emanated from me, I think it will be allowed that the title of *originator of The Miser's Daughter* should be conferred.'[2]

'Labouring under a singular delusion' is quoted from Ainsworth's letter to the editor in response: 'Mr. Cruikshank appears to labour under a singular delusion in regard to novels he has illustrated; it is not long since he claimed to be the originator of Mr. Dickens's *Oliver Twist*.'[3]

From here, the war of words had escalated until the editor announced that 'We can publish no more letters on this subject', hence Cruikshank's pamphlet, in which he argues that he 'originated' the stories of *Oliver Twist, The Tower of London, Old St Paul's* and *The Miser's Daughter* by a sequence of drawings produced in advance of the actual writing, as he had done in *Life in London*, his illustrations providing a loose storyline to which Egan added text.

The success of *The Tower of London* had left booksellers clamouring for a similar sequel, and Ainsworth had written to Crossley in early December that 'I commence a new Romance with the New Year, under the title of *The Plague of London*. If you have any other tract relating to the period, or to the Fire, I shall feel obliged by the loan of it,' indicating he was already quite advanced in his preparations, having been studying Defoe's *Journal of the Plague Year*, which he had borrowed from his old friend.[4] In *George Cruikshank's Life, Times, and Art*, Robert L. Patten speculates that as no written agreement existed and that Cruikshank had merely proposed an idea already in the mind of the author (as the letter to Crossley indicates), Ainsworth saw nothing wrong in following the money. Alternately, suggests Patten, Ainsworth might have believed that Cruikshank's present contracts with Bentley meant that he simply did not have the time to immediately embark on another *Tower of London*-sized project or, perhaps, he was finding Cruikshank's editorial suggestions increasingly intrusive. But whatever Ainsworth's reasons, the first Cruikshank heard of it was when the advertisements appeared, leading him to exclaim that 'Ainsworth has deserted me'. In *The Artist and The Author*, Cruikshank wrote that, on hearing that 'another artist was working out my pet subject, which I had nursed in my brains for many years, and which I had long intended to have placed before the public with my own hands', he decided to wash his hands of Ainsworth and start his own periodical, the *Omnibus*.[5] But the ageing artist's chronology is out. After *Old St Paul's* commenced, Ainsworth and Cruikshank were still collaborating on the novelisation of *Guy Fawkes*. Also, as Patten notes, Cruikshank was committed to Tilt and Bogue for the *Omnibus* by February 1841, so Ainsworth's relationship with Franklin, which didn't start until December, had nothing to do with Cruikshank's decision to start his own magazine. The two men also collaborated on *Ainsworth's Magazine* from February 1842 until Ainsworth sold it to his publisher (much to Cruikshank's annoyance) the following year. Cruikshank therefore illustrated *The Miser's Daughter* and *Saint James's* after the *Old St Paul's* disagreement. Ainsworth also offered Cruikshank the job of illustrating the complete novel before Franklin, but Cruikshank was by then too committed to other projects and declined. His reply, however, shows that he was still very hurt:

> I do assure you my Dear Ainsworth I sincerely regret – that I cannot join you in this work, but what was I to think – what conclusion was I to come to but that you had *cut* me – at the latter end of last year you announced that *we* were preparing a 'New Work' – in the early part of December last – I saw by an advertisement that – your 'New Work' – was to be published in the 'Sunday Times' – you do not come to me – or send for me nor send me any explanation – I meet you at Dickens's on 'New Years Eve'. You tell me then that you will see me in a few days and explain everything to my satisfaction – I hear nothing from you – in your various notes about the 'Guy Fawkes' you do not even advert to the subject –
>
> I purposely keep myself disengaged refusing many advantageous offers of work – still I hear nothing from you – at length you announced a New Work as a *companion to the 'Tower'* without my name – I then conclude that you do not intend to join *me* in *any* New Work – and therefore determine to do something for myself – *indeed I could hold out no longer* – To show that others besides my self considered that you had left me – I was applied to by Chapman & Hall – to join with them & Mr. Dickens in a speculation – which indeed I promised to do should the one with Mr. Tilt be abandoned – However I have still to hope that when you are disengaged from Mr. Bentley that some arrangements may be made which may tend to our mutual benefit.[6]

Patten surmises from the reference to Bentley that Ainsworth may have had to avoid another collaboration with Cruikshank to facilitate his escape from the *Miscellany* (much as Dickens had previously done). After the success of *The Tower of London*, it would have been difficult to keep Bentley out of a similar deal. Such fallings-out were not uncommon in the hectic environment of Victorian publishing, the dramas often rivalling any fiction being produced. As far as Cruikshank was concerned, though, Ainsworth had thrown him under the bus. Ultimately, whatever the reasons, it was neither man's finest hour.

Meanwhile, *Old St Paul's* was unfolding to a very receptive audience, despite the lack of illustrations. As Ainsworth's letters to Crossley suggest, it was the latter's Defoe collection that was the real inspiration for the new project. This is freely acknowledged in the 'Advertisement' that prefaces the novel:

> THE portion of the ensuing Tale relating to the Grocer of Wood-street, and his manner of victualling his house, and shutting up himself and his family within it during the worst part of the Pestilence of 1665, is founded on a narrative, which I have followed pretty closely in most of its details, contained in a very rare little volume, entitled, *'Preparations against the Plague, both of Soul and Body'*, the authorship of which I have no hesitation in assigning to DEFOE. Indeed, I venture to pronounce it his masterpiece. It is strange that this matchless performance should have hitherto escaped attention, and that it should not have been reprinted with some one of the countless impressions of the *'History of the Plague of London'*, to which it forms an almost necessary accompaniment ...
>
> For my acquaintance with this narrative, as well as for the suggestion of its application to the present purpose, I am indebted to my friend, Mr. JAMES CROSSLEY, of Manchester.[7]

The attribution of *Due Preparations for the Plague* (1722) to Defoe is an astute piece of literary scholarship, as its authorship is nowadays unquestioned. This gave Ainsworth the idea for the character of Stephen Bloundel, the Puritan grocer who seals his house, while his principal source of reference was Defoe's *Journal of the Plague Year* (also 1722). Defoe's book is a remarkably immediate account of the summer of 1665, a sleight of hand attributed to a first-hand witness ('H.F.'), but in fact written from contemporary accounts and records, embellished with fictional episodes that the author insists are all real. Defoe presents his

Journal as a true history, but it is rather a historical novel. Anticipating Scott, Defoe, through a relatively neutral narrator, examines the effect on basic humanity of such a dehumanising experience. 'H.F.' is not a hero so much as a camera, turned upon an entire city in decay and despair.

Ainsworth's rewrite of Defoe (adding the closure of the Fire of London) was generally applauded by reviewers, the best of which he appended to the advertisement for the launch of *Ainsworth's Magazine* and the novelised version of *Old St Paul's*. *Bell's Life of London* notes the Defoe connection and Ainsworth's dramatic development:

> Although the horrors of the Plague and the Fire have already
> been described by various writers, and especially by Defoe,
> Mr. Ainsworth has in these volumes clothed those events in
> a manner the most exciting.

The *Courier* similarly applauds Ainsworth's talent for weaving an engaging story out of the historical record without taking too many liberties with the facts:

> In this work, Mr. Ainsworth has portrayed many of the
> horrible incidents of the Great Plague with historical
> fidelity. He places his principal characters in the midst
> of that dreadful scourge, and makes the plot depend in
> a great measure for its progress and development on the
> circumstances common to the time. The scenes described
> are all founded on well-authenticated accounts, presented
> by Mr. Ainsworth with a forcible semblance of reality,
> which his pen can so well accomplish.

The *Atlas* appreciates the horror, as well as the narrative pacing:

> Two of the most appalling events in the history of London
> have been drawn into the work before us – the Plague and
> the Fire, and treated in Mr. Ainsworth's usual graphic style.
> It argues in favour of the skill with which these scourges
> of the great city are treated, that several of the descriptive
> passages made us literally shudder … Mr. Ainsworth
> does not fatigue his readers with long accounts of places,

and scenes, and events. He always mixes up his descriptions with vivid action, and never lets his narrative pause for a moment. This is one of the secrets of his success.

And the *Observer* pays a huge compliment:

We are glad to meet Mr. Ainsworth again in the region of historical romance, a department of literature in which he has already distinguished himself above almost every author of the day … He has interwoven historical facts into a web of most pleasing fiction, thereby investing history herself with new attraction.

Even old adversary the *Athenaeum* revised its earlier opinions:

We prefer the two first volumes of 'Old St. Paul's' to any previous work of their author. Treated as a tale of adventure, the test of which is the hold retained on the reader, these volumes have great merit. The reader who has once opened them will hardly be disposed to lay them down again.

Finally, the *Court Journal* paid the highest tribute possible: 'Mr. Ainsworth is the Defoe of his day.'[8]

While such accolades have vanished into obscurity, R.H. Horne's predictable rejection of the novel endures:

'Old St. Paul's, a tale of the Plague and the Fire,' is a diluted imitation of some parts of Defoe's 'Plague in London', varied with libertine adventures of Lord Rochester and his associates. It is generally dull, except when it is revolting.[9]

In short, some people just don't get Gothic horror, and contemporary reviews of Hammer films in the 1950s and 60s often took the same tone.[10] Once again, the literary elite failed to understand popular fiction.

Old St Paul's is a 'disaster story' worthy of Hollywood, where an all-star cast is introduced merely to be decimated by the plague, the fire and each other in an apocalypse of biblical proportions, again based around a famous national monument. It is divided into six books, each separately dated from April 1665 to September 1666. Manchester man Leonard Holt, a grocer's apprentice, is in love with his master's daughter, Amabel Bloundel. His rival is a young aristocrat, Maurice Wyvil (later revealed to be John Wilmot, 2nd Earl of Rochester), whom she meets in secret in the cathedral. Bloundel's hypochondriac servant, Blaize, offers some comic relief through his faith in a variety of quack remedies.

As the plague progresses, the cathedral is turned into a pesthouse and London becomes an eerie necropolis where victims of the illness are preyed upon by unscrupulous and opportunist characters such as the coffin-maker Anselm Chowles and Mother Malmaynes, the plague nurse, who hasten their patients' ends in order to loot their properties. Bloundel decides to seal his family within their house, and Leonard finds himself wandering the wasteland, finally catching, but surviving, the plague. Rochester, meanwhile, tricks Amabel into a phoney marriage and deflowers her. On learning the truth, Amabel falls into a fever and dies. The beautiful daughter of a blind piper, Nizza Macascree, falls for Leonard and this initially unrequited love grows after Amabel's death. Nizza is actually Lady Isabella Argentine, so marriage seems out of the question. After an interlude of nine months, religious zealots fire the city, and Leonard saves the life of King Charles II. He is rewarded with a title and marries Isabella. The Bloundels survive their ordeals, while Chowles and Malmaynes die horribly in the vaults of St Paul's as it burns in a sea of molten lead. Leonard lives to see St Paul's rebuilt by Wren.

The *Book of Revelations* is as much present as Defoe's *Journal*, the destruction of London often articulated in biblical terms by characters. The first book therefore opens with a sermon on the day of judgement. This would appeal to the middle-class Victorian audience, who could take the moral high ground while enjoying the licentiousness. Although Rochester's filthy poetry is not cited, the debauchery begins well with the Earl and his cronies playing cards for each other's wives while the city falls apart, before being relegated to a subplot like a Restoration comedy played out in parallel with the main through line, suddenly and surprisingly turning nasty at its conclusion. Ainsworth again uses prophecy to turn the history into tragedy, the fanatical Solomon Eagle – another historical figure – screaming 'The wrath of Heaven is at hand' from the roof of St Paul's, a flaming brazier on his head.[11]

Protagonist Leonard Holt witnesses the city's death and rebirth. As he wanders the urban desert, much like Defoe's observer, civilisation increasingly unravels before his eyes:

> As Leonard passed Saint Michael's church, in Basinghall-street, he perceived, to his great surprise, that it was lighted up, and at first supposed some service was going on within it, but on approaching he heard strains of lively and most irreverent music issuing from within. Pushing open the door, he entered the sacred edifice, and found it occupied by a party of twenty young men, accompanied by a like number of females, some of whom were playing at dice and cards, some drinking, others singing Bacchanalian melodies, others dancing along the aisles ...

Holt is appalled, but when he calls on the revellers to repent, one of them replies, 'Do you know whom you address? These gentlemen are the brotherhood of Saint Michael, and I am the principal.'[12]

Everywhere Holt goes he encounters chaos, violence and death. The beast that lives beneath the veneer of civilised society is loose. If people fall in the street, passers-by step over them; Malmaynes and Chowles rob and murder the sick with impunity; law and order is replaced by mob violence; the churches have closed; and the aristocracy has withdrawn into orgy to await the end. Foreshadowing Poe's 'The Masque of the Red Death' (1842), the cathedral hosts the *danse macabre*:

> In the midst of the nave ... stood a number of grotesque figures, apparelled in fantastic garbs, and each attended by a skeleton. Some of the latter grisly shapes were playing on tambours, others on psalteries, others on rebecs – every instrument producing the strangest sound imaginable ...[13]

Old St Paul's is not so much Gothic as darkly carnivalesque. The world is turned upside down and nurses kill their patients, undertakers their clients; grocers hoard food, sex results in death not life, monks blaspheme, and the dead throw their own wakes. Pain, despair, death and decay are celebrated in their every aspect.

The chapter entitled 'The Dance of Death' immediately precedes the heart of the novel, the central image of the plague pit. Despite himself, Holt is grimly fascinated; like Defoe's observer, he must look:

> Strange and fantastic thoughts possessed him. He fancied that the legs and arms moved, – that the eyes of some of the corpses opened and glared at him – and that the whole rotting mass was endowed with animation.[14]

But reality is even worse than the supernatural fantasy, and he is brought back to his senses by the workmanlike dumping of more bodies. London is a vast graveyard, and, unlike the Tower of London, even St Paul's is not inviolate; it burns like everything else.

The plague pit is symbolic of human misery on a scale more recognisable to a modern reader. The mass grave is a twentieth-century icon, a symbol of war, famine, toxic spills, terrorist attacks, and ethnic cleansing. The horror of Ainsworth's imagery throughout the three historical novels of 1840–41 reminds us that there is not a single civilisation, including the British Empire, that is not built upon a foundation of human bones. *Old St Paul's* concludes on an image of rebirth, but it is the plague pits that remain longest in the memory.

Chapter 13

Our Library Table

While *Old St Paul's* ran its course, Ainsworth was still editing *Bentley's Miscellany*. More easygoing and less worried about his reputation than Dickens had been, Ainsworth knew how to cater to the public and sales remained high. However, as had been the case with Dickens, it was the success of the magazine that caused problems between editor and proprietor. Ainsworth's original contract did not allow for either an increase in salary or more editorial control, and Bentley was not inclined to change it. This was a mistake. After the monumental success of *The Tower of London* in particular, he did not see fit to pay his editor and headline writer what he was now clearly worth. Instead, he tried to drive him harder, claiming that Ainsworth had promised to write two additional stories in addition to his regular contributions. Ainsworth denied any such commitment and refused to write the stories. Bentley insisted, and in December 1841, Ainsworth resigned, taking Cruikshank with him to begin their own magazine. Cruikshank was at that point producing a monthly magazine of his own, which he called the *Omnibus*. His after-dinner joke at the time was that he had 'driven his *Omnibus* into *Ainsworth's Magazine*'.

Ainsworth had by now learned the hard way that the best way to profit by his writing was to sell it himself. To this end, he invested heavily in this new project, in terms of both energy and money. His publisher was Hugh Cunningham of St Martin's Place, Trafalgar Square, who had published the novelised version of *Old St Paul's*. The first issue appeared at the start of February 1842, with a jaunty 'Preliminary Address' harking back to the playfulness of the *Pocket Magazine* letters, in which Ainsworth wrote:

> In introducing Ainsworth's Magazine to the public, he whose name it bears pledges himself only upon one point — that

at the end of the many volumes yet unformed, to which he confidently anticipates his new venture will extend, nobody shall be able to convict him of breaking a single promise; for he does not intend to make one.

Also, 'Of its productions in the various fields of romance, the most conspicuous, in the earlier numbers, will be a New Tale by the Editor.'[1]

This 'New Tale' was *The Miser's Daughter*, another historical novel, although this time about ordinary and by and large fictional characters with some excellent world-building. It is a comedy in the classical sense, in which two lovers are destined to be together but are beset by obstacles that keep them apart until the third act. Set in 1744, the protagonist, Randulph Crew, travels to London from Cheshire after the death of his father to visit his maternal uncle, Abel Beechcroft. An honourable young man, Crew has surrendered his inheritance to his father's creditors. Also seeking out Scarve (the miser), an old friend of his mother's, Randulph falls for the beautiful Hilda, the miser's daughter. Scarve opposes the match; not only is Randulph poor, the miser despises him for settling his father's debts rather than hanging on to the estate. Scarve also plans to marry Hilda off to his nephew, Philip Frewin. Abel disapproves of the union too. He hates Scarve for stealing his sweetheart (Hilda's mother) when they were young.

The novel also has a 'Life in London' strand to it, as Abel's younger brother introduces his provincial nephew to the fashionable society of Lady Brabazon – a real historical figure – the elderly rake Sir Singleton Spinke, the dandy Beau Villiers and the actress Kitty Conway. This allows Ainsworth to recreate the great Georgian pleasure gardens of Marylebone, Ranelagh and Vauxhall, which he does with imagination and a vivid style supported, as ever, by detailed research. Randulph also meets the Jacobite plotter Cordwell Firebrass (another historical figure), although in his preface to the novelised edition Ainsworth admits this doesn't go anywhere, writing:

It was part of my original scheme to describe the secret proceedings of the Jacobites in Lancashire and Cheshire prior to the Rebellion of '45, with Prince Charles's entrance into Manchester in that memorable year, and the subsequent march to Derby. But I found these details incompatible with

142

my main plan, and I was therefore obliged to relinquish them; contenting myself with a slight sketch of a conspiracy in London.[2] [He would later achieve this aim in *The Manchester Rebels* in 1873.]

Inheritance and wills play a major part in the story, moving the plot forward and representing a deeper theme on how the law affects individuals (as Dickens would later do in *Bleak House*). As a recovering lawyer, this was a subject that Ainsworth knew well. Frewin persuades Scarve to leave him his fortune, but in the story's climax, Randulph kills Frewin in a duel. After Scarve's lonely death, Randulph and Hilda are able to marry and inherit his estate. Although a rollicking, trolloping adventure through the London of Boswell and Johnson, the author, still mindful of the Newgate Controversy, intends, he writes, to 'convey a useful lesson', being 'To expose the folly and wickedness of acuminating wealth for no other purpose than to hoard it up, and to exhibit the utter misery of a being who should thus voluntarily surrender himself to the dominion of Mammon'.[3]

Unusually, Cruikshank finished his illustrations in watercolour, giving them additional depth. The serial was well received, launching *Ainsworth's Magazine* with style and buoyant sales. Even John Forster was impressed, writing to Ainsworth that 'I like the notion of your story. Come and tell me about it — and about your magazine. And let us have a chop together as soon as you can.'[4] Forster and Dickens also both wrote to advise that, at eighteen pence a copy, Ainsworth wasn't charging enough. He later put it up to 2/6. *The Miser's Daughter* was dramatised by Edward Stirling at the Adelphi in October 1842, and in November by T.P. Taylor at the City of London Theatre. Also, at the end of the year, as the serial neared completion, it was published as a triple-decker novel by Cunningham and Mortimer. Ainsworth dedicated it 'To my Three Dear Daughters'.

In addition to the serial, *Ainsworth's Magazine* kicked off strongly with some serious talent, including Thackeray, Talfourd, Hunt, the philosopher Martin Farquhar Tupper, the poet and translator – and later infamous QC – Dr Edward Kenealy,[5] Shirley Brooks (later editor of *Punch*), Coventry Patmore (he of 'The Angel of the House'), John Hughes ('Mr Buller of Brazennose'), R.H. Horne, Laman Blanchard, Charles Ollier, G.P.R. James, and Alexandre Dumas (serialising *The Count of Monte Cristo* in English for the first time). The dramatist Richard Brinsley Peake, author of the play *Presumption; or, the Fate of Frankenstein*, the first theatrical version of Shelley's novel, was also on board.[6] Ainsworth also found a slot for his cousin, W. Francis Ainsworth. In addition, there were also an unusually high number of distinguished female contributors, such as the poet Caroline Anne Southey (the second wife of Robert), travel writer and historian Louisa Stuart Costello (her brother, Dudley, also writing for the magazine), the fledgling historical novelist Catherine Gore, and Countess Harriette D'Orsay (wife of the dandy Count). Unfortunately, the latter's involvement kept Lady Blessington from contributing as the women loathed each other. There was also a loosely editorial section of the magazine called 'Our Library Table', where letters from contributors were printed, along with reviews and a cheery engagement with readers. Notably it was *our* library table, and the first instalment was accompanied by an illustration by Cruikshank of Ainsworth and the artist working together on the magazine in the library at Kensal Manor House, adjoining Kensal Lodge, which Ainsworth had purchased in 1841, while retaining rooms at the lodge, where Eliza still lived.

The first issue was, however, marred by the inclusion, after Ainsworth's 'Preliminary Address', of 'A few Words to Richard Bentley', a spiteful attack on his former publisher by Cruikshank, which was later removed from the collected first volume. This was in part mocking Bentley for his vanity in becoming 'Her Majesty's Publisher in Ordinary', a largely meaningless title that he nonetheless flaunted. Cruikshank was also aggrieved at Bentley continuing to advertise the *Miscellany* as illustrated by him when he was only contracted now to begrudgingly produce one etching a month, while Bentley conflated his contribution with that of his nephew, who was a minor wood engraver, albeit with a famous surname. It was a mean-spirited broadside and Bentley was obliged to respond, which he did through his champion, 'Father Prout' (the irascible Irish humourist Francis Mahoney). Oddly, the fire was directed at Ainsworth in a satiric poem called 'The Red-Breast of Aquitania', about a bird who, soaring to heights where his powers could not sustain him, collapsed and fell 'nor uprose again', with a L'envoi directly addressing Ainsworth as 'Author of the admirable "Crichton"' and 'subsequent chronicler of "Jack Sheppard"':

> Thus sadly I thought
> As that bird unsought
> The remembrance bought
> Of thy bright day.[7]

This returns, again, to the days of *Jack Sheppard*, when Mahony had been one of the critics who had admired *Crichton* but felt that its author had betrayed his literary gifts and standards to write for the vulgarities of fame and profit. John Hughes responded in the April edition of *Ainsworth's Magazine*, with a 'humble ballade' called 'The Magpie of Marwood', in which the magpie (Prout) entices two friendly birds into his garden and then asks Bentley to shoot them. To this, Ainsworth appended his own L'envoi, lambasting Bentley for putting his man up to berating a serial that he himself had published and done rather well out of. Thomas Hood called this a 'paper war', and at a dinner held at Greenwich celebrating Dickens's return from America, six guests were put between Ainsworth and Mahony to avoid a scrap. Meanwhile, the animosity between Cruikshank and Bentley that had started the whole thing was soon forgotten.

In an open letter to Ainsworth in the magazine, Hughes advised restraint. 'The Padre is breathing vengeance,' he wrote, 'but I agree with you, it is best to content ourselves with one tarring and feathering, since our friends agree that the plumage sticks on appropriately; and to let him peck away without further molestation.'[8] Ainsworth duly left well alone; not so Mahony, whose response was brutal, even by the standards of Paternoster Row. In a long ballad entitled 'The Cruel Murder of Old Father Prout by a Barber's Apprentice: A Legend of Modern Literature', Mahony took Ainsworth apart in a vicious personal attack covering the Newgate Controversy, leaving Bentley's employ, and rumours about discord between contributors in the new magazine, implying Ainsworth had deliberately played Lady Blessington off against Countess D'Orsay. He attacked Ainsworth's regional background, as well as his writing, rehashing many of the Newgate critics' slurs on the quality of his books:

> 'Twas true, this lad from MANCHESTER, of jokes had few,
>   if any.
> Yet at twisting 'tales' he was a sort of story-spinning-jenny;
> But, as the tongues of giddy youth too much indulgence
>   loosens,
> His 'stories', which came thick and thick, at last became a
>   nuisance.
> The shop frequenters often wished he'd hold his peace,
>   or alter

The staple of his tedious yarns, all ending in a halter.
Soon, one by one they dropped away — for life cannot afford us
Sufficient time with maudlin tales of cut-throats to be bored thus ...[9]

He also published old and private correspondence from Ainsworth in footnotes, in which the young author had asked for favourable reviews for *Rookwood* and *Crichton*. But Mahony had overplayed his hand. Everyone knew the two men had been friends for years, and when Mahony had been struggling, one of his sources of a regular meal had been Ainsworth's table at Kensal Lodge. And as well as being ungracious, this reaction was completely disproportionate to the original quarrel, which amounted only to some nonsense from Cruikshank that Ainsworth had indulged because Cruikshank was, with him, the main selling point of the magazine. For literary London, Mahony's publication of private correspondence had gone completely beyond the pale.

Ainsworth went high and did not respond. Only in his December issue was there a minor reference to it in a reply to a query about the provenance of a poem Bentley had recently published as original in the *Miscellany* but was, in fact, an older piece recycled from the *Monthly Magazine* with a different title and added notes by Mahony. 'The long and stupid notes attached to it would seem to emanate from the Jesuit scribe who publishes his friends' private letters,' wrote Ainsworth.[10] Mahony left 'The Murder of Old Father Prout' out of *The Reliques of Father Prout* in 1860, as did his posthumous editor, Charles Kent, who was appalled by it, in *The Works of Father Prout* (1881). Towards the end of his life, Ainsworth corresponded with Kent, being, as the latter noted in his 'Biographical Introduction', one of only two surviving 'Fraseriansy' who could speak of Mahony from experience. 'I always regret the misunderstanding that occurred between myself and Mahony,' he wrote, 'but any offence that was given him on my part was unintentional':

I cannot help thinking he was incited to the attack he made upon me by Bentley. Be this as it may, I have long ceased to think about it, and now only dwell upon the agreeable parts of his character. He was an admirable scholar, a wit, a charming poet, and generally — not always — a very genial companion ... I should like very much to see a new edition of his works.[11]

As the magazine continued successfully into the New Year, 'Our Library Table' was restricted to reviews. Going against the industry grain, these were generally favourable, and always affable, although R.H. Horne got a deserved mauling for 'sham-review and mock honour' and 'the spirit of a jealous and injurious misrepresentation' in a long take-down of *A New Spirit of the Age*.[12] But in the main, as Ainsworth told his readers, 'We make no fierce war on books or authors, but seek rather to find out what is good and honest and pleasant in rivals and contemporaries, giving our readers the benefit of the discovery.'[13] So no grudges were borne, the successful were not envied, and the inexperienced encouraged. He was, wrote Ellis of this period, 'Truly a character of singular amiability and charm'.[14]

Chapter 14

Devils and Kings

Ainsworth was working around the clock. While writing *The Miser's Daughter* he was also labouring on a parallel serial about the court of Henry VIII entitled *Windsor Castle*. Close friends worried about his health, Mrs Hughes writing to Mrs Southey that 'Were I an absolute monarch I should for the love I bear him put him in handcuffs, or any confinement which would prevent his writing more than for limited time every day.'[1]

Mary Ann Hughes was the wife of the Reverend Thomas Hughes, Canon of St Paul's and tutor to the younger sons of George III. She was the mother of *Ainsworth's Magazine* stalwart John Hughes and grandmother of Thomas Hughes, author of *Tom Brown's Schooldays*. Ainsworth was a regular guest at Mrs Hughes's residence at Kingston Lisle, and *Guy Fawkes* is dedicated to her.

Windsor Castle was originally intended to appear in monthly parts like *The Tower of London*, its launch date advertised as 29 March 1842. This plan was interrupted by the death of Ainsworth's mother, Ann, on 15 March, aged sixty-four. Among the many condolences from friends, one letter is particularly interesting, showing a side of John Forster he rarely exhibited:

> How deeply I sympathize with the sorrow you are suffering –
> I hope I need not say. This is the grief that of all others,
> in this world of grief and losses, falls heaviest on a true-
> hearted man. So much of all one's life is in it – so many
> of those thoughts of life's beginning which last beyond all
> others. But you have many consolations, my dear friend, and
> not the least that you have attended your poor mother to the
> close, and that she died with your love beside her. Is there
> anything I can do for you? I imagine that you will defer

the *Windsor Castle* this month – but should you not do so, I might be of some assistance to you. I have all my Henry VIII books here, and if you told me some particular thing you wanted – it may be horrible conceit – but somehow I think I might be of some beggarly service to you. At all events, in that or lesser matters, try if for old affection's sake you can discover anything for me to do for you ... I will go to you at any time you wish. Forgive my naming such a thing now, but it is from the fear you may think me careless in the matter of your magazine.

Ever, my dear Ainsworth,
Your affectionate friend,
JOHN FORSTER.[2]

Ainsworth declined the offer, and *Windsor Castle* commenced instead in the July issue, the cover price being raised by sixpence. The French artist Tony Johannot provided the first four illustrations, being replaced by Cruikshank at the completion of *The Miser's Daughter*. W. Alfred Delamotte also contributed eighty-seven woodcuts depicting forest scenes and architectural features and three plans of Windsor Great Park and the castle in 1530 and 1843. As R.H. Horne had it, 'It is a picture-book, and full of very pretty pictures.'[3] Like *The Tower of London*, *Windsor Castle* was equipped with a full index when published as a three-volume novel by Colburn in 1843. Despite the somewhat hasty composition, *Windsor Castle* was another great success, its popularity keeping it in print in England (along with *Old St Paul's*), until the late 1960s. In its own day, a French translation appeared daily in *Le Messenger* and a play inspired by the romance, entitled *Herne the Hunter*, did the rounds in London.

Windsor Castle is divided into six short books; the first five take place in 1529, the sixth is a coda set in 1536 to conclude Anne's story with her execution and replacement by Jane Seymour. Book the Third is a long digression covering the history of the castle itself. The plot demonstrates the emerging pattern of Ainsworth's historical novels, comprising a significant historical event from the point of view of the main players (usually monarchs), fictionalised romantic subplots, and intervention by a supernatural agency. The main story arc follows Henry VIII's attempts to replace Catherine of Aragon with Anne Boleyn. Cardinal Wolsey tries to subvert Henry's plans, using the king's obvious attraction to the beautiful Mabel Lyndwood to make Anne jealous. (Apparently the grandchild of a forester, Mabel is really Wolsey's daughter.) When this fails, he gives Catherine information regarding Anne's relationship with Thomas Wyat. Wolsey's plan again comes to nothing, as we know it must, and he is dismissed from court, dying shortly afterwards. Catherine surrenders to the inevitable but predicts that Henry will tire of Anne as he has her, and this prophecy is fulfilled at the novel's conclusion. The demonic Herne the Hunter, who haunts Windsor Forest with a band of ghostly followers, provides the Gothic/supernatural dimension, often helping characters to gain their souls. Wyat and Mabel fall in love while imprisoned by Herne, but Mabel is drowned during an escape attempt. The king tries unsuccessfully to destroy Herne, and the spirit remains at large at the end of the novel.

As the writers of the play *Herne the Hunter* understood, the horned god is the most interesting character in the novel, representing Ainsworth's continuing interest in the Faustian pact. Herne is a legendary figure dating from the reign of Richard II, although the pagan imagery of the stag's horns on his head suggests a much longer lineage. Shakespeare uses the legend for laughs in *The Merry Wives of Windsor*, when Falstaff dresses as Herne for an assignation with Mistress Ford by Herne's oak in Windsor Forest. (Herne's oak was still alive in Ainsworth's day, until it was blown down in 1863.) Shakespeare's is the first printed reference to Herne although, as with Robin Goodfellow, he was tapping into a much older vein of myth and folklore. Ainsworth offers his own version of the story in a chapter entitled 'The Legend of Herne the Hunter', a complete invention that is nonetheless often cited in popular histories.

As told to a group of servants by Hector Cutbeard, the clerk of the castle kitchen, Herne was one of King Richard's gamekeepers, highly skilled in all aspects of woodcraft. Much to the satisfaction of his many (inferior) rivals, Herne was mortally wounded saving the king from a wild hart. Richard promises to make Herne the head keeper of the forest and offers a reward to anyone who can save his life. A 'tall dark man, in a strange garb' (Philip Urswick) comes forward, flays the head of the hart and has the gory skull tied to Herne's head, before having him carried to his hut in the woods. In private, Urswick asks the present chief keeper, Osmond Crooke, what it would be worth to him to stop Herne taking his position. A compact is made obligating the rival keepers to Urswick in return for

Herne losing all his woodland skills. 'If thou canst accomplish this thou art the fiend himself!' cries Crooke, which Urswick does not deny.[4]

Herne recovers but his skills have deserted him. In despair, he rides wildly into the forest, returning 'with ghastly looks and a strange appearance – having the links of a rusty chain which he had plucked from a gibbet hanging from his left arm, and the hart's antlered skull … fixed like a helm on his head'.[5] He is soon found hanging from an old oak tree, his body disappearing shortly after discovery. A terrible storm blows up, and the fatal oak is struck by lightning. The other keepers lose their hunting skills and are told by Urswick that they are cursed by Herne and must go to the old oak with horse and hound. Herne appears, followed by Urswick, who declares him Lord of the Forest, whom the keepers must serve as his hunt. Many of the king's deer are slaughtered until Richard himself goes to Herne's oak and asks, 'Why dost thou disturb the quietude of night, accursed spirit?' Herne demands vengeance, and when one of the keepers confesses, Richard has them all hanged. Herne is seen no more during Richard's reign, but appears with a fresh band every time a new monarch holds the castle, and none have ever driven him from the forest.

When Cutbeard concludes his yarn, a deep voice from the darkness responds with, 'Nor will the present monarch be able to drive him from the forest … As long as Windsor Forest endures, Herne the hunter will haunt it.'[6] This is a wonderful piece of Gothic stagecraft. Everybody in the room jumps, and no one recognises the speaker, who could be Herne himself. The 'tall archer' commends Hector on the telling but offers some amendments, adding a lost love whom Mabel uncannily resembles (hence her later kidnap). In common with most folk tales, everyone seems to know a slightly different version. But there is one constant. As the Duke of Richmond tells the Earl of Surrey, 'the spirit by which the forest is haunted is a wood demon, who assumes the shape of the ghostly hunter, and seeks to tempt or terrify the keepers to sell their souls to him.'[7]

Everyone Herne strikes a deal with comes to a sticky end. Wyat gets neither Anne nor Mabel, and as he later leads a failed rebellion against Mary I (as told in *The Tower of London*), we know his fate is sealed. Henry Norris also makes a pact for the love of Anne and ends up in the Tower for his trouble. Herne also has the last word in the novel:

'There spoke the death-knell of Anne Boleyn!' cried Herne, regarding Henry sternly, and pointing to the Round Tower.

'The bloody deed is done, and thou art free to wed once more. Away to Wolff Hall, and bring thy new consort to Windsor Castle!'[8]

The implication is clear. Henry has surrendered his soul to marry Jane Seymour. Written in conjunction with *The Miser's Daughter*, it is obvious from some rough edges that both novels suffered compositionally from their hasty production. *Windsor Castle* is no *Wolf Hall*, but that said, it isn't so far off the bodice-ripping TV series *The Tudors* created by Michael Hirst. As John Moore wrote in his introduction to a Literary Heritage reprint of *Windsor Castle*, capturing the essence of all of Ainsworth's histories: 'The kings were kingly and majestic, the queens were queenly and beautiful; and whether the historians had assigned them to the pigeon-hole labelled "Good" or the one labelled "Bad", they were always in a sense Great.'[9]

Ainsworth returned to the devil's bargain in the incomplete romance *Auriol, or The Elixir of Life*, a tale of alchemy, immortality and satanic pacts that ranged from the sixteenth to the nineteenth century and would have been fascinating if adequately completed. After *Windsor Castle* ended, the magazine's next serial was not by Ainsworth but the prolific novelist Catherine Gore. *Modern Chivalry, or a New Orlando Furioso* – her fortieth book – was only edited by Ainsworth. This afforded him a much-needed break after several years of writing like a steam engine. He took the opportunity to travel, visiting friends, and serving on the funding committee for the Scott Monument in Edinburgh. At the end of 1843, Ainsworth sold his magazine to his publisher, John Mortimer, for £1,000, retaining the editorship for a high salary. Although far from destitute, Ainsworth had overspent on his magazine, largely by paying contributors much higher fees than was normal at the time – his maximum being sixteen guineas a sheet. When Mortimer took over the purse strings, Ainsworth had to apologetically inform his stable of writers that the going rate was now one guinea.

His next serial, *Saint James's or The Court of Queen Anne, An Historical Romance*, appeared in *Ainsworth's Magazine* from January to December 1844 and was published by Mortimer in three volumes the same year. Although the recent period comedy-drama *The Favourite* shows that there is something interesting to say about the reign of Queen Anne, Ainsworth did not say it. Instead, the story is a rather plotless account of the Tories' successful strategy to curb the political influence of the Duke and Duchess of Marlborough, led by Harley and St John, with none of the flair of *The Tower of London*, *Old St Paul's* or *Windsor Castle*. This was the first novel not to become an instant and international bestseller. It is notable only as the last Ainsworth's romance to be illustrated by Cruikshank. *Auriol*, such as it was, then followed.

Auriol could have been one of the great Rosicrucian Gothic novels of the nineteenth century, alongside Percy Shelley's *St Irvyne; or, The Rosicrucian: A Romance* (1811) and Lytton's *Zanoni* (1842).[10] But in 1845, before the story was completed in *Ainsworth's Magazine*, Ainsworth fell out with his publisher over an unpaid £60 'editorial honorarium' and promptly resigned. Legal action for breach of contract was threatened but not pursued, and Ainsworth purchased the *New Monthly Magazine* from Colburn soon afterwards for £2,500, later writing that he was 'thus establishing one interest, one will, and one undivided purpose'.[11] Clearly, he had been reminded of this old lesson by Mortimer and by the end of the year he'd bought back *Ainsworth's Magazine* as well and begun publishing it with Chapman and Hall. He continued to edit both titles, although his cousin William Francis Ainsworth, as 'sub-editor' of the *New Monthly*, took on some of the heavy lifting until he eventually became editor himself in 1871. *Auriol* did not, however, move with him, although the fascinating first instalment, in which a young Catholic renegade – Auriol Darcy – drinks an Elizabethan alchemist's *elixir vitae* and becomes immortal, was given away with the *New Monthly* as the first and, as it turned out, only part of a series entitled *The Revelations of London* as a 'gratuitous supplement', leading Mr Punch to remark:

> Says Ainsworth to Colburn,
> 'A plan in my pate is,
> To give my romance as
> A supplement, gratis.'
> Says Colburn to Ainsworth,
> ''Twill do very nicely,
> For that will be charging
> Its value precisely.'[12]

Apparently, readers and critics were not ready for a story that opened like the first act of a Hammer film. *Auriol* was not published as a novel until twenty years later, and then only as a slim volume with an obviously hurried conclusion and expanded to an acceptable size by the inclusion of two early short stories and Phiz's superbly atmospheric illustrations. Ainsworth considered it a 'fragment of a romance' and left it out of his bibliography altogether. Nonetheless, the villain, the Rosicrucian Rougemont, is another of Ainsworth's Mephistophelian characters:

'Some men would call me the devil!' replied Rougemont, carelessly. 'But you know me too well to suppose that I merit such a designation. I offer you wealth. What more could you require?'

'But upon what terms?' demanded Auriol.

'The easiest imaginable,' replied the other. 'You shall judge for yourself.'

And as he spoke, he opened a writing-desk upon the table, and took from it a parchment.

'Sit down', he added, 'and read this.'[13]

After the cliffhanger ending of the original first instalment, the 'novel' unravels over forty new pages until Auriol wakes up wearing his Elizabethan clothes, the story ending with his conclusion that '"I am satisfied I have lived centuries in a few nights."'[14] So it was all a dream. Yet this intriguing misfire, along with *Windsor Castle*, still serves as a preface to Ainsworth's finest piece of occult writing: *The Lancashire Witches*.

Chapter 15

Open House

Installed in his new house, Ainsworth remained as convivial as ever through the 1840s. The need for more space for his girls, now young women, had prompted the move to Kensal Manor House, originally a large bungalow. Ainsworth had it renovated and another storey was added, and it now boasted a huge dining room at the back of the house with access to the garden and the paddock, and a glorious view of the fields and woodland beyond. Pastoral but still close to London, it was a perfect house for dinner and garden parties, which was exactly what its new owner wanted.

He, of course, threw a big housewarming party, which Dickens attended, bearing gifts, having written to accept the invitation:

> My dear Ainsworth
>
> With all imaginable pleasure. I quite look forward to the day. It is an age since we met, and it ought not to be.
>
> The artist has just sent home your 'Nickleby' ... I will bring it together with the 'Pickwick' to your house-warming with me.
>
> Faithfully yours always,
> Charles Dickens.[1]

Guests included Forster, Thackeray, Blanchard, Talfourd, Barham, Lytton, Knight Browne, Maclise, Cruikshank, Captain Marryat, G.P.R. James, Douglas Jerrold, Dr Kenealy, Shirley Brooks, Edwin Landseer, Dudley Costello, William Macready, Lord Albert Conyngham MP, and many old Fraserians and *Ainsworth Magazine* alumni. And now that Ainsworth's daughters were of an age, these gatherings were no longer for men only; 'I will joyfully present myself at six', wrote Dickens in

September 1842, 'and bring my womankind along with me,' referring to his wife, Kate, and sister-in-law Georgina Hogarth.[2] There appears to have been none of the rancour one might have expected after the Newgate Controversy, and Dickens was evidently the life and soul, Ainsworth writing to Dr Thomas Pettigrew (inviting him and his wife to a Christmas party) that 'Dickens has promised to bring his conjuring apparatus with him'.[3] Other correspondence indicates that Dickens also supplied the drink on occasion, and that even ill health could not discourage him from a Kensal Manor House get-together:

> My dear Ainsworth,
>
> I want very much to see you, not having had that old pleasure for a long time. I am at this moment deaf in the ears, hoarse in the throat, red in the nose, green in the gills, damp in the eyes, twitchy in the joints, and fractious in the temper from a most intolerable and oppressive cold, caught the other day, I suspect, at Liverpool, where I got exceedingly wet; but I will make prodigious efforts to get the better of it to-night by resorting to all conceivable remedies ...[4]

Georgina Hogarth lived until 1917 and told S.M. Ellis:

> The parties at Mr. Ainsworth's hospitable house are among the most pleasant remembrances of my girlhood. The guests were generally all the best-known people in literature and art, and the evenings were most social and informal. They were always dinner-parties — succeeded by games and music, and very often winding up with a dance, in which the three young daughters joined. Mr. Ainsworth was a most kind friend of mine, and I was very fond of his three daughters. Mr. Dickens and Mr. Ainsworth were greatly attached to each other, and on most intimate terms.[5]

A nice sketch of the festivities also appears in Serjeant Ballantine's memoir, *Some Experiences of a Barrister's Life*:

> The name of Mr. Landseer brings to my memory that of another gentleman and of a scene, a very pleasant one,

that occurred, alas! many years ago. Its locality is a house in the neighbourhood of Kilburn, spacious and elegantly furnished; the time is early summer, the hour about eight o'clock in the evening; the dinner has been removed from the prettily decorated table, and the early fruits tempt the guests, to the number of twelve or so, who are grouped around it. At the head there sits a gentleman no longer in his first youth, but still strikingly handsome; there is something artistic about his dress, and there may be a little affectation in his manners, but even this may, in some people, be a not unpleasing element. He was our host, William Harrison Ainsworth, and whatever may have been the claims of others, and in whatever circles they might move, no one was more genial, no one more popular.[6]

As well as being remarkably pleasant, as many Victorian memoirists attest, these gatherings were also culturally significant. Even William Wordsworth visited when he was in London. Ainsworth loved to surround himself with his family and friends, and this infectious sociability turned Kensal Manor House into the most popular meeting place for the creative elite, just as Lady Blessington's famous soirees had brought them together in the thirties.

And in addition to the formal gatherings, Ainsworth kept an open house in which friends were always welcome to join him for dinner. This can be seen in a letter from Forster inviting himself over on a sunny day:

> Will you give me pot luck to-day at the Manor House? It is such delicious weather, and an engagement I have to dine with Fox vanishes in that blaze of sunshine which welcomes this brilliant notion. Say 'yes' — if you have no overpowering claim upon you — say 'yes' — and expect on the utterance of the word.
>
> Your affectionate
> John Forster.[7]

Ainsworth's house was a favourite haunt for friends in the summer months, and literally a breath of fresh air after a hard day's quill-driving in dark rooms in an increasingly smoggy London. Thackeray, who at that time still lived in lodgings and was then 'writing for his life', loved Ainsworth's garden. He would often walk to the Manor on Sundays, share an early dinner and then accompany Ainsworth and his daughters to evensong at Willesden Church. Like Ainsworth, Thackeray had had three girls – Anne Isabella, Harriet Marian, and Jane, who died at eight months old. His wife suffering from suicidal depression and in and out of professional care, Thackeray seemed to take great solace from Ainsworth's family, and many of his letters inquire after 'those pretty young ladies'. Like Georgina Hogarth, Anne Isabella Thackeray, later Lady Ritchie, lived a long life and was therefore able to tell S.M. Ellis in person that 'I can quite imagine how glad my father must have been to be with kind people, and to join in their family life. He always loved children and peaceful home doings.'[8]

But it was not just the great and the good who were welcomed. Ellis tells the story of one Mr Perry, a printer's boy who later emigrated to America and died during the Civil War. Perry's job had been to take proofs to Ainsworth and wait while these were reviewed and corrected. While he waited, he was spoiled in the servants' hall with unaccustomed treats, as were all visiting tradespeople. Ainsworth took cuisine very seriously, and to a low-paid, working-class kid, those sweet cakes and oyster patties must have tasted like heaven. On one such occasion, Ainsworth worked on his proofs late into the night. Unwilling to let the boy take the long, lonely walk back to London in the dark, a bed was immediately made up for him. Perry never tired of telling this tale, about the night he spent in the house of the man who wrote *Jack Sheppard*.

Chapter 16

Live at the Witch Trials

Following the collapse of *Auriol*, Ainsworth's next completed work was *James the Second, or The Revolution of 1688; An Historical Romance*, which ran in *Ainsworth's Magazine* from January to December 1847, appearing as a three-volume novel from Colburn the following year. Both serial and novel were illustrated by Robert William Buss, one of the *Pickwick* illustrators best known nowadays for his painting *Dickens's Dream*. The serial was described as 'edited' by Ainsworth, but the novel was attributed to him alone, despite a false rumour at the time that Crossley was the author, which resulted in some teasing from his friend. In this team, Crossley did the history, Ainsworth the creative writing. That May, the cover of *Reynolds's Miscellany of Romance, General Literature, Science, and Art* was a full-page illustration of Ainsworth, Dickens and Lytton as 'The three most popular writers in England'.[1]

James the Second deals with the decline and fall of the unpopular monarch, and his replacement by William of Orange in the Glorious Revolution, resulting in the removal of his Jacobite descendants from the royal lineage. In common with most of Ainsworth's historical plots, the novel also tells the story of the romance between Charles Moor, a loyal Jacobite, and the Huguenot Sabine Saint Leu. The pair are eventually able to marry when Charles proves that he is the rightful Lord Mauvesin, a title usurped by an impostor who is killed when an angry mob fires the house of the Spanish ambassador in London. The highwayman Will Davies ('The Golden Farmer') is sneakily included, but his presence does not save the narrative, which is only marginally more interesting and well-constructed than *Saint James's*.[2] After a couple of rather flat novels, it is oddly only the incomplete *Auriol* that gives an indication of the epic romance with which Ainsworth was to conclude the decade.

The Lancashire Witches is set on and around Pendle Hill in early seventeenth-century Lancashire, with an 'Introduction' set in 1536.

The Cistercian monk Borlace Alvetham is falsely accused of witchcraft by his rival, Brother John Paslew, and condemned to a lingering death. Alvetham escapes by selling his soul to Satan. During the Pilgrimage of Grace, he returns as the warlock Nicholas Demdike to witness the execution of the now Abbot Paslew for treason. Paslew dies cursing Demdike's daughter and 'that infant and her progeny became the Lancashire Witches'.[3] The rest of the story is set a century later, when the ancient witch Mother Demdike wields tremendous power over the area, her evil family challenged only by the rival witches Mother Chattox and Alice Nutter. The elaborate plot centres on the fate of two lovers, the pious Alizon Device (raised by the Demdike clan, but in fact the long-lost daughter of Alice Nutter), and the young aristocrat Richard Assheton. In Book I, Alizon discovers her birth mother is Alice Nutter and resolves to save her soul. Book II chronicles the rivalry between Demdike, Chattox and Nutter, Demdike's attempts to corrupt Alizon, and the eventual destruction of Demdike and Chattox in a fire on Pendle Hill. Book III follows Alice Nutter's penitence, a visit from James I, and the final struggle between heaven and hell for the souls of Alice and her daughter, culminating in a violent confrontation with Alice's demon familiar. Both women praying fervently, the mark of Satan fades from Alice's brow but Alizon is killed by the demon. Richard Assheton, who has been cursed repeatedly by various witches, pines away and the lovers are buried in a single grave.

This is the first of Ainsworth's 'Lancashire novels', and his love for the county of his birth is present on every page. While sharing the Faustian archetype of the less polished *Windsor Castle* and *Auriol*, *The Lancashire Witches* was subject to much more detailed preparation. The project commenced in 1845, three years prior to the first published instalment. In dedicating the novel to James Crossley, Ainsworth acknowledges that both the source material and the original idea came from his friend:

> To James Crossley, Esq., (of Manchester), President of the Chetham Society, and the learned editor of 'The Discoverie of Witches in the County of Lancaster', – the groundwork of the following pages, – this romance, undertaken at his suggestion, is inscribed by his old and sincerely attached friend, the author.

160

Ainsworth's references to the new novel in correspondence date from the Chetham Society's 1845 reprint of Thomas Potts's record of the 1612 trial of the so-called 'Lancashire Witches', which Crossley edited, and document three years of research and several visits to the ruins of Whalley Abbey and the 'Witch Country', which Ainsworth made Gothic and sublime:

> This glen was in very ill repute, and was never traversed, even at noonday, without apprehension. Its wild and savage aspect, its horrent precipices, its shaggy woods, its strangely-shaped rocks and tenebrous depths, where every imperfectly-seen object appeared doubly frightful – all combined to invest it with mystery and terror.[4]

In Ainsworth's magical forest, notions of fact and fantasy blur just as they seemed to in wild, mysterious reality. As Crossley wrote in his introduction to Potts's *Discoverie*: 'The "parting genius" of superstition still clings to the hoary hill tops and rugged slopes and mossy water sides, along which the old forest stretched its length, and the voices of ancestral tradition are still heard to speak from the depth of its quiet hollows.'[5] *The Lancashire Witches* succeeds precisely because of this tangible tension between the real and the unreal that surrounds the complex folklore of the author's native county.

In early 1848, Ainsworth wrote to Crossley, 'I hope you like the "Witches". They find favour here; and satisfy the Sunday Times.'[6] Crossley approved, and the novel was popular with public and publisher alike, although the distorted 'creepy' typography used on the advertisements caused Thackeray to remark that 'I thought I was drunk when I saw the placards in the street'.[7] Ainsworth had received £1,000 from *The Sunday Times* for the complete serial (copyright to revert to him on completion), which was the same deal he had accepted from them in 1841 for *Old St Paul's*. The new serial was just as much of a hit as the old, as was the complete novel upon its release the following year. It remained unillustrated until the third edition of 1854, which contained twelve drawings by Sir John Gilbert, all of which contribute to the fairy-tale qualities that are often apparent in the text by depicting the witches as pointy-hatted hags with flying broomsticks.

There were two famous cases of supposed witchcraft in Lancashire in the first half of the seventeenth century. The first was prosecuted in

1612, as chronicled by Master Potts, and forms the basis for Ainsworth's novel. The second occurred in 1633, and like the first, the most damning testimony came from children. In this case, however, the judges were considerably less credulous, and four of the seven accused were acquitted after the matter was referred to Charles I. The key witness, an 11-year-old boy named Edmund Robinson, confessed many years later to having been induced by his father to give false evidence against women towards whom he bore a grudge. The 1634 play *The Late Lancashire Witches* by Thomas Heywood and Richard Broome took much of its supernatural material from Robinson's account, and it was later reimagined by Thomas Shadwell in his comedy of 1681, *The Lancashire Witches, and Tegue O Devilly The Irish Priest*. Paradoxically, both Ainsworth and Shadwell ridicule the beliefs of the witch-finders of the day while still representing these beliefs as actually true.

In 1612, the 'nineteene notorious witches' of Potts's account were made up of three separate cases – the Pendle Forest group, the Samlesbury witches, and two independents from Padiham and Windle. The Pendle witches present at the August Assizes at Lancaster Castle were Anne Whittle (alias Mother Chattox), Elizabeth, James and Alizon Device (this is Potts's spelling and is probably pronounced 'Davies'), Anne Redfern ('Nance' in Ainsworth's version), Alice Nutter, Katherine Hewitt and John and Jane Bulcock. 'Old Mother Demdike' (Elizabeth Southerns) did not appear, having died in custody. Jennet (Janet) Device, the nine-year-old daughter of Elizabeth, was a key witness for the prosecution and was herself not accused. As Potts tellingly writes of the Magistrate Roger Nowell, 'by his great paines taken in the examination of Iennet Deuice, al their practises are now made knowen'.[8] Jennet was later hanged in the 1633 fiasco.

The Pendle problems began when the licensed beggar Alizon Device was accused of laming by witchcraft a peddler from Halifax called John Law after a dispute over some pins. Law suffered a stroke and his son took up his cause, leading to Roger Nowell's examination of the entire Device family and their friends, many of whom were Catholics, which would have contributed to the magistrate's reported fervour. Demdike, Chattox, Redfern and Alizon Device were immediately detained in the dungeons of Lancaster Castle. Understandably concerned, friends and relatives held a meeting at Malkin Tower on Good Friday and reports of this 'sabbat' resulted in further arrests. At the

Assizes, all but Elizabeth Device confessed to witchraft under torture. Their statements form the body of Potts's account and Ainsworth takes many of the supernatural events in his novel from these testimonies. The Pendle witches were hanged together at Lancaster Castle on Thursday, 20 August 1612, early victims of James I's Witchcraft Act of 1604 and the increasing influence of the continental Inquisition.

Because of Potts's report, this is the most precisely documented witch trial in English history, but there are still many popular versions of the story that have more in common with the imagination of Ainsworth than the detailed accounts left us by Master Potts. In his non-fiction account of the history of witchcraft, *The Devil and All His Works* (1971), for example, Dennis Wheatley wrote:

> In Pendle Forest, a lofty ruin known as Malkin Tower was a favourite place for holding sabbats. Two rival witches, Mother Demdike and Mother Chattox, caused so much trouble in the neighbourhood that a local magistrate had them arrested. On the night of Good Friday, 1612, their covens met at the Tower to cast spells, with the object of freeing their leaders ... all that group of witches were seized and went to the stake.[9]

Malkin Tower was an unremarkable farm near Blacko rather than the impregnable fortress described by Ainsworth and unproblematically accepted by Wheatley. The rivalry between Demdike and Chattox is also an Ainsworthian plot device rather than part of the original account, and the stake was the European punishment for 'witchcraft'; England employed the gallows. Similarly, the Roughlee boundary dispute between Alice Nutter and Roger Nowell, so often cited as the catalyst for the accusations, again comes from the novel. Nowell lived in Read, which is approximately 10 miles south-west of Roughlee, with several properties in between. Once again, the forgotten novelist has supplanted history.

Ainsworth had finally achieved a narrative that had space to develop and contain his unique synthesis of history, romanticism and magic realism. In his presentation of powerful women, who have by social necessity embraced the word of Satan over God, Ainsworth offers his best and, perhaps, the ultimate, romance of fall and redemption. His Faustian protagonists are not modelled after those of Goethe or

Byron, nor are his witches Shakespearian, but return to source: to Eve herself. They are Miltonic, and by further rewriting *Paradise Lost*, *The Lancashire Witches* is both a return to the radical ideals of Romanticism and a quirky precursor to Victorian feminism.

Many Romantics had adopted Satan as the true hero of Milton's epic, favouring the parallel narrative arc of *Paradise Lost* in which Lucifer rebels over the story of Adam and Eve. Also, in the Gothic tradition, the creature of Mary Shelley's *Frankenstein* tells his creator that after reading *Paradise Lost*, 'Many times I considered Satan as the fitter emblem of my condition.'[10] The male Romantics (Blake being the only exception) were not as interested in Eve as they were Satan, often taking their implicitly female muse completely for granted. (When the male Romantic poet stares into a female face, he invariably sees his own, narcissistic reflection.) Ainsworth's narrative may not have the subtlety and depth of *Frankenstein*, nor the overt feminism of the three Brontë sisters, but he is in the same camp, and arguably always was. The powerful and sexually active women of *Jack Sheppard*, for example – Poll Maggot and Edgeworth Bess – are radically different from their sacrificial counterparts in Dickens's fiction and are the only denizens of Ainsworth's Georgian underworld left standing at the conclusion of the novel. The year 1848 also saw the publication of fellow Mancunian Elizabeth Gaskell's *Mary Barton*, in which the fallen woman, Esther, fares no better than Dickens's Nancy. Against such a familiar frame, Ainsworth's witches are trailblazing in their self-emancipation.

The feminist literary critics Sandra Gilbert and Susan Gubar read *Paradise Lost* as a distillation of the endemic, institutional misogyny of Western literary culture, arguing that 'if Eve is in so many negative ways like Satan the serpentine tempter, why should she not also be akin to Satan the Romantic outlaw'. Eve, therefore, 'is the only character in *Paradise Lost* for whom a rebellion against the hierarchical status quo is as necessary as it is for Satan'.[11] Although Adam is subordinate to God, he is still the master of Eden, and Eve. Eve, however, dreams of flying:

> Forthwith up to the clouds
> With him I flew, and underneath beheld
> The earth outstretched immense, a prospect wide
> And various.[12]

Parallels between Satan and Eve abound in *Paradise Lost* and, note Gilbert and Gubar, 'not only is Milton's Satan in certain crucial ways very much *like* women, he is also – enormously attractive to women'.[13]

Ainsworth's novel would seem to offer a similar reading, with his witches representing, in Blake's terms, the various 'emanations' of Eve. In his previous narratives of temptation and fall, the protagonists were all flawed male Faustian figures prosecuting the destruction of female innocents, with only 'Mary Stukeley' in *December Tales* depicting a female tempter. In *The Lancashire Witches*, Ainsworth's previously passive female victims become suddenly very active. The Demdike dynasty is one based upon matriarchal rather than patriarchal authority, the implication being that the peasant women have fallen into grace rather than out of it, from a social hell of repressive fathers, husbands, priests and landlords into a heaven of self-realisation and determination. This can be seen quite clearly in the story of the landed and independent Alice Nutter:

A proud, poor gentleman was Richard Nutter, her late husband, and his scanty means not enabling him to keep up as large an establishment as he desired, or to be as hospitable as his nature prompted, his temper became soured, and he visited his ill-humours upon his wife, who, devotedly attached to him, to all outward appearance at least, never resented his ill-treatment.

All at once, and without any previous symptoms of ailment, or apparent cause, unless it might be over-fatigue in hunting the day before, Richard Nutter was seized with a strange and violent illness, which after three or four days of acute suffering, brought him to the grave. During his illness he was constantly and zealously tended by his wife; but he displayed great aversion to her, declaring himself bewitched, and that an old woman was ever in the corner of his room, mumbling wicked enchantments against him. But as no such old woman could be seen, these assertions were treated as delirious ravings.[14]

Ainsworth wryly concludes that 'Mistress Nutter gave the best proof that she respected her husband's memory by not marrying again.'

Alice later tells Alizon that Richard's violent domestic abuse was 'hidden from the eyes of men', but not the women, who had their revenge.[15]

The innocent Alizon, of course, represents the young, prelapsarian Eve, and resists all temptations to the dark side, being the only one of Elizabeth Device's family to do so. The witches are Eve 'fallen', free, empowered and unrepentant (the dream of flying now a reality), with only Alice ultimately adopting a feminine role that Victorian readers would find more acceptable, that of reformed and contrite sinner. The original Alice was a mysterious figure from the first trial of whom little is known, which gives the author particularly free reign with the character. As she is independent of the Demdikes and the Devices, she is not subject to the abbot's curse and has thus chosen freely to sign the dreaded parchment in return for the power she is seen to wield at the sabbat at the conventual church, where the other witches 'bent so lowly at her coming, and rose so reverentially at her bidding'.[16] Alice, however, moves from the 'queen witch' of Book I to the 'penitent' in Book III, brought to feelings of remorse by 'her newly-awakened affection for her daughter, long supposed dead, and now restored to her' and the question 'Was it, she asked herself, too late to repent? Was there no way of breaking her compact?'[17] On her forehead, she bears the mark of Satan, and as long as it remains we know she is damned, and one cannot help but feel that Bram Stoker had this in mind when Mina Harker was similarly branded by Van Helsing's crucifix in *Dracula* (1897). The finale comes in a battle between Alizon and her mother's former familiar in which Alizon gives her life for Alice's soul. Alice is burned at the stake with all the rest, but her passing is serene. Like Viviana in *Guy Fawkes*, Alizon sacrifices her life for a repentant sinner, and both achieve a state of grace as a result. The rebellion is over, and the hell's angel is once more the angel of the house.

The ostensibly Christian conclusion to *The Lancashire Witches* does little, however, to dispel the overall impression that it can be good to be bad. The story of Alice and Alizon merely confirms that the rewards of virtue are largely spiritual, whereas the witches are seen actively to enjoy their mortal existence. The novel concludes:

> Jennet was the last of the Lancashire Witches. Ever since then witchcraft has taken a new form with the ladies of the county – though their fascination and spells are as potent as ever. Few can now escape them – few desire to do so.

But to all who are afraid of a bright eye and a blooming
cheek, and who desire to adhere to a bachelor's condition –
to such I should say, 'Beware the Lancashire Witches'.[18]

Witchcraft is now a metaphor for female sexuality, which is really what
it always was historically. While celebrating the ladies of Lancashire,
Ainsworth is also suggesting that the sexual/supernatural power of
women that informed his novel may have been transmuted, but that
female magic is merely dormant rather than completely absent, at least
in his home county.

Ainsworth always sympathised with his outlaws, obviously preferring
the freedom they seemed to symbolise compared to the social norm. His
own position as a literary outsider might also be read allegorically within
the pages of this book. Finally, and most significantly, Ainsworth's witch-
women seem to anticipate what is to come in mid-Victorian women's
writing. In 1848, the year of European revolution, Ainsworth may not
have appreciated the full implications of his narrative; he also put the
genie firmly back into the bottle at its conclusion, throwing it onto the
fire for good measure (as Charlotte Brontë did Bertha Mason in *Jane
Eyre*). Nevertheless, his well-established love of outlaws and powerful
women still places this work in the Romantic tradition that, in turn,
leads to the writers who succeeded him – most notably the Brontës – in
redefining the satanic and the Gothic once more. His women at least
know how to fly.

Like the traditional Gothic narrative, Ainsworth's vogue was now
passing. A letter he wrote to his brother-author G.P.R. James during this
period seems to signal their mutual departure from the mainstream as
the new generation of Victorian novelists come of age:

My dear James

Anything I can do for you at any time you know you may
command, and I shall only be too happy in the opportunity
of making kindly mention in *The New Monthly Magazine* of
your *Dark Scenes of History*. The times are not propitious to
us veterans, and literature generally has within the last two
years suffered a tremendous depreciation –
    Do you know, I took it into my head you were the author
of *Jane Eyre*, but I have altered my opinion since I read a

portion of *Shirley*. Currer Bell, whoever he or she may be, has certainly got some of your 'trick', and I began to think you were coming upon us in fresh and more questionable shape. But *Shirley* has again perplexed me.

I hope when you are next in town you will come and dine with me. It will really delight me to see you.

Ever cordially yours,
W. Harrison Ainsworth.[19]

Ainsworth, like his beloved highwaymen, seems suddenly out of time and place; the last of a line, a fantasist in an age of fact and the last of the original English Gothic novelists, soon to be pensioned off by Palmerston.

Pendle Hill is still associated with witchcraft, and every Halloween there is a gathering on the hilltop. Within the last twenty years, two petitions have been presented to Parliament (the first in 1998 and the second in 2008) calling for the Pendle 'witches' to be pardoned, with another campaign launched in 2012, the 400th anniversary of the original case. The anniversary was marked by a series of high-profile civic and cultural events, culminating in the unveiling at Roughlee of a haunting life-size statue of Alice Nutter in chains, sculptured by local artist David Palmer.

The Lancashire Witches was to be Ainsworth's last major national success and marks the end of his literary celebrity, at least in the south of England, although a further twenty-eight novels were yet to be written. It is also, however, the first of an irregular series of works devoted to the history of his birthplace, which would result in the epithet of which he was so proud, that of 'The Lancashire Novelist'.

Chapter 17

The End of an Era

As well as seeing revolutions across Europe, the last Chartist petition and the publication of *The Communist Manifesto*, 1848 also marked a sea change in English literature. The year was prefaced by the publication of *Jane Eyre* in October 1847, followed by *Wuthering Heights* in December. *Dombey and Son* finished its serial run in April and was published as a novel in one volume, heralding Dickens's mature style. Anne Brontë's *The Tenant of Wildfell Hall* was published in June. *Punch's Vanity Fair* serial likewise concluded and was published as a novel by Bradbury and Evans in July, and Thackeray was already writing *Pendennis*. Finally, Mrs Gaskell's *Mary Barton* was published by Chapman and Hall in October, heavily supported by Dickens. This was the high watermark in English fiction. Often before, significant individual novelists had emerged, but now there was a generation.

Popular fiction was also evolving, as seen in Mayhew's vast social study, *London Labour and the London Poor*. In the section entitled 'The Literature of Costermongers', the great social explorer explains that:

> It may appear anomalous to speak of the literature of an uneducated body, but even costermongers have their tastes for books. They are very fond of hearing one read aloud to them, and listen very attentively ... What they love best to listen to – and, indeed, what they are most eager for – are Reynolds's periodicals, especially the 'Mysteries of the Court'. 'They've got tired of Lloyd's blood-stained stories', said one man, who was in the habit of reading to them, 'and I'm satisfied that, of all London, Reynolds is the most popular man among them. They stuck to him in Trafalgar-square, and would again. They all say he's "a trump", and Feargus O'Connor's another trump with them.'[1]

Edward Lloyd was a prolific penny dreadful publisher of titles like *The History of Pirates, The History of and Lives of the Most Notorious Highwaymen, Footpads and Robbers, The Calendar of Horrors* and *The String of Pearls: A Romance*, which introduced the character of Sweeney Todd, the Demon Barber of Fleet Street. G.W.M. Reynolds was a prolific writer and publisher, best known for his epic serial *The Mysteries of London* and a name, wrote Dickens, 'with which no lady's, and no gentleman's, should be associated'.[2] Like Ainsworth, Reynolds was Dickens's other leading commercial rival. Reynolds was also a Chartist and resented Dickens's popular image as a man of the people, feeling that his own voice much more accurately reflected the plight of the urban poor, who from Mayhew's interviews, clearly supported him. Feargus O'Connor was the firebrand Irish leader of the Chartist movement who had presented their third and final petition to Parliament in 1848. Mayhew concludes:

> The tales of robbery and bloodshed, of heroic, eloquent, and gentlemanly highwaymen, or of gipsies turning out to be nobles, now interest the costermongers but little, although they found great delight in such stories a few years back. Works relating to Courts, potentates, or 'harristocrats', are the most relished by these rude people.[3]

The 'harristocrats' were corrupt and debauched politicians and royals from recent history fictionalised in Reynolds's politically charged and sensational *Mysteries*. Ainsworth, of course, was much more reverent with Dame History and largely apolitical aside from his charmingly outdated Jacobitism. Dick Turpin and Jack Sheppard were no longer proletarian icons. They had been replaced by the more tangible figures of O'Connor and Reynolds as the working classes found their political voice in Chartism.

Despite the success of *The Lancashire Witches*, Ainsworth's letter to G.P.R. James indicates he was aware by this point that his time was passing. His inability to understand Brontë was a further indication of his increasing literary stagnation. He had also misunderstood Dickens's growing sophistication, writing to Crossley that *Dombey and Son* was 'infernally bad'.[4] Ainsworth's fiction was fast becoming a fossil of another age, although after buying back his copyrights from Bentley, cheap reprints of his early historical romances published by Chapman and Hall in 1849 sold extremely well. *Windsor Castle* alone shifted 30,000 copies in a couple of weeks, while Ainsworth wrote to Charles Ollier that 6,000 copies of *Rookwood* had sold in London in a single day. Nonetheless, his decline was becoming apparent and he knew it.

Meanwhile, the success of *Vanity Fair* had, predictably, gone to Thackeray's head. Writing to his friend (and possibly lover) Jane Octavia Brookfield, the literary hostess, of dining with Ainsworth in Paris, he said that the older writer showed a 'friendly disposition and a desire to forgive' him 'his success', but although there was 'a good-humoured acquiescence', Thackeray concluded that he really didn't care what his 'old friend' thought.[5] Mrs Brookfield then replied with the following anecdote:

> I am amused at your having Mr. Ainsworth at Paris – he was at Venice when we were there, and was always called 'Tiger or Tig' by Uncle Hallam, who did not know who he was till he came up one day and proffered the hand of fellowship to uncle H. on the ground of their mutual authorship. 'I am Mr. Ainsworth', as if he had been Herschel at the least, and we sat together in the Place St. Mark, eating ices and discussing you, and I recollect saying you had 'such an affectionate nature', which Mr. Ainsworth made me repeat about 3 times, pretending not to hear, and I felt I had thrown pearls before swine and been unnecessarily frank in my praise of you, and began to think he might very possibly have a feeling of jealousy about you as an author, tho' it would be ludicrously presumptuous in him – as of all detestable writing his is the worst, I think.[6] [Henry Hallam was a British historian.]

After Thackeray's treatment of his 'old friend' over the years, we can hardly blame Ainsworth for letting his guard slip. It is also never easy to be superseded by one's protégés, and for Ainsworth this was becoming a depressingly regular occurrence. Thackeray would later write to his mother that 'there has been a sort of coolness since I have got on in the world & he has got off'.[7]

Ainsworth's correspondence with Crossley shows that the next project was to be a sequel to either *Windsor Castle* or *The Tower of London*.

171

It would seem, however, that reading Currer Bell had made an impression as he instead followed *The Lancashire Witches* with a radical departure from his normal style and subject matter with the semi-autobiographical *The Life and Adventures of Mervyn Clitheroe*, written after a lengthy break in which Ainsworth enjoyed the summer of the Great Exhibition and then returned to Paris, later visiting Germany. Crossley was supposed to go with him to France but cried off at the last moment.

Mervyn Clitheroe is also set in Ainsworth's native county, but there any similarity with *The Lancashire Witches* ends. Following a contemporary fashion for *bildungsroman* ('novels of formation') and fictional autobiography, Ainsworth for the first time wrote a story set entirely in his own century. The first book of *Mervyn Clitheroe* was serialised by Chapman and Hall from December 1851 to March 1852, covers designed by 'Phiz'. What makes this a particularly significant text is that, as Ainsworth's oldest friends immediately spotted, the central character is very recognisably the author himself. As he wrote to Charles Ollier:

> Having chosen an everyday subject, I have endeavoured to be as natural as possible, and most of the characters and incidents of this part of the story are taken from life and actual occurrences. The schooldays of 'Mervyn' are a mere transcript of what happened to me at the Free Grammar School at Manchester. 'Dr Longdale' and 'Mr Cane' are no exaggeration. 'John Leigh' is unchanged even in name.[8] Almost all the incidents at Nethercrofts happened to myself; and the old farmer and his wife stood in the same degree of relationship to me that they are supposed to stand to the autobiographer ... The farmhouse and its occupants are, I think, true to nature. And even 'Mrs. Mervyn', who may appear overdrawn, is taken from life, and lives at Kersal Cell ('The Anchorites'), near Manchester.[9]

Ainsworth was obviously enjoying himself, having had, by all accounts, a very happy childhood. Other characters were equally personal. The reserved and scholarly 'John Brideoake' was based on Ainsworth's brother Gilbert before the accident; 'Cuthbert Spring' was old friend Gilbert Winter; 'Colonel Clitheroe' was Captain John Ainsworth, the author's uncle; and the plump and balding bibliophile 'Dr Foam' was Crossley. The protagonist's name is a combination of region and family, 'Mervyn' comes from the Touchets, and 'Clitheroe' (along with several other character names such as 'Massey', 'Malpas', 'Mobberley' and 'Sale') is taken from the map of Lancashire and Cheshire. 'Apphia', the story's heroine, was the Christian name of Ainsworth's great-grandmother. 'Cottonborough' was, of course, Manchester, and *Mervyn Clitheroe* is dedicated to 'My contemporaries at the Manchester School'.

Ainsworth felt that *Mervyn Clitheroe* was 'better than anything I have written'.[10] Friends and critics alike seemed to warm to *Mervyn Clitheroe*, but Ainsworth's audience was not so ready to accept this new direction, wishing instead for another horrible history, the author writing to Mrs Hughes that 'Though, in some respects, he resembles his father more than the rest of his brethren, he is so little like *them*, that the public scarcely seem to recognise him as one of the family'.[11] His disappointment is palpable in his final letter to Crossley on the subject: 'I cannot understand why it has not found favour with the general public, because I have written it carefully, and I think there is interest in the story. But I could not go on at a loss, when that loss might be serious if increased monthly. It is certainly vexatious.'[12] As with *Auriol*, the serial story of *Mervyn Clitheroe* therefore ended abruptly and without resolution with the fourth issue in March 1852. The novel was not completed and published until 1858, when Crossley finally nagged him into it. This time it was reasonably well received, but regrettably, the author, once bitten, did not subsequently pursue the new style.

The young Mervyn Clitheroe – Ainsworth's David Copperfield – is an orphan. The death of his mother in the opening chapter is the change in the status quo that engages the story's engine, and he has never met his father, an army officer lost somewhere in India and presumed dead. He is raised by an elderly relative, Mrs Mervyn, whose great-grandfather died for the Stuart cause in 1715, her grandfather keeping up the family tradition by being killed in the second uprising of 1745. (Everyone she knows can proudly boast of having ancestors executed as Jacobites in various grisly ways.) Mervyn also spends time at Nethercrofts, the farm of his rich great-uncle and aunt, the Mobberleys. Here, he meets and falls foul of the Mobberleys' grandnephew, Malpas Sale. He attends the Free Grammar School, where he befriends the impoverished but brilliant

John Brideoake, whose proud mother has fallen upon hard times. Mervyn falls for his friend's sister, Apphia, but the course of true love does not run smoothly. Expected to inherit Nethercrofts, Mervyn is wrongfully accused of killing a family pet and is disinherited. Mobberley repents and makes a new will, but it is stolen by a corrupt barber-surgeon called Simon Pownall. Playing both sides off against the middle, Pownall and his gypsy henchmen use the secret will to threaten Malpas, who is due to inherit the Mobberley estate upon coming of age, and to torment Mervyn. Worse, Malpas has ingratiated his way into the hearts of the Brideoakes and the Mervyns. Mervyn hears of this while travelling in Europe, and unable to master his temper (his fatal flaw), he writes a hasty and strongly-worded letter to Mrs. Mervyn; when he returns to England he is disavowed by both families. With the help of his few remaining friends, a disparate group of *Pickwickesque* characters including the mysterious Major Atherton (who turns out to be his father in disguise), and the dotty occultist Hazilrigge, he eventually secures his inheritance. Malpas is killed in a riding accident, and the Brideoakes are revealed to be Jacobite nobility and their fortunes restored. Mrs Brideoake forgives Mervyn and he is finally able to marry Apphia, while best friends John Brideoake and Cuthbert Spring pair off with the daughter and sister of Hazilrigge.

The literary historian George J. Worth uses *Mervyn Clitheroe* as an example of a conventional Ainsworth plot. And with its lost inheritance, melodramatic villain and a thwarted love story that turns out well in the third act, this is true. Only the near-contemporary setting and dearth of great historical figures marks it out, and, most importantly, the autobiographical content. Although not based on a real person, Norbury Radcliffe Hazelrigge (or 'Old Hazy') is also worth noting as an ostensibly familiar figure in an Ainsworth plot, the brooding occultist. What's unique is that Ainsworth plays him entirely for laughs, as the Gothic writer J.S. Le Fanu (who admired Ainsworth) did with Spiritualists in his novel *All in the Dark* (published by Bentley in 1866), despite being famous for his ghost stories. Old Hazy firmly believes himself to be a powerful necromancer but is in fact nothing of the sort. 'He seems to have the organ of credulity rather extensively developed,' observes Mervyn, and through a humorous deconstruction of Hazelrigge's dearly held beliefs, Ainsworth appears to enjoy himself negating many of his own stock Gothic devices.[13]

Finally, there is the vivid depiction of industrial Manchester, dominated by giant warehouses and ornate public buildings, in contrast with the most appalling slums and industrial pollution, reflecting an obscenely wealthy mercantile class who had left the cramped city centre to their new workforce. As a middle-class Mancunian, however, Ainsworth/Mervyn does seek to find a balance that is generally absent from better-known contemporary accounts of this potent symbol of Victorian capitalism:

What a wondrous town is Cottonborough! How vast – how populous – how ugly – how sombre! Full of toiling slaves, pallid from close confinement and heated air. Full of squalor, vice, misery: yet also full of wealth and all its concomitants – luxury, splendour, enjoyment. The city of coal and iron – the city of the factory and the forge – the city where greater fortunes are amassed, and more quickly, than in any other in the wide world. But how – and at what expense? Ask yon crew of care-worn men, wan women, and sickly children, and they will tell you. Look at yon mighty structure, many-windowed, tall-chimneyed, vomiting forth clouds of smoke, to darken and poison the wholesome air. Listen to the clangour and the whirl of the stupendous and complicated machinery within. Count the hundreds of pale creatures that issue forth from it at meal-times. Mark them well, and say if such employment be healthy. Yet these poor souls earn thrice the wages of the labourer at the plough, and therefore they eagerly pursue their baneful taskwork. Night comes; the mighty mill is brilliantly lighted up, and the gleam from its countless windows is seen afar. It looks like an illuminated palace ... There Mammon has set up his altars: there his ardent votaries are surest of reward. Ugly and black is Cottonborough, shrouded by smoke, tasteless in architecture, boasting little antiquity, and less of picturesque situation; yet not devoid of character strongly impressive, arising from magnitude, dense population, thronged streets, where the heavy wagon with its bales of goods takes place of the carriage, vast warehouses, and a spacious and bust 'Change – the resort of the wealthiest merchants of the realm. Active and energetic are its inhabitants, enterprising, spirited, with but one thought – one motive – one aim, and one end – MONEY. Prosperous is Cottonborough – prosperous beyond all other cities – and long may it continue so; for, with all its ugliness, and all its faults – and they are many – I love it well.[14]

In common with the Manchester of Gaskell's *Mary Barton*, Ainsworth makes much of the contrast between countryside and city life. Although Mervyn asserts his love of this city of contrasts, he cannot help but return again and again to the squalor that surrounds him (the corrosive air, ankle-deep sludge and creeping black snow are also particularly memorable details), and he is happy to escape into the preserved Georgian haven of Mrs Mervyn's household. That said, lacking an obvious political agenda, Ainsworth's 'Cottonborough' is one of the most objective accounts of Manchester from this period.

But back in 1851, Ainsworth had produced, in commercial if not critical terms, his first real flop. This must have been a very nasty surprise, especially given his personal investment in the work. Just as critical pressure had killed off a very promising run of innovative outsider novels, public pressure had once more pulled Ainsworth back into the clutches of the historical romance, at a time when he appeared, along with his contemporaries, to be breaking away into a new creative area. But, as he'd indicated to Crossley, he couldn't afford to invest in a failure. Years of excessive entertaining and a careless attitude to his businesses – he still paid his writers too much – had seriously depleted his finances, while his own serial novels no longer commanded the high sales they once had. He had to start downsizing, so, in the summer of 1853, he sold his beloved Kensal Manor House, got rid of his horses and most of his servants and moved to a smaller house in Brighton, which he purchased from his friend Charles Hervey, another *Ainsworth's Magazine* contributor.

No. 5, Arundel Terrace, Kemp Town, was a tidy, seafront property within easy walking distance of the Downs, on which Ainsworth took a turn more days than he did not. With this move, the old circle of Forster, Dickens, Thackeray *et al* broke up, and although Ainsworth continued to privately entertain, the great literary gatherings were over. Life became much quieter.[15]

After *Mervyn Clitheroe* was mothballed, Ainsworth began two conventional historical romances, which were written side by side in 1853/4. *The Flitch of Bacon* was serialised in the *New Monthly* while *The Star Chamber* appeared in the *Home Companion*. The Star Chamber was an English court that sat at the royal Palace of Westminster, established in the fifteenth century to ensure the fair enforcement of laws against people so powerful that ordinary courts would hesitate to convict. The melodramatic novel is set during the reign of James I, with some wonderful descriptions of Jacobean London, when the Star Chamber was at the height of its almost Inquisitional power and the king and his favourites abused it to extort money and suppress political rivals. The story concerns the ruination of the family of Sir Ferdinando Mounchesney at the hands of the corrupt and unscrupulous noblemen Sir Giles Mompesson and Sir Francis Mitchell. Sir Ferdinand's son, Jocelyn, recovers the family fortune and gets the girl at the end.

The Flitch of Bacon or The Custom of Dunmow is subtitled 'A Tale of English Home' and that's exactly what it is. Set in 1750, this rather rambling tale of simple country folk – enlivened by some very good ballads – is based around the old custom of awarding a flitch of bacon to married couples who can swear to having not regretted their union for a year and a day. Dating back to the fourteenth century – Chaucer mentions it in *The Canterbury Tales* – the tradition survived in Little Dunmow in Essex until the mid-eighteenth century, and the main plotline concerns two couples competing to prove theirs is the most blissful marriage. The novel is lightweight but rather fun and was very popular. It was translated into several languages, being especially well received in Russia, with whom Great Britain was then at war in the Crimea. The novel was greatly loved in Dunmow, to the extent that locals decided to revive the tradition, inviting Ainsworth to present the award. As the custom originated at Dunmow Priory before the English Reformation, local clergy strongly objected to what they viewed as a Papist ceremony being revived at the original site (now a church). Hostile pamphlets were circulated, and the Lord of the manor forbad the event to take place on his lands, leading to its relocation to the town hall at Great Dunmow. Many claims were made and tested, the committee finally deciding upon the brickie James Barlow and his wife, Hannah, of Chipping Ongar. Ainsworth had dedicated the book to his friends Baron and Baroness von Tauchnitz, who published, among other things, English Classics in Leipzig, and whom Ainsworth believed to be the happiest couple he had ever met. He put in a good word for them at Great Dunmow, and it was agreed that two flitches would be awarded. Much was made of the event, and special trains were laid on from London.

The ceremony took place on Thursday, 19 July 1855. Unfortunately, it chucked it down, but the locals remained enthusiastic and several tourists from the capital also braved the weather. Ainsworth took the chair and made an epic speech on the tradition itself and the nature of wedded bliss, and the couples then presented their cases as if in court, with the journalist Dudley Costello and Robert Bell, editor of the *Atlas*, acting as counsels for the defence and prosecution. The German publishers took on the Essex builders and in the end, everyone won. The sun came out and there was then a medieval floral procession through the streets of the town, the presentation taking place in a field marquee in front of an estimated 7,000 people. There were more speeches, followed by much drinking and dancing. A full account of the proceedings was published in *Bentley's Miscellany* and the *Illustrated London News*. 'Flitch Trials' are still held in Great Dunmow to this day.

The reason that *Bentley's* covered the event was because by then Ainsworth had quietly acquired it. This had all happened very quickly, Bentley approaching Ainsworth with the deal. Cutting short another European trip, Ainsworth had written to Crossley in October 1854:

> I have just concluded an arrangement for the purchase of Bentley's Miscellany, so with The New Monthly I shall have two powerful magazines in my hands. I have given a long price (£1,700 for the copyright of Bentley's Miscellany), but I hope in the end it will fully repay me. It was this matter which brought me back from the Continent sooner than I desired ... Do not mention this circumstance, especially in any literary circles, as I do not intend to have any ostensible connection with the magazine, which will continue to be published by Bentley.[16]

He also wrote to Shirley Brooks that:

> My acquisition of The Miscellany was a very sudden matter, and made without much consideration. I hope I shall

have a good bargain, but if I see my money back in three years, it is as much as I expect. I was just starting for Paris when I received Bentley's offer of the magazine, and on the day after my return I called upon him, and the matter was settled.[17]

The sale had been a 'sudden matter' because Bentley was desperate. His empire had crumbled since losing Dickens and Ainsworth, and the *Miscellany* had become a showcase for his other publications rather than the culturally literate organ of the 1840s. As modern publishing expanded, along with every other business in the British industrial free market, competition in the industry of which Bentley had been a founding father had become ferocious and he had failed to keep up. His new sixpenny newspaper, *Young England*, had floundered after fourteen issues, and cheap editions of his back catalogue in 'Bentley's Shilling Series' and the 'Parlour Bookcase' had similarly failed to take off. Worst of all, changes in copyright law in 1849 had resulted in Bentley losing his monopoly on the many American titles he had acquired over the years; a formerly steady income that often kept his company afloat. Increasingly in debt, Bentley had embarked on a fire sale of his copyrights and Ainsworth was an easy mark, known for impetuous financial decisions and less business sense than he was born with.

From Ainsworth's point of view, it was a chance to cut the mooring line with the increasingly unprofitable *Ainsworth's Magazine* and control the two biggest titles in mid-Victorian periodical publishing. Although Ainsworth was not a vindictive man, it perhaps also felt good to best Bentley and snag the magazine that had so ill-used him in the past. Ainsworth had maintained the high standard of the *New Monthly*, but at the expense of the magazine that bore his name, in which he had resorted to re-running his old serials, backed-up with weaker new material by relative unknowns who did not go on to achieve any literary prominence. He thus bought it quietly to a close at the end of the year on Volume XXV, while starting a new serial, *The Spendthrift*, in *Bentley's*.

Set in the mid-eighteenth century, *The Spendthrift* was a competent but unremarkable historical novel with an interesting premise that fails to deliver a strong dramatic climax. In a nice class reversal, a servant grows rich at his rakish young master's expense by goading him into reckless gambling and increasingly extravagant living.

The manipulative steward, Fairlie, also pushes his unwilling daughter, Clare, into a romance with his master, Gage de Monthermer, even though he is already betrothed to the aristocratic Lucy Poynings. Clare falls for Gage but also befriends Lucy and the two become allies, trying to save the clueless young man. The stress of Clare's conflicted emotions and her failure to stop her father's schemes drives her into an early grave, but before she passes, she writes a long letter to Fairlie. At the verge of supplanting his flawed and now ruined master, Clare's last message impels Fairlie to restore Gage's fortune before dying himself. The penitent spendthrift is thus able to marry Lucy, the novel concluding with the moral that 'A reformed rake makes the best husband'.[18] As ever, there is some impressive world-building, from the gambling hells of Georgian London to the races at Newmarket Heath and the family seat in Suffolk, 'Monthermer Castle' (modelled after Hengrave Hall, a Tudor manor near Bury St Edmunds). The serial was further dignified by eight wonderful illustrations from 'Phiz'.

The Spendthrift was followed in the same year with *Ballads: Romantic, Fantastical, and Humorous*, a collection of the best of the songs from Ainsworth's novels, published by Routledge and nicely illustrated by John Gilbert. And the year after that, 1856, Ainsworth was awarded a Civil List Pension of £100 per annum for his services to English literature on the recommendation of Lord Palmerston, which must have been a relief on one hand, but on the other a little like being put out to pasture. 'It was a great misfortune to me that Disraeli went out,' he would later write to Crossley. 'He would have given me something better than a pension.'[19]

Dickens, Forster and Ainsworth dined together one more time, at the National Club, Whitehall Gardens, in June 1854. Dickens relocated from London to Gad's Hill Place in 1856, and without any apparent enmity, he and Ainsworth seemed to just drift apart as friends sadly often do in later years, as there is no further record of them ever meeting again. Thackeray tried to organise a Kensal Manor 'reunion' dinner involving himself, Maclise, Dickens and Ainsworth in March 1857, but everyone was too busy to agree a date, Dickens by then committed to extensive and lucrative reading tours. 'Something tells me that it may be long before the banquet in question takes place,' Thackeray told Maclise, and he was right; the event never happened.

Chapter 18

Semi-Retirement

Ainsworth ended the fifties with a scholarly work. *The Combat of the Thirty* is his own translation from the French of an epic medieval ballad chronicling a strange episode in the Breton War of Succession. *Le Combat des Trente*, 1351, was an arranged battle between thirty select combatants on each side representing the interests of King Philip VI and Edward III, fought to determine control of the Duchy of Brittany. After a close and bloody fight, the Franco-Bretons carried the day. Medieval chroniclers celebrated both English and French champions as symbols of the highest ideals of chivalry. Ainsworth's text is based on an original medieval ballad he found and transcribed in the Bibliothèque du Roi. The story is further enhanced by his translation and application of a recently discovered lost chapter of Jean Froissart's fourteenth-century *Chroniques* of the Hundred Years War. The work, which he published in *Bentley's Miscellany* and as a separate pamphlet, is prefaced by a learned introduction, showing Ainsworth's skills as both a historian and a linguist. 'I want to get it known,' Ainsworth wrote to Charles Kent, 'and it is difficult to make the public look at a poem nowadays.'[1] The year 1859 also saw the loss of old friend, the publisher Charles Ollier, the only man in whom Ainsworth confided almost as much as he did Crossley. Leigh Hunt – who Dickens had sent up as the freeloading Harold Skimpole in *Bleak House* – also died that year; Ainsworth wrote of him that he was 'one of the shrewdest and kindliest of critics – a man who always tried to see good in everything'.[2]

The sixties began with a new romance in *Bentley's Miscellany*, *Ovingdean Grange, A Tale of the South Downs*, which ran from November 1859 to July 1860. Of his later historical romances, *Ovingdean Grange* is one of Ainsworth's better efforts and his descriptions of the sweeping Downs are particularly effective. The story is largely concerned with the escape of Charles II after defeat at the Battle of Worcester in 1651, told in parallel with that of fleeing fictional Royalist Clavering Maunsel, who also takes refuge at the Grange and is hunted by the relentless Roundhead captain, Stelfax. As ever, the novel ends with the hero's marriage. In terms of Ainsworth historical chronology, *Ovingdean Grange* picks up Charles's flight where the later novel *Boscobel* (1872) concludes. Scott's *Woodstock* (1826) covers much the same ground and Ainsworth's plot is often quite similar. Having fallen in love with the South Downs, Ainsworth was looking for a historical narrative set there. The legend that Charles had visited Ovingdean Grange gave Ainsworth his plot, although it is unlikely that the king made the detour in reality. Ainsworth now walked to Ovingdean Church every Sunday, and he dedicated the book 'To the Rev. Alfred Stead, Rector of Ovingdean, by One of his Flock'. Every location in the story was familiar to him, and in this sense *Ovingdean Grange* is another very personal work.

Money was once more a problem, and Ainsworth was forced to sell the house in which he was born in Manchester for £5,500. (King Street was soon to become prime real estate as a new business district, and had Ainsworth sold a couple of years later he would have made a small fortune.)[3] He was also very eager to sell his other family house in Manchester, 'Beech Hill', to provide some much-needed financial security as he grew older, and to escape the yoke of constant literary production, writing to Crossley:

> For several years I have been obliged to work exceedingly hard, and the strain is almost too much for me, and I may break down. It is only prudent therefore to relax these excessive exertions, but as I now stand I cannot do so. Of course I should be glad to get more for the property, But I will take £3,000 for it … I shall consider what you do for me in this matter as a *great act of friendship*, and I feel sure you will be glad to serve me, and to help lighten my labours.[4]

Crossley sold the house for the required amount in June 1854, which Ainsworth invested in Indian Railway shares, losing the lot.

Ainsworth continued to write at least one middling serial a year throughout the sixties. *The Constable of the Tower* (*Bentley's Miscellany*, 1861) sits chronologically between *Windsor Castle* and *The Tower of London*. It begins with the death of Henry VIII and follows the coronation and brief reign of Edward VI. Xit, Og, Gog and Magog from *The Tower of London* therefore return as secondary characters. The story concerns the ultimately thwarted pursuit of power by Henry's brother-in-law, Thomas Seymour, who woos both Princess Elizabeth and Catherine Parr, before finally being betrayed by a subordinate and executed. In the real world, Ainsworth's youngest daughter, Blanche, married Francis Swanson, an Anglo-Indian Royal Artillery captain, in August 1861.[5]

The Lord Mayor of London (*Bentley's Miscellany*, 1862) trod much the same ground as *The Spendthrift*. This is another redemptive tale of an extravagant eighteenth-century rake called Tradescant Lorimer, son of the mayor, who cleans up his act after a series of escalating crises, marries and joins the family business. *Cardinal Pole* (*Bentley's Miscellany*, 1863) is a sequel to *The Tower of London*, covering Mary's marriage to Philip of Spain and sharing many of the same characters. The secondary storyline concerns the doomed romance of Osbert Clinton and Constance Tyrrell. *Cardinal Pole* concludes with the death of Mary. In 1862, Ainsworth also donated first editions of his favourite works to the Chetham's Library, after a request by the chief librarian.

Before *Cardinal Pole* had concluded, Ainsworth was already working on *John Law* (*Bentley's Miscellany*, 1864). John Law was an early eighteenth-century Scottish financier who went to the French court. He was a brilliant speculator and established the Bank of France until his bubble eventually burst and he died in poverty. Ainsworth follows his life in France, which is told in parallel with the fictional Laborde family, who are ruined by the speculative mania incited by Law's paper money and Mississippi schemes. *The House of the Seven Chimneys* (*Bentley's Miscellany*, 1865) concerned the adventures of Charles I, then still Prince of Wales, as he travelled to Madrid to claim the hand of the Infanta Maria, fighting brigands and attending balls and bullfights along the way. The title refers to the house in Madrid where Charles lived in secret. (It was changed to *The Spanish Match* when published as a three-volume novel by Chapman and Hall at the end of 1865.)

The following year, Ainsworth was delighted to be included in *Modern Songs and Ballads of Lancashire*, edited by Crossley's friend John Harland, which anthologised 'The Mandrake' (from *The Lancashire Witches*), 'Black Bess' (*Rookwood*), and 'Old Grinrod's Ghost' (*The Flitch of Bacon*). The 'completed' *Auriol* followed, then the *Crichtonesque* serial *The Constable de Bourbon* (*Bentley's Miscellany*, 1866), set in 1523 when Charles de Bourbon, Constable of France, joined forces with Emperor Charles V and Henry VIII in an attempt to overthrow François I. The story covers the Siege of Marseilles and the Battle of Pavia, and concludes with Bourbon's death during the Sack of Rome in 1527.

Old Court (*Bentley's Miscellany*, 1867) was, like *Mervyn Clitheroe*, set in the present day and is at once a tale of fashionable life, a Gothic novel and a very Victorian melodrama, and is as close as Ainsworth came to the 'sensation' novels of Wilkie Collins and Charles Reade. In the story, Sir Hugh Chetwynd and his brother Clarence love the same girl. Hugh accidentally kills his rival, and in atonement he hopes to bequeath the family seat, Old Court, to his nephew. Young Clarence loves Hugh's daughter Lucetta, but she rejects him for Captain Rainald Fanshaw. Meanwhile, the shadowy Vandeleur La Hogue is revealed to have witnessed the murder. He blackmails Sir Hugh at first, then finally kills him, before dying trapped in Old Court as it burns. Clarence survives and pairs off with Fanshaw's sister.

The same year, ever-decreasing sales forced Ainsworth to move to another cheaper property. After fourteen happy years in Brighton, he 'retired' to a smaller house in Tunbridge Wells at No. 1, St James's Villas. Ainsworth became increasingly insular, having few local friends and rarely appearing in public. He ceased to entertain anyone outside the family at home, seeing friends only at his club, the Carlton, when in London. This social withdrawal was likely the result of an even more significant event that year, the birth of another daughter, Clara Rose, with the mysterious Sarah Wells, thirty years his junior. S.M. Ellis, ever the Edwardian gentleman, cites a 'private marriage (some years earlier)' but says no more.[6] Public records, however, tell a more interesting story.

In the 1861 census for Ainsworth's household, Sarah Wells is listed as a 'housemaid', aged twenty-six. By 1871, Jane Wells – Sarah's mother – has entered the household as a 'general domestic

184

servant' while a 'Sarah Williams', aged thirty-six, is listed as 'housekeeper' along with her daughter, 'Clara Williams', aged five. By the 1881 census, under 'William Harrison Ainsworth – author, novelist', appears 'Sarah Ainsworth – wife', aged forty-six, and 'Rose Ainsworth – daughter', aged fifteen. And, although not acknowledged in the 1871 census, Ainsworth and Sarah had, indeed, married, in Braintree, in September. Clara Rose was born on 28 July of the next year, although apparently not publicly acknowledged until towards the end of her father's life.

Still compelled to write, Ainsworth's last contribution to *Bentley's Miscellany* was the serial *Myddleton Pomfret*, published in 1868. Again set in the present day, 'Myddleton Pomfret' is the assumed name of the debt-ridden Julian Curzon, who fakes his own death by drowning in Lake Windermere (in front of his new bride, Sophy), before absconding to India and making a fortune. He returns to England years later to find Sophy married to the oily womaniser Captain Scrope Musgrave, who knows his true identity. In the story's climax, Curzon kills Musgrave in a duel. Once the serial concluded, Ainsworth sold the increasingly moribund magazine back to Bentley for £250. An increasing lack of funds had resulted in the necessity of reducing contributors' fees over the last few years, and the talent had gone elsewhere. As had been the case with *Ainsworth's Magazine*, sales had fallen, and Bentley merged it with *Temple Bar Magazine*. It ceased publication in 1906. Ainsworth's second involvement with *Bentley's Miscellany* had nonetheless had a significant impact on popular Victorian literature through his discovery and promotion of the popular authors 'Ouida' (Louise de la Ramé) and Mrs Henry Wood.

The young writer 'Ouida' – named from a childhood mispronunciation of 'Louise' – knew Francis Ainsworth, who encouraged her to submit work to one of his cousin's magazines. Her first contribution was the short story 'Dashwood's Drag; or the Derby and what came of it', which was published in *Bentley's Miscellany* in 1859 when she was nineteen. Ainsworth was so impressed that he published a further seventeen of her stories over the next year, writing in his 'Epilogue' of 1860 that:

> We offer not our own opinion, but that of a host of critical commentators, when we say that few periodical writers have suddenly achieved a greater success than the contributor

who has chosen the fanciful designation of 'Ouida', whose sketches of society, both in England and on the Continent, are as graceful as they are accurate.[7]

'Accurate' was something of an overstatement, as 'Ouida's' early short fiction was already establishing her intense bodice-ripping style, always set against a somewhat artificial background of military and Society life. After a succession of stories with titles such as 'Belles and Blackcock', 'Coaches and Cousinship' and 'Taming of the Pythoness', 'Ouida' was ready for a novel. Under the encouragement and tutelage of Ainsworth, she wrote her first long work for the *New Monthly Magazine*, the serial *Granville de Vigne*, which ran from 1861 to 1863 and is better known as her first novel, *Held in Bondage*. This she followed with *Strathmore* (*New Monthly*, 1863–65), then *Idalia* (*New Monthly*, 1865–67). The title of the latter was suggested by Ainsworth, who disapproved of her original in a telling piece of editorial advice. 'I do not like the title *The Lady of his Dreams*,' he wrote to her. 'It might do very well as the title of a poem, especially of the Tennysonian school, which I abominate, but it is too lackadaisical for a novel. If you can find nothing better, give it the name of the hero or heroine.'[8] 'Ouida' was a suitable successor to Ainsworth. She went on to write forty-five novels, the most successful being *Under Two Flags* (1867), a tale of the Foreign Legion. She remained popular until the early 1890s, and although a period of relative poverty followed, she was granted a Civil List pension and died in reasonable comfort in 1908. Like Ainsworth, she is not much read nowadays.

Mrs Henry Wood (born Ellen Price) contributed short stories to both *Bentley's Miscellany* and the *New Monthly Magazine* anonymously for some years before she became anxious to write a serial novel. Ainsworth was resistant at first, but Wood persuaded him by refusing to contribute any further short fiction unless he also accepted a longer work. As, by his own admission, the magazine could not have survived without her short stories, Ainsworth accepted *East Lynne* as a serial for the *New Monthly*, and it ran from January 1860 to September 1861. Mixing piety, sentimentality and melodrama in roughly equal measure, the saga of Lady Isobel Vane was something of a slow burner at the time. As *East Lynne* ultimately made Mrs Wood world famous, it is often forgotten that she could not originally give it away to a publisher in its novelised form. *East Lynne* was first offered to Chapman and Hall, who turned it down flat on the recommendation of their reader, George Meredith, despite Ainsworth's protestations. Ainsworth continued to lobby his old publishers and, at his suggestion, Chapman and Hall returned the manuscript to Meredith for reconsideration, but it was again dismissed out of hand. Smith and Elder returned *East Lynne* unread, and Bentley finally took it on, the novel going on to be one of the best sellers in the history of his publishing house. Mrs Wood, now suddenly rich and famous, did not forget Ainsworth's support, and she wrote *The Shadow of Ashlydyat* for the *New Monthly* (serialised from 1861 to 1863), accepting only a fee of £60, her standard rate before she became a literary celebrity.

Ainsworth concluded the sixties with *Hilary St Ives* (1869) in the *New Monthly Magazine*. This was another contemporary serial, and the devices of the historical romance, melodramatic dialogue, formal courtship, transparent disguises and supernatural occurrences seem absurdly out of place in the polite society of Victorian Guildford. The plot involves the young artist Hilary St Ives, who turns out to be the long-lost son of Colonel Seymour Delacombe and the housekeeper, Mrs Sutton.

The year 1869 was a sad one for the family though, seeing the passing of Eliza Touchet, aged seventy-seven. 'Drink as much old port as you can, while there is yet time, and rejoice us of old,' Ainsworth wrote to Crossley.[9] For the first time, he seems to have sensed his own mortality. 'You seem to be flourishing like an oak, and to set time at defiance, while I find myself growing older,' he told his friend, adding fatalistically, 'I am obliged to be careful.' Shattered after *Hilary St Ives*, he concluded, 'I am just putting the finishing touches to a story on which I have been engaged for the last nine months. Whether I shall write another, Heaven knows!'[10]

Restless and bereaved, Ainsworth left Tunbridge Wells at Christmas and returned to his beloved South Downs, moving to 'Little Rockley' at Hurstpierpoint. Here he lived with his two single daughters, moving between the new house and Hill View Lodge, Reigate, the home he had purchased for his brother. 'Gilbert is in excellent health,' he reported to Crossley. 'He takes long walks in this beautiful country twice a day with his attendant.'[11] Ainsworth now had no desire to socialise. He took long, lonely walks with his King Charles spaniels, and endeavoured to avoid people as he slogged across the Downs. As Dickens's friend Percy Fitzgerald later told Ellis:

> I recall a dinner at Teddington, in the sixties, given by Frederic Chapman, the publisher, at which were Forster and Browning. The latter said humorously,
> 'A sad, forlorn-looking being stopped me today, and reminded me of old times. He presently resolved himself into – whom do you think? Harrison Ainsworth!'
> 'Good Heavens!' cried Forster, 'is he still alive?'[12]

Ainsworth was, however, destined to outlive almost all his contemporaries. On hearing of Dickens's death in 1870, he poignantly wrote to Charles Kent, 'I was greatly shocked by the sudden death of poor Dickens. I have not seen him of late years, but I always hoped that we might meet again, as of old.'[13] Of Richard Bentley, who died the following year, he wrote to Crossley, 'Did you notice Bentley's death in the papers – aged 77? I thought he had been older. He was a great rascal.'[14]

As soon as he had cut the mooring line with *Bentley's Miscellany*, Ainsworth threw in his lot with John Dicks's new periodical *Bow Bells: A Magazine of General Literature and Art*. Dicks had started out as a penny dreadful publisher and had worked closely with G.W.M. Reynolds back in the day. He had been a clerk of George Vickers, who had published *The Mysteries of London*, and had gone into business with Reynolds after a rift between author and publisher, producing *Reynolds's Miscellany* and *The Mysteries of the Court of London*, a major source of stories about 'Courts, potentates, or "harristocrats"' cited by Mayhew as greatly loved by working-class readers. He now published affordable popular fiction for the masses, such as 'Shilling Shakespeares' and cheap editions of Scott and other well-known but passé authors including Lytton and G.P.R. James. Established in 1862, *Bow Bells* had assimilated *Reynolds's Miscellany* the year before Ainsworth joined it. This was to be the destination of most of Ainsworth's remaining literary works.

His first serial for Dicks was *The South Sea Bubble* (1868), something of an English version of *John Law*. Framed by the audacious rise of the South Sea Company and subsequent crash in 1720, Margaret Harpledown establishes her parentage, recovers the will of her murdered father, and marries the love of her life, Trevor Craven. *Talbot Harland* appeared in *Bow Bells* next in 1870. This 'Tale of the days of Charles II' was contemporary with J. Hain Friswell's scathing attack in *Modern Men of Letters*, and he singled it out for criticism because of the inclusion of the French highwayman Claude Duval. Had this been conceived and written in the 1830s it would probably have been a masterful Newgate novel; as it is, Talbot Harland is a dreary hero and 'Claude Duval' turns out to be an imposter. In the same year, Ainsworth passed the editorship of the *New Monthly Magazine* to his cousin Francis, remaining the owner until 1879, when Chapman and Hall took over. It ceased publication in 1884.

In October 1870, Ainsworth was invited to dinner in Manchester by the trustees of the Grammar School as a distinguished old boy. As the south forgot Ainsworth, his native north was increasingly embracing him as something of a regional treasure. Similarly, as his books became progressively peripheral to English literature, they remained popular in the United States (although unlicensed editions meant that the author never saw a penny). Tickled by a letter from an American reader, he copied it out and sent it to Crossley, 'as I do not want to part with the original':

To Mr. Ainsworth from Mr. Latrobe,

Permit me, as a stranger to you, to express the pleasure with which I have read the very excellent series of historical romances by which you have so admirably illustrated many of the localities and edifices of England, together with the manners, customs, and superstitions of their most interesting epochs ... I am an American residing in the city of Baltimore, Maryland, The United States, visiting England for the first time ... In my visits to Windsor Castle and the Tower of London, your volumes were my companions, and vastly enhanced the pleasure of the visits.

Yours very respectfully
Benjamin H. Latrobe.[15]

Ainsworth, of course, had taken the time to reply in person, as he always did with his fans, taking great joy in positive feedback from any source. Mr Latrobe's letter also gives a context for Ainsworth's work apparently overlooked in his own country; that of the heritage industry.

Tower Hill, another history that fills in the gaps between *Windsor Castle* and *The Tower of London*, was the next *Bow Bells* serial, appearing in 1871. This is a return to form for Ainsworth and tells the story of Anne of Cleves and Catherine Howard. Catherine uses her influence over Henry VIII to aid the Catholic cause in England, but she is exposed as the lover of Francis Dereham by Archbishop Cranmer and the story ends with her execution on Tower Hill. *Boscobel, or The Royal Oak. A Tale of the Year 1651* followed in the *New Monthly* and was published in three volumes by the Tinsley Brothers in 1872. William and Edward Tinsley were interesting businessmen. The sons of a gamekeeper from a family of ten children, they were taken out of school to work in the fields scaring birds as kids. The brothers were nonetheless inveterate bookworms, and as a young adult William tried his hand at second-hand bookselling before going into business as a publisher in 1858, encouraging Edward to quit his job on the railways and join him. They started out with virtually no capital and even less knowledge of the industry but caught the sensation fiction wave and hit it big with *Lady Audley's Secret* by Mary Elizabeth Braddon in 1862. They published Thomas Hardy's early novels but lost out on *Far from the Madding Crowd* to the *Cornhill Magazine* through an unwillingness to raise his fee.

Like *Tower Hill*, *Boscobel* represents Ainsworth at his best again, recalling in standard the great historical romances of the 1840s, and of his later works it is still well worth seeking out. As a *New Monthly* project, Ainsworth would have been more inclined to keep the bar high. This was another Jacobite romance, the tale of Charles II's attempts to elude Cromwell's forces and escape to France after the Royalists were defeated at the Battle of Worcester. It covers the king's flight to White Ladies Priory in Brewood Forest, then on to Madeley Court and Boscobel House disguised as a woodsman, and the famous story of his hiding in a pollarded oak in Boscobel Wood, guarded and guided to safety by loyal foresters, the Penderel brothers. It concludes with his arrival at Heale House, setting up the events of *Ovingdean Grange*. Narrative pace is positively page-turning, as one resourceful escape is followed by another, Cromwell's trackers never far behind.

Merry England; or, Nobles and Serfs (*Bow Bells*, 1874) goes back to 1381 and the Peasants' Revolt. Aside from *The Combat of the Thirty*, it is Ainsworth's only medieval history. Chaucer appears as an incidental character, and Wat Tyler, John Ball and Jack Straw are depicted as revolutionary conspirators much like Fawkes, Catesby and Garnet, with Straw portrayed as a Robin Hood figure and Tyler as the villain. *Merry England* is a powerful story of the feudal class war, interspersed with a subplot concerning Editha Tyler, supposedly Tyler's daughter but in fact of noble birth. The novel was published as a triple-decker by the Tinsley Brothers.[16] With dizzying speed, Ainsworth next gave *Bow Bells* the raunchy tale of Jane Shore, *The Goldsmith's Wife*, the same year. The real Jane Shore (née Milverton) was a Nell Gwyn-like figure, who became a mistress of Edward IV while married to the goldsmith Alban Shore. In Ainsworth's story, she tries to save the king's sons after his death, but the history of the princes in the Tower dictates that they are murdered by order of the Duke of Gloucester on his way to becoming Richard III.

In 1875, the chief librarian of Chetham's College died, and Ainsworth considered applying for the post, writing to Crossley, 'I really think the office would suit me, and I shall give the matter consideration.'[17] The compulsion to keep writing remained too strong, however, and he never followed up. The same year, in a cute rerun of Ainsworth's youthful correspondence with Charles Lamb, a young hopeful called James George Joseph Penderel-Brodhurst, then just fifteen, wrote for advice about his manuscript historical novel, *Destined to Win Her*. That he was a lineal descendant of the Penderels that had saved Charles II was probably enough to get him a reply and the two exchanged several letters until the boy's story was picked up by Dicks and published in *Bow Bells*. On a career in writing, Ainsworth offered the following counsel: 'I do not advise you to enter upon a literary career. It is a very hazardous profession ... I am certain you will find your old avocation more profitable than literature.' (The 'old avocation' was an earlier ambition to become a lawyer, Ainsworth's abandoned profession.) But if he must, Ainsworth concluded, 'You may possibly succeed if you connect yourself with the newspapers.'[18] This Penderel-Brodhurst did, later working as a journalist on the *St James's Gazette* and the *Evening Standard*. He was the editor of the *Guardian*, the leading organ of the Church of England, from 1905 to 1922, and consulting editor until his death in 1934.

In April 1876, Ainsworth's only sibling, Gilbert, whom he had been watching over since the death of his mother, died suddenly aged sixty-nine. He was buried in the family vault Ainsworth had purchased at Kensal Green Cemetery for his mother. 'Just before the coffin was lowered in to the vault,' he wrote to Crossley, 'I had a glimpse of my poor Mother's coffin, which I have not seen for thirty-four years. It was in perfect preservation.'[19] Ainsworth and Crossley collaborated on a memoir for the *Manchester Courier*. 'I am certain', wrote Ainsworth, 'if Gilbert had retained his mental powers, he would have been a distinguished writer.'[20] The loss of Gilbert seemed to shock Ainsworth out of his solitary existence, and at the age of seventy-one he became a patron of the Sussex Bicycle Association and an enthusiastic cyclist, flamboyantly presenting signed copies of his works as prizes at race meetings. He continued to write, telling Crossley, 'I do not mean to lay down the pen.'[21]

In 1878, Ainsworth presented a full-length portrait of himself, painted by H.W. Pickersgill in 1841, to his beloved Chetham's Library. In the same year, Routledge published the only standard edition of his novels, and the library got a set of those too. 'I myself regard the series with some surprise,' he later confessed to Crossley.[22] This reminded the reading public of his existence enough to warrant a charming interview in the *World* entitled 'Celebrities at Home. No. LXXXIV. Mr. W. Harrison Ainsworth at Little Rockley' by Edmund Yates. 'Time has dealt kindly with Mr. Harrison Ainsworth', begins Yates, 'and laid its finger but lightly on his handsome head. There is no difficulty in recognising in the well-preserved gentleman of threescore and twelve the Adonis of the D'Orsay period, whom Maclise loved to paint.'[23] Ainsworth now moved to his late brother's house in Reigate, living with Sarah Wells and his young daughter. Here, his health finally began to decline. Later writing to his cousin, Dr James Bower Harrison, Ainsworth explained, 'For myself, I live here very quietly, but I shall draw nearer London in the summer. I suffer awfully from neuralgic pains. As you will perceive, I cannot give a very satisfactory report of myself. My handwriting will show you how desperately shaky I am.'[24]

Only two novels remained to be written.

Beau Nash was published by Routledge in three volumes in 1879. The novel is a jaunty account of Bath in the eighteenth century and the adventures of the famous dandy of the title, while also painting a picture of a morally corrupt aristocracy. In the story, Mrs Aylmer Mallet, 'the Beauty of Bath', elopes with Sir Thomas Carew, who subsequently kills her husband in a duel. His distraught lover enters a convent as Sister Helena, eventually dying there. Mallet's nephew,

Frank Farington, meanwhile, courts the contrary Edith Wilmot with the help of his friend, Beau Nash, eventually winning her hand after a series of intrigues, obstacles and reversals of fortune. For quite an old-fashioned historical novel, the book sold reasonably well, indicating that Ainsworth's base had stuck with him. His final serial, *Stanley Brereton*, was contemporary in setting and ran in the *Bolton Weekly Journal* in 1881. It is essentially provincial melodrama, with perhaps a bit of a sensational twist. Sir Thomas Starkey elopes to France with a mistress, and his wife's cousin, Lionel Darcy, restores family honour by killing him in a duel. Starkey's nephew, Stanley Brereton, inherits the estate and weds Mildred Warburton, who is no better than she should be. In a reflection of earlier events, Mildred runs off with Darcy, whom Stanley kills in a duel. Stanley takes Mildred back, but she is killed in a riding accident, leaving Stanley to marry Rose Hylton, the girl who truly loves him. Again, the novel was published in three volumes by Routledge. As a swansong it is a good book, but not a great book, and a long way from the glory days of *The Tower of London* and *The Lancashire Witches*. What is most important about it is that it represents its author writing to the end. And what better epitaph for a novelist can there be than that?

Chapter 19

The Lancashire Novels

But this isn't the whole story.

In later life, Ainsworth's thoughts turned more and more towards his native Manchester, and a wish to chronicle its history in much the same way that he had so successfully done with London. As soon as he completed *Boscobel*, Ainsworth therefore wrote to his historical advisor Crossley:

> I have an idea of opening the new tale with a picture of Manchester in 1745, during the stay of Prince Charles. Doctor Byrom and a good many other personages might be introduced, with Colonel Townley, the Deacons, Jenny Dawson, Syddall, and the Jacobite clergy. I think the period is better than 1715. Written in a quiet sort of style, I think a sketch of Manchester in 1745, with the society of the period, would be interesting.[1]

This project became *The Manchester Rebels of the Fatal '45*, published in three volumes by the Tinsley Brothers in 1873 for a fee of £150, demonstrating the fickle nature of the writing life and outliving your own fashion.[2] Nonetheless, Ainsworth had certainly rediscovered his creative voice, as the novel maintains the standard set by *Tower Hill* and *Boscobel*. It was dedicated to Ainsworth's old friend from the D'Orsay days, Benjamin Disraeli, 'with every sentiment of respect and admiration'.

The real Manchester Rebels were a rich source of regional history. Northern Jacobites had already paid dearly for their involvement in the previous uprising of 1715. Nonetheless, in the equally doomed uprising of 1745, Manchester raised a regiment loyal to the Stuart cause and the city was occupied by the Young Pretender himself.

194

Bonnie Prince Charlie had landed at Eriskay with a tiny band of followers in June 1745. After an initially muted response from the now cautious Highland clans, he remarkably managed to capture Perth and Edinburgh, declaring the Union dissolved. Charles went on to defeat Sir John Cope at Prestonpans, his now 5,000-strong army beginning to represent a genuine challenge to George II. He crossed the border, took Carlisle and headed for Lancashire. Despite his enthusiastic welcome, the rest of the English Jacobites stayed away and his forces got no further south than Derby, where his officers convinced him to retreat or be defeated. This was a terrible choice, between humiliating withdrawal or military disaster. The disaster came anyway, as government troops pursued the retreating army, growing smaller by the day as soldiers deserted. The loyal few were slaughtered at the Battle of Culloden in April 1746. Charles escaped to France, where he drank himself to death in 1788. State reprisals were brutal, bloody and absolute, and the Jacobite cause was broken forever. This story forms the backdrop for Scott's seminal historical novel *Waverley*.

The *Manchester Rebels* is Ainsworth's Mancunian *Waverley*, the story following the fortunes of prominent Jacobite citizens and their children. In Book I, while Charles and his Highland army march on Manchester, the older generation argue about the implications of pledging allegiance to the Stuarts once more, while their children fall in love with the romance of the cause and each other. Book II covers the occupation of Manchester, and Books III to V chronicle the rebel army's march to Derby, the retreat, the siege of Carlisle and the final rout. Like Scott before him, Ainsworth does not describe the final battle at Culloden. Book VI follows the defeated Jacobites to their inevitable fate and they are hanged, drawn and quartered on Kennington Common. The political moral of the story, voiced several times by authorial voice and characters alike, is that the prince failed tactically by not attacking Cumberland's forces at Lichfield, and that even a glorious defeat would have been preferable to a retreat without engagement. A subplot deals with the tragic love story of Helen Carnegie and Sergeant Erick Dickson. Erick is sentenced to death by court martial for killing a superior officer, the dastardly Captain Lindsay, who is obsessed with Helen, who, in turn, throws herself in front of the firing squad and dies with her lover. Ainsworth presents Athertone Legh as 'our hero', although the dashing Jacobite Captain Jemmy Dawson seems a more likely contender for the novel's true protagonist. In a typical Ainsworth plot device, Legh is really Conway Rawcliffe, dispossessed of his birthright by his wicked uncle when still a baby. Conway is the only leading Jacobite character to survive the narrative. He is pardoned by the Duke of Cumberland and marries his beautiful cousin, Constance, the happy couple taking up residence at Rawcliffe Hall.

By his own admission, Ainsworth was retelling the stories of elderly relatives and family friends, upon whom Mrs Mervyn and her circle had already been based in *Mervyn Clitheroe*. *The Manchester Rebels* is therefore the story that is ever present but not told in the earlier novel. Ainsworth describes his inspiration and process in the preface:

> All my early life being spent in Manchester, where I was born, bred, and schooled, I am naturally familiar with the scenes I have attempted to depict in this Tale.
>
> Little of the old town however, is now left. The lover of antiquity – if any such should visit Manchester – will search in vain for those picturesque black and white timber habitations, with pointed gables and latticed windows, that were common enough sixty years ago. Entire streets, embellished by such houses, have been swept away in the course of modern improvement. But I recollect them well. No great effort of imagination was therefore needed to reconstruct the old town as it existed in the middle of the last century.
>
> When I was a boy, some elderly personages with whom I was acquainted were kind enough to describe to me events connected with Prince Charles's visit to Manchester, and the stories I then heard made a lasting impression upon me. The Jacobite feeling must have been still strong among my old friends, since they expressed much sympathy with the principal personages mentioned in the Tale – for the gallant Colonel Townley, Doctor Deacon and his unfortunate sons, Jemmy Dawson, whose hapless fate has been so tenderly sung by Shenstone, and, above all, for poor Tom Syddall. The latter, I know not why, unless it be that his head was affixed on the old Exchange, has always been a sort of hero in Manchester.[3]

The author's longing for the old city is prominent within the text, comparisons made constantly between Manchester as it was (not only in 1745 but in Ainsworth's own youth) and the dirty, industrial metropolis it had become. This nostalgia is further informed by romantic tales recollected from childhood. As Scott had in *Waverley*, Ainsworth has invested much of himself in this work, writing to Crossley that 'No one I think could have written it but myself, and though I am not altogether satisfied with what I have done, I believe that the tale will become popular in Manchester.'[4] It was indeed, Manchester Public Library statistics showing it to have matched *The Tower of London*, *The Lancashire Witches*, *Old St Paul's* and *Windsor Castle*. In a retrospective on Ainsworth written for the *Manchester Evening Chronicle* in 1904, the local journalist Edward Mercer explained the novel's enduring appeal:

> We doubt whether Ainsworth ever told a tale more interesting to a Manchester born reader – As a plot it is smooth and straightforward as the alphabet; as history its main incidents are true; as a description of Manchester and Manchester life at the time it is the more realistic as the scenery is, so to say, allowed to draw itself, and the characters were all real men and women with well-known figures, traits and dispositions. Ainsworth's style is here at its lightest, and its very simplicity adds so much to the verisimilitude of the dialogue that he might have seen and heard all he relates, might have been an actual participator in the events that happen. Perhaps the secret of this is that he was born in the town and personally knew every street in it, and – that he often heard (from lips repeating what eyes had seen and ears had heard) the doings in Manchester at first hand.[5]

The Manchester Rebels remains, however, strangely out of place in national literary history. Written almost sixty years after *Waverley*, it is something of an anachronism. As Constance Rawcliffe exclaims to Atherton Legh in the novel, 'With such exalted sentiments, 'tis a pity you did not live in the days of chivalry.'[6] By this point, she might as well have been addressing her author.

Ainsworth continued the Lancashire Jacobite project with what was to become *Preston Fight, or The Insurrection of 1715*, as always, running the idea past Crossley in advance:

> I have already commenced a new story which I intend to call *The Last Lord Derwentwater*. It will relate, as you will at once comprehend, to the Rebellion of 1715. 'Preston Fight' may be made very effective I think. Lord Derwentwater, Lord Widdrington, General Forster, and Brigadier Mackintosh are well contrasted. Dr. Hibbert-Ware's *Lancashire during the Rebellion of 1715* will furnish me with ample material. Can you suggest a better title for the new story than the one I have selected?[7] [Hibbert-Ware's history was a Chetham Society publication.]

When George I acceded to the British throne in 1714, he did not immediately endear himself to his subjects. He never bothered to learn English and clearly preferred Hanover to Britain. Jacobite resistance in both Scotland and Ireland was still lively, although the Highland uprising collapsed after defeat at the Battle of Killiecrankie in 1689 and James Edward Stuart, the Old Pretender, who had been hanging around in Ireland, finally fled to the Continent after a decisive defeat at the Battle of the Boyne in 1690. More alarming for the new monarch, James had tried, unsuccessfully, to invade Scotland with French troops in 1708, and the English Tory party had continued to maintain a flirtatious contact with him across the water.

The Hanovarian succession had ended any political chance of a peaceful Stuart restoration, and open Jacobite rebellion broke out in 1715. It was a desperate gamble. The cause received no support from Louis XIV, or his successor the Regent Orléans, and the British government, knowing what was coming, suspended *habeas corpus* and reinforced the army. The original conspirators, mostly Anglican Tories, had already failed in the south when rebel leaders met at Greenrig, near the seat of Lord Derwentwater, hoping to march on Newcastle. Their intention was to raise revolts in the West Country and the north of England, where there remained a concentration of old Catholic families loyal to the Jacobite cause. (Ainsworth had already explored this political geography in *Guy Fawkes*.) But Sir William Blackett, a principal plotter, panicked and surrendered to the authorities, alerting them to the plan. Not sure how to respond, the insurgents rode rather aimlessly around Northumbria, recruiting when and where they could. Eventually, they entered Scotland, where the Earl of Mar had recently rallied the Highland clans by prematurely declaring 'James III' at Braemar.

Still unsure how to proceed, the insurgents wasted valuable time waiting at the border, trying to decide if they should march north to support Mar or move into Lancashire and Cheshire. They chose the latter, and marched into Preston, where they met a greatly superior government force under General Wade. Despite inflicting almost ten times as many casualties as they suffered in the ensuing battle, the Jacobite army was betrayed by its leaders, who lost heart and surrendered in much the same way as their successors were to do in 1745. With the tactical acumen that seems to characterise Jacobite actions, James landed in Scotland in January 1716. By February his followers were sick of the sight of him, and he left for France, never to return. Twenty-six insurgents were executed, including the Earl of Derwentwater. Almost fifty estates were confiscated in Lancashire and Cheshire, and two Registration Acts were passed. Such a heroic failure appealed to Ainsworth, doubly so given the location of the final battle.

Preston Fight begins at Dilston Hall, Lord Derwentwater's ancestral seat in Northumberland, and an apocryphal visit by the Old Pretender. The story follows the historical record reasonably closely from then on, describing the Braemar rising and the subsequent ill-fated advance to Preston, where Derwentwater and his co-conspirators are captured and sent to London as traitors. The battle itself is a romantic depiction of the kind of military action that the English seem to love, in which the underdogs, outnumbered and outgunned, bravely face a superior enemy. As with the inglorious Derby retreat of the second rebellion, blame for the outcome is laid at the door of overly cautious and gutless generals rather than the heroic rank and file. The Earls of Nithsdale and Wintoun escape, Jack Sheppard-style, from the Tower of London, while other Jacobite friends break out of Newgate. The tale concludes with Derwentwater's execution on Tower Hill where, according to legend, the aurora borealis burned blood red that night. *Preston Fight* was issued in three volumes by the Tinsley Brothers in May 1875. This time, the fee was £125 – worth around £8,000 today, so not terrible, but not great either for a year's work.

Ainsworth followed *Preston Fight* with another foray into Lancashire history, returning to the Civil War and the siege of Manchester in 1642 in *The Leaguer of Lathom, A Tale of the Civil War in Lancashire*, again published by the Tinsley Brothers. The story principally concerns the brave defence of Latham House against parliamentary forces by Charlotte de la Tremouille, Countess of Derby, during the absence of her husband. Ainsworth also covers the storming of Lancaster and Bolton and the surrender of Warrington. The narrative concludes with the martyrdom of the gallant Cavalier Derby at Bolton in 1651. Ainsworth once again used Chetham Society publications as his primary sources.

After the unintentionally opportunistic *Chetwynd Calverley* (1876), in which the poisoning of the hero's father by his wicked stepmother uncannily mirrors the sensational 'Balham Mystery' (a connection Ainsworth urged the Tinsley Brothers to exploit), and a story set in Norwich during Kett's Rebellion in 1549, with *The Fall of Somerset* (1877), Ainsworth returned, once more, to Manchester.[8] His letters reveal that he had two projects in mind – *Beau Nash*, and something based on the Jacobite trials in Manchester in 1694. Crossley preferred the latter idea. 'I shall take your advice,' wrote Ainsworth, outlining the plan for the new work:

> I shall commence with the Jacobite Trials in Manchester then introduce the assassination and invasion plots, and Sir George Barclay, the Duke of Berwick, and Sir John Fenwick. The arrests, trial, and execution of the latter will form the staple of the story.
>
> I shall give William III at Kensington, and James II at St. Germain.
>
> If I can manage all this satisfactorily I shall do very well.[9]

Beatrice Tyldesley is set against the historical background of James II's dispossession, his defeat in Ireland and retirement to the Château de Saint-Germain-en-Laye, just outside Paris. While his supporters attempt to restore James to the throne, the Jacobite Beatrice Tyldesley is maid of honour to Queen Mary of Modena at Saint-Germain. Meanwhile, her lover, Walter Crosby, is stuck at the court of William and Mary despite also being a staunch Jacobite. Eventually, love conquers all and Beatrice and Walter are reunited and able to marry. *Beatrice Tyldesley* was serialised in *Bow Bells* (illustrated by Frederick Gilbert, brother of Sir John Gilbert RA) and published in three volumes by the Tinsley Brothers in April 1878, again for £125. A sixpenny edition was later issued by John Dicks.

And so ended Ainsworth's irregular series of Lancashire novels. They did not pay well but seem to have been written as much for the author's own pleasure as for profit. Despite the huge success of his earlier works, it was these books of which Ainsworth was most proud.

Chapter 20

The Lancashire Novelist

By now, Ainsworth was pretty much the last of his literary generation. Some had gone early. Samuel Laman Blanchard killed himself in 1845, a year after the death of his wife. R.H. Barham died the same year after a long and painful illness. Driven out of England by gossip, Lady Blessington had died of a heart attack in Paris in 1849, D'Orsay following in 1852. Valued school friend Gilbert Winter died in 1853, Henry Colburn in 1855, and G.P.R. James in 1860. Thackeray had died suddenly of a stroke in 1863, aged only fifty-two. Dickens had also died of a stroke in 1870, his final novel, *The Mystery of Edwin Drood*, left unfinished; Maclise also died that year. Richard Bentley had died in 1871, having never recovered after breaking his leg badly falling off a railway platform. Lytton had died just short of his seventieth birthday in January 1873, of complications arising from an ear infection. Forster had gone in 1876, while working on the second volume of his *Life of Swift*. Cruikshank went in 1878. After his death, it was discovered that he had fathered eleven illegitimate children with a former servant, Adelaide Attree, who lived close to his family home in North London. John Dicks and Disraeli, whose health had been bad for some months, died early in 1881. Only Crossley and the indestructible R.H. Horne were left.[1]

Although still writing, Ainsworth was a ghost, at least in the south. In 1881, the sensation novel was past its prime, although Elizabeth Braddon and Wilkie Collins were still active, and Modernism was stirring – Ibsen's *Ghosts* was written that year and Henry James published *A Portrait of a Lady*. The Gothic novel was yet to be revived by Robert Louise Stevenson and Bram Stoker. But despite being increasingly left behind by trends in popular and literary fiction, at the very end of his life Ainsworth's contribution to English letters was celebrated by the city of his birth, in a public display of love and respect that had so often eluded him since the glory days of *Rookwood*. In July 1881, the Lord Mayor of Manchester, the Right Honourable Thomas Baker, formally invited Ainsworth to a civic banquet in his honour to be held at the Manchester Town Hall. The once-dazzling socialite, now sole survivor of the D'Orsay set, was going to have one last party.

The 'Complimentary Dinner to William Harrison Ainsworth, Esq., by Thomas Baker, Mayor of Manchester. As an expression of the high esteem in which he is held by his Fellow-townsmen and of his services to literature' took place on Thursday, 15 September, and was impressively heralded by the Town Hall bells as if welcoming royalty. As the great and the good of Manchester, old friends, writers and journalists mingled in the reception room, each was presented with a commemorative brochure containing a short biography, a bibliography and an original illustration from *Rookwood, Crichton, Jack Sheppard, The Tower of London, Old St Paul's, The Miser's Daughter, Windsor Castle, The Lancashire Witches* and *Mervyn Clitheroe*. Among the guests were Dr Ralph Ainsworth, representing the family; Crossley, of course; the journalists William Axon and John Evans; Edmund Yates, editor of the *World* and former editor of *Tinsley's Magazine* and *Temple Bar*; Colonel Henry Fishwick, Mayor of Rochdale and author of *A History of Lancashire*; George Milner, President of the Manchester Literary Club; Leo Grindon, author of *Lancashire: Brief Historical and Descriptive Notes*; Charles Sutton, Chief Librarian of the Manchester Free Library; R.C. Christie, Chancellor of the Diocese; and the cotton merchant and philanthropist John Rylands, whose fortune gave Manchester the beautiful neo-Gothic library that bears his name. Mrs Stanford Harris and the novelists Mrs G. Linnaeus Banks and Miss Jessie Fothergill represented the literary ladies of Manchester, Victorian decorum requiring that they dined separately from the men in the company of Ainsworth's cousin Mabel Harrison and the Lady Mayoress. The women were allowed into the banqueting hall only for the after-dinner speeches.

After the extravagant banquet, formal proceedings began with the Lord Mayor offering a toast to the queen and the Royal Family, before giving the welcoming address in honour of Ainsworth:

> I have now to ask your attention while I propose the health of the gentleman in whose honour we are met – (applause) – distinguished as being a fellow-citizen with us, his immediate ancestors having for several generations resided

within a very short distance of the spot whereon we are now assembled, and distinguished also for the possession of the highest literary ability of any living native of Manchester. (Applause.) My personal acquaintance with Mr. Ainsworth, though it dates back some forty years, has, unfortunately for myself, not been of an intimate character. But the mental intimacy which I have with Scott, and Bulwer, and Southey, and Thackeray, all men of my day whom I did not know, has in his case the vitality of just so much personal knowledge as has enabled me, while I was reading his books, to picture to myself the personal appearance of the author of them. (Hear, hear.) … It forms no part, gentlemen, of my duty to-night to offer any criticisms upon Mr. Ainsworth's voluminous works. I may, however, remark that he has embodied in them just so much of historical matter to give great interest to his stories; in point of fact, to make them most delightful reading. (Hear, hear, and applause.) He has also done another thing which gives him a claim to the gratitude of every native of this county, by introducing into his works the legends and the characters of past times in this county – (hear, hear) – and by making the folk-lore and speech of Lancashire a distinctive literature. (Applause.) … In our Manchester public free libraries there are 250 volumes of Mr. Ainsworth's different works. (Applause.) During the last twelve months those volumes have been read 7,660 times – (applause) – mostly by the artisan class of readers. (Hear, hear.) And this means that twenty volumes of his works are being perused in Manchester by readers of the free libraries every day all the year through. (Applause.) My statistics would be incomplete if I did not tell you which of his books are most read. It would be a pleasure to me if I could only read Mr. Ainsworth's mind and know what the conviction is on this point which he entertains. (Hear, hear.) Whether I shall astonish him, or whether the result of my inquiry agrees with the result which prevails in his own mind, I really cannot tell. But I give you six of his most popular works, and in the order in which they are most read. The first is – what? (Laughter.) *The Tower of London.* (Loud applause.)

The next is – what? The ladies can tell me. (Laughter.) It is *The Lancashire Witches*. The third is *Old St. Paul's*. Then comes *Windsor Castle*, *The Miser's Daughter*, and *The Manchester Rebels*. (Applause.) I think now, gentlemen, I have said enough to make you agree with me in saying that we may consider ourselves very proud in having such a man as Mr. Harrison Ainsworth among us. (Applause.) We may consider ourselves very proud in having him here tonight to tell him how much we appreciate his genius and his industry. (Applause.) And he, too, will, I think, be gratified to hear that he has given and is giving so much pleasure and instruction to the reading part of the community of England. (Applause.) ... I ask you to drink the health of Mr. William Harrison Ainsworth. (Loud applause.)[2]

The toast was accepted with great enthusiasm, and cheers greeted Ainsworth as he rose to reply:

With those ringing cheers in my ear, I scarcely know how to thank you; but I can assure you that I really think this is the most gratifying moment of my life. I feel proud, and beyond measure indebted to my excellent friend the Mayor, for the kindly welcome he has given me. In the course of my life many compliments have been paid me, but none that has gratified me so much as the present one. If, however, a compliment is to be paid me, it is here in Manchester – in my native city – that I would have it. (Hear, hear and applause.) Nothing has delighted me more than to be styled, as I have been, the 'Lancashire novelist'. (Hear, hear.) You have heard it said to-night that the most popular of my works is *The Tower of London*. It may be so, but I can assure you that my desire has really been to write a Lancashire novel, a novel that should please the whole county, and I don't care whether it pleased anyone else. (Applause.) If I really thought that the designation which I have latterly received of the 'Lancashire novelist' were justified, I should indeed feel proud. I hope I may deserve it; I hope it may attach to my name. My great ambition has been to connect my name as an author with the city of my birth, and with this aim I have chosen certain subjects that would give me a chance of doing so...

At this point, Ainsworth described the 'Lancashire Novels', continuing:

> I have been honoured by the Chief Magistrate of my native city, who has bidden me to a Banquet at which I have been received with a warmth I shall never forget. (Applause.) I thank you again most heartily for the reception you have accorded me. I shall ever look back with pride and pleasure to this day. (Applause.)

He then delivered a eulogy to the late Gilbert Winter – 'one of the best specimens of the Manchester men of the last generation; a model of kindly hospitality, a man of business, a man of the strictest honour, and untiring in his zeal to serve a friend' – before moving on to 'another old friend of mine, for whom I have an equally strong regard, and whom I am happy to see beside me to-night':

> I allude to Mr. James Crossley. (Applause.) I need not expatiate on Mr. Crossley's social qualities, on his learning and scholarship, on his varied and extensive reading. It is not an extravagant compliment to say that he may be compared to the great Dr. Johnson himself. (Hear, hear.)

He concluded:

> As I cannot doubt that the honour paid me by the Mayor is due to my having gained some distinction as a chronicler of Lancashire, I may congratulate myself on obeying the impulse that prompted me to select that particular walk. (Hear, hear.) I believe my task to be well nigh accomplished, and can scarcely hope to write another tale, but should I do so I shall return to the old ground, and strive to maintain the honourable distinction I have acquired as the 'Lancashire novelist'. (Applause.) Mr. Mayor and gentlemen, I am thankful to have lived to see this day. (Applause.)[3]

A standing ovation of several minutes followed.

Crossley appropriately spoke next. His speech was particularly charming (following the time-honoured tradition of opening with a joke), as he alluded to the close relationship between the author and himself when it came to material and inspiration for the novels, without ever once even thinking of taking a little credit. He also took the party back to the banquet given some forty years since to celebrate the completion of *The Tower of London*, offering the assembly a unique glimpse into the literary past while reminding them, as had the mayor, of Ainsworth's stature as an early Victorian writer:

> I was very forcibly struck on coming into this room with the recollection of another dinner in honour of Mr. Ainsworth which took place just forty years ago in London, and at which I had the good fortune to be present. It was given in celebration of his popular, and deservedly popular *Tower of London* ... and the party that was congregated on that occasion was a fair and full representation of those who as authors, as critics, as artists, as publishers, were in the first rank in the metropolis at that time. Amongst them was, then in the full bloom of authorship, delighted and delighting, Charles Dickens – and with him his friend and subsequent biographer – I cannot say successful biographer – John Forster ... Amongst the party were several of that group of Fraserians of whom I believe Mr. Ainsworth is now the sole survivor, but who still sit around their table perpetuated and pictured by the admirable sketches of Maclise. Nor was there wanting on that occasion that capital artist, whose bark will ever
>
> > Attendant sail,
> > Pursue the triumph and partake the gale,[4]
>
> with the works of the distinguished authors whom he so admirably illustrated. Need I say I refer to George Cruikshank? The Chairman, in proposing the toast of the evening, did full justice to the work which had been the means of calling that party together; and in his happiest terms gave his estimate of the literary merits of Mr. Ainsworth. That estimate was a very

high one, and it was enthusiastically seconded and adopted by the party present ... The characteristic of the remaining part of the evening was the grand geniality and the utter impossibility of anything like a jar. There were rival authors present, but they did not quarrel; there were hostile critics, but their challenges were limited to champagne; there were men of different schools, but they broke down the partition in order to make the harmony perfect. There was a case of mortal feud, but it was arranged by an armistice which lasted, at all events, that evening. I believe everybody spoke – whether accustomed or unaccustomed to public speaking, who was able and capable in his turn of assisting that grand social exhibition ... The proceedings were carried out with admirable spirit and success to the end. I cannot tell you – I have referred to my diary, but it does not assist me – at what time we broke up; but from inquiries I made I ascertained that every guest present awoke a wiser and better man in the morning, but without the disagreeable headache which generally accompanies that discovery. I have always considered that that meeting settled, by a decisive and conclusive verdict, the position of Mr. Ainsworth amongst the novelists of his time.[5]

As always, Crossley was content to step back and let his friend get all the glory, yet this event was as much in honour of the much-loved historian as the much-loved novelist; they were, after all, always something of a matched pair. Several other long speeches followed, and Ainsworth's subsequent correspondence suggests that the cheers were ringing in his ears for what remained of his life.

Before leaving Manchester, Ainsworth took a walk through her dear, dirty streets, saying goodbye as he knew by this point that his health was failing fast. We can only hope that this final moment of glory gave the old survivor of Victorian literature a suitable sense of closure. After attending a service in Manchester Cathedral on Sunday, and another, more modest dinner with Thomas Baker at his home in Old Trafford, Ainsworth left Manchester for the last time.

In London, *Punch* remembered the novelist with whom it had shared a love-hate relationship throughout the 1840s and 1850s and commemorated the Manchester banquet with the last in a long line of affectionate caricatures. This wonderful drawing by Edward Linley Sambourne depicts the elderly Ainsworth in Elizabethan dress, sitting at his writing desk, the pen of romance in one hand, a short dagger in the other. An axe rests casually against his leg, and a highwayman doll sits upon a hobbyhorse at his feet, flintlock drawn, with the caption: 'To the greatest axe-and-neck-romancer of our time, who is quite at the head of his profession, we dedicated this block. *Ad Multos Annos!*'[6] This was not far short of the truth and Ainsworth loved it, commending the cartoon to Crossley in a letter that is also careful to remark that a recent article in the *World* compares Crossley's scholarship to that of Coleridge.[7]

In gratitude to Thomas Baker, Ainsworth dedicated the Routledge edition of *Stanley Brereton* to him:

My Dear Mr. Mayor,

As I deem the banquet given by you in my honour, in my native city of Manchester, one of the most important events of my life, I shall endeavour to evince my sense of it by inscribing this tale to you. To you, moreover, and to the friends assembled on the occasion, I owe the gratifying title conferred upon me of 'The Lancashire Novelist', and I assure you I feel extremely proud of that distinction …

Your deeply obliged
W. Harrison Ainsworth.

With an honest, almost childlike response to praise that he had exhibited all his life, Ainsworth uses this dedication to blow his own trumpet as much as that of the mayor. It must have been nice to be briefly famous once more. Nonetheless, Ainsworth also remembered to include Crossley, quite rightly, in the glory, writing to him that 'this Banquet will form an important festival in your own biography as well as mine'.[8]

His last letter to Crossley was as upbeat yet matter of fact as usual, giving nothing away of his faltering health:

My Dear Crossley,

I have the pleasure to send you a copy of *Stanley Brereton*, and shall address the packet to the Chetham's Library. Like all the Tauchnitz editions, it is very charmingly printed.

The Mayor was good enough to send me the *Manchester Courier* containing the report of his re-election, at which I am rejoiced – for he is a most excellent fellow. I have written to offer him my hearty congratulations. It certainly is very gratifying to me that he has been complimented on this Banquet and his re-election.

Let me hear what you think of *Stanley Brereton* when you have read the book.

Give my kind regards to Evans, and thank him for sending me the *Guardian*.[9] I hope Routledge's edition will soon be published.

Give my kind regards to Ralph.[10] When he dined with me the other day at the Queen's Hotel, I gave him one of the *best* bottles of claret to be had at the house, but he didn't seem to understand it. Hinde thought the same wine superb.[11]

Always yours
W. Harrison Ainsworth.[12]

Ainsworth's final letter, written just after Christmas, was to his cousin, Dr James Bower Harrison. Here he gives a more honest account of his health, having been plagued since the previous winter with severe neuralgia, bronchitis and insomnia brought on by the constant pain and asthma. 'I cannot give a very good report of myself,' he confessed, 'for the fogs with which we have been troubled during the last week have affected me a good deal, and I have been obliged to call in Dr. Holman, our chief medical man ... Dr. Holman thought me much wasted since I last saw him.'[13] Holman later told Ellis that in those final days he found his patient 'pleasantly chatty and inclined to talk of old times'.[14]

Five days later, on Tuesday, 3 January 1882, Ainsworth died at home aged seventy-six, his cause of death ascribed to 'congestion of the lungs fatally affecting weak action of the heart'.

The Times published a lengthy obituary beginning, 'In him there has passed away a novelist who at one time might have boasted that he had as many readers as Dickens, and had but few equals as an antiquarian,'[15] while the *Daily Telegraph* marked the passing of the 'veteran novelist'.[16] The *Graphic* commemorated him with a portrait, and 'The literary world mourns the loss of W. Harrison Ainsworth,' intoned the *Manchester Evening News*.[17] Obituaries from the London and Manchester dailies were reproduced across the country, acknowledging Ainsworth's status in English literature even if his peers often hadn't. Over and over again he was described as the 'popular novelist', the 'famous novelist', the 'great novelist', and the 'Lancaster Novelist'; he was the author of *Rookwood, The Tower of London, Windsor Castle, Old St Paul's* and *The Lancashire Witches*, and the 'reviver of the flitch'; he was the author that had outsold Dickens.

His four-horse, open carriage funeral procession – along the Strand, Fleet Street, over Blackfriars Bridge, along the Embankment, Pall Mall, Piccadilly, Park Lane, Edgware Road and, finally, out of the city to his last ride along the Harrow Road – was reported in detail, down to the white silk lining of his oak coffin and the brass shield bearing his name.

His estate quickly became a matter of news, divided as it was between his daughters at Hurstpierpoint and his wife at Reigate. 'It is understood that Mr. Harrison Ainsworth has not died very rich,' reported the *Liverpool Daily Post*, 'but has left behind a valuable possession in the shape of manuscript … Ainsworth was in the set over which Sir Walter Scott towered, and the intimate acquaintance with eminent workers in literature commenced then has continued ever since.'[18] His properties were a treasure trove of autograph papers, his own and those of Dickens, Cruikshank, Thackeray and his many other famous friends and collaborators, celebrated as almost holy relics, as well as thousands of rare books and first editions.[19] These were auctioned by Sotheby, Wilkinson and Hodge in London in July, raising enough for his widow and daughters to live out their lives independently, Hinde managing the royalties that still came in from the classic novels, the copyrights of which Ainsworth had wisely bought back in the forties.[20]

Ainsworth was buried at Kensal Green Cemetery in the family vault with his mother and his brother, close to his beloved Kensal Manor House and having, among others, Henry Mayhew, Anthony Trollope, Wilkie Collins, Shirley Brooks, Cruikshank (though his remains were later moved to St Paul's), Forster, Maclise, Barham, Thackeray and Dickens's other unsung rival, G.W.M. Reynolds, for company in the earth. James Crossley was too frail to make the journey south for the funeral and he died, aged eighty-three, nineteen months after his best friend on 1 August 1883. 'On Tuesday he seemed to be conscious that his end was near, though his sufferings were comparatively slight,' recorded the *Manchester Guardian*. 'Up to the last his intellect was as bright as ever, and he conversed freely on many of his favourite and familiar topics. He passed away quietly, as we have said, yesterday afternoon at a quarter before one o'clock.'[21] Crossley ascribed his longevity to having never married.

L'envoi

Failure is, of course, always more interesting than success. Although he left some small properties and a private library so large it once brought a ceiling down, by the standards of his class and his profession, Ainsworth died a poor man. He also went out virtually pen in hand, a jobbing writer living hand to mouth, as writers often do, who kept his family afloat by his labours to the end of his life, approaching each new project with an infectious enthusiasm and incredible energy, whether it became an international bestseller or a serial in a provincial newspaper. And in his heyday, Ainsworth *was* an international bestseller, his novels routinely translated into German, French, Dutch and Russian, with unlicensed reprints hugely popular in America. Wild West outlaws Frank and Jesse James even signed their letters to the *Kansas City Star* 'Jack Sheppard'.

Ainsworth's career, then, represents all the stages of the literary life for the vast majority of writers, who do not become millionaires or cultural icons. He was the young hopeful, who through enthusiasm, hard work and tenacity bluffed his way into the lower echelons of the publishing landscape and then fought his way up, eschewing the easy life of the provincial solicitor that fate had in store for him. He took risks, invested in his art, and was rewarded by a loyal public and a string of very successful novels, before falling foul of the Victorian literary establishment and victim to a disproportionate public shaming from which his reputation never fully recovered. And he forgave and continued to encourage every friend who had turned on him so savagely. Finally, he lived through a long professional decline, as public tastes moved on and he grew older, still writing, only now for few laurels, less money and an ever-dwindling readership. In the artistic pantheon, many are called but few are chosen. And if not on your industry's A-list, creative work can be decidedly blue-collar. In this regard, Ainsworth's biography is a true portrait of an artist.

But, as Malcolm Elwin wrote of him, 'Of all the Victorian novelists, his literary life is among the most important and most interesting.'[1] In Ainsworth's long life, we can see not only the struggle and commitment that necessarily comes of laying down one's life for literature, but in his professional and personal relationships with friends and foes alike, the entire literary and cultural milieu of his age. And beyond this, there is the evolution of the English novel itself, from Romanticism to Realism, from Scott to Dickens. Writers like Ainsworth and his forgotten friends represent the transition, a dynamic period of literary production that was neither Regency nor Victorian but something in between, in which genres were born, merged and abandoned with dizzying speed. *Rookwood*, for example, was written two years after the first Reform Act and during the brief reign of William IV, *between* Regency and Victorian. Ainsworth was not Scott or Dickens, nor did he wish to be, and judging any writer against the fathers of the nineteenth-century English novel is likely to find them wanting. But this was not the real reason for his critical annihilation, at the hands of influential friends who should have behaved better. Ainsworth was pilloried because of *what* he wrote, not *how* he wrote it, the charge of 'bad writing' a baseless but convenient way for the emerging Victorian establishment to reject the previous generation, and to clear the way for *their* people.

Throughout his life, the memory of the Newgate Controversy allowed increasingly stiff Victorian critics to exclude Ainsworth from a literary history that he had helped build. True, his novels were not great literature, but they commanded a massive audience in the 1830s and 1840s and had a vast influence on popular and literary narratives, both in fiction and more importantly in legend. And at his best, Ainsworth's storytelling could be magical; at his worst, he was usually fun to read. As he cheerfully admitted: 'If the design of Romance be, what it has been held, the exposition of a useful truth by means of an interesting story, I fear I have but imperfectly fulfilled the office imposed upon me; having, as I will freely confess, had, throughout, an eye rather to the reader's amusement than his edification.'[2]

Although hardly the only Victorian author to prefer adventure stories to moral fables, literary criticism has been harsher on Ainsworth than on any other. His work is thus the reflection of the Victorian literary novel cast in the black and lurid tarn, a figure Dickens once felt he must define his own work *against*. William Harrison Ainsworth, like his greatest heroes, remains a literary outlaw; but, in the words of Dick Turpin, 'England, sir, has reason to be proud of her highwaymen!'

Notes

Prologue

1. Crossley, James & Evans, John (1881), *Specially Revised Accounts of the Recent Banquet to William Harrison Ainsworth, Esq.*, privately printed, Manchester, p. 2.

Introduction

1. Drabble, Margaret (ed.) (2006), 'Ainsworth, William Harrison (1805–82)', *The Oxford Companion to English Literature*, Oxford University Press, p. 12.
2. Joshi, S.T. (2014), *Unutterable Horror: A History of Supernatural Fiction*, Vol. I, Hippocampus, New York, p. 195.
3. Horne, R.H. (1844), *A New Spirit of the Age*, 2 vols, Smith, Elder & Co, London, I, p. 220.
4. Friswell, J. Hain, *Modern Men of Letters Honestly Criticised*, Hodder & Stoughton, London, 1870, p. 257.
5. Friswell, p. 266.
6. Sanders, Andrew (1978), *The Victorian Historical Novel, 1840–1880*, Macmillan, London, p. 46.

Chapter 1

1. Ainsworth, W.H. (1837), *Rookwood: A Romance, Revised, Corrected and Illustrated with A New Preface, and Notes*, Richard Bentley, London, 'Preface to the 4th Edition', p. xxxviii.
2. There is now an excellent biography of Crossley by Stephen Collins, *James Crossley: A Manchester Man of Letters*.

3. De Quincey, Thomas (1986), *Confessions of an English Opium Eater*, Penguin, London, p. 36. (Original work published 1821).

4. Ainsworth, *Mervyn Clitheroe*, 11, Ainsworth, W.H. (1858), *Mervyn Clitheroe*, George Routledge & Sons, London, p. 11.

5. Ainsworth, W.H. (1821), *Ghiotto; or Treason Discovered. Pocket Magazine of Classics and Polite Literature* VIII, John Arliss, London, pp. 181–2.

6. Ainsworth, *Ghiotto* p. 257.

7. Qtd. in Ellis, S.M. (1911), *William Harrison Ainsworth and His Friends*, 2 vols, John Lane, London, I, p.56.

8. Ainsworth, letter to James Crossley, 22 May 1876.

9. Qtd. in Smith, The Rev. Jeremiah Finch (1874), *The Admission Register of the Manchester School* Vol. III, Chetham Society, Manchester, p.131.

10. Ainsworth, W.H. (1821), *The Rivals: a Serio-Comic Tragedy. Pocket Magazine* VII, John Arliss, London, p. 293.

11. Qtd. in Popova, Maria (2017), 'The Doom and Glory of Knowing Who You Are: James Baldwin on the Empathic Rewards of Reading and What It Means to Be an Artist', *Brainpickings*, available at: https://www.brainpickings.org/2017/05/24/james-baldwin-life-magazine-1963/ (accessed 7 March 2018).

12. Ainsworth, W.H. (1821), 'Horæ Dramaticæ No. I', *Pocket Magazine*, VIII, John Arliss, London, p. 35.

13. Ainsworth, 'Horæ Dramaticæ I', pp. 38–9.

14. Ainsworth, W.H. (1821), 'On the Writings of Richard Clitheroe', *New Monthly Magazine and Literary Journal: Original Papers*, I, p. 123.

15. Arliss, John (1821), 'Editor's Note', *Pocket Magazine* VIII, John Arliss, London, p. 36.

16. Ainsworth, W.H. (1821), 'Horæ Dramaticæ No. III', *Pocket Magazine*, VIII, p. 314.

Chapter 2

1. Anon. (1821), 'Hymn to Christopher North, Esq.', *Blackwood's Edinburgh Magazine*, IX (49), p. 62. For the full story of Scott and Christie, see my article 'Duel at Chalk Farm Tavern: A Regency Tragedy', available at: https://www.geriwalton.com/duel-chalk-farm-tavern-regency-tragedy-2/.

2. Poe, Edgar Allan (1840), 'The Signora Zenobia' (AKA 'How to Write a Blackwood Article'), *Tales of the Grotesque and Arabesque*, 2 vols. Lea & Blanchard, Philadelphia, I, p. 218.
3. Galt, John (1821), 'The Buried Alive', *Blackwood's Edinburgh Magazine*, X (56), p. 262.
4. Hunt, Leigh (1819), 'A Tale for a Chimney Corner', in Ollier, Edmund (ed.), *Essays of Leigh Hunt* Chatto &Windus, London, p. 74.
5. Ainsworth, W.H. (1821), 'Sir Albert's Bride', *Pocket Magazine* VIII, John Arliss, London, p. 239.
6. Ainsworth, W.H. (1821), 'The Dying Laird', *Pocket Magazine* VIII, John Arliss, London, p. 268.
7. Ainsworth, W.H. (1821), 'The Baron's Bridal', *European Magazine, and London Review*, LXXX, p. 538.
8. Ainsworth, 'The Baron's Bridal', pp. 539–40.
9. Ainsworth, 'The Baron's Bridal', p. 540.
10. Ainsworth, W.H. (1822), 'The Spectre Bride', in Mitsuharu Matsuoka, *Victorian Ghost Stories*, available at: http://www.lang. nagoya-u.ac.jp/~matsuoka/ghost-stories-ainsworth.html (accessed 23 March 2018).
11. Ainsworth, W.H. (1823), 'The Half-Hangit', *European Magazine, and London Review*, LXXXIV, p. 404.
12. Morgan, Peter ed. (1973), *The Letters of Thomas Hood*, University of Toronto Press, p. 78.
13. Ainsworth, letter to Crossley, 22 August 1822.
14. Ainsworth, W.H. (1821), 'To the Editor of the Edinburgh Magazine', *Edinburgh Magazine and Literary Miscellany: A New Series of the Scots Magazine,* IX, p. 589.
15. Anon. (1821), 'Foscari: A Tragedy', *Edinburgh Magazine*, IX, p. 596.

Chapter 3

1. Ainsworth, W.H. (1822), 'What shall I write?', *Edinburgh Magazine*, XI (July), p. 39.
2. The flamboyant and profligate Wainewright was transported in 1837 for an audacious fraud against the Bank of England committed thirteen years earlier. He was, however, also suspected of fatally poisoning

his uncle for an inheritance, and his sister-in-law and mother-in-law to collect on multiple life insurance policies. Although these charges were unproven, it is highly likely that the old case was used as a credible way of transporting him for life for the murders.

3. Talfourd, Thomas Noon (1849), *The Letters of Charles Lamb*, Edward Moxon, London, p. 295.
4. Anon. (1823), '*The Maid's Revenge, and A Summer Evening's Tale and Other Poems* by Cheviot Ticheburne', *Monthly Review*, CII, pp. 98–9.
5. Anon. (1823), '*The Maid's Revenge, and A Summer Evening's Tale and Other Poems* by Cheviot Ticheburne', *The Literary Chronicle for the Year 1823*, Davidson, London, 282.
6. Ainsworth, W.H. (1823), 'The Church-Yard', *December Tales*, G. & B.W. Whitaker, London, pp. 84–8.
7. Ainsworth, 'The Englisher's Story', *December Tales*, p. 63.
8. Anon. (1823), '*December Tales*', *Monthly Review*, CI, pp. 442–3.
9. I have published academically on Ainsworth's fiction, so for a critical reading of *December Tales* and the major novels, please see *The Life and Works of the Lancashire Novelist William Harrison Ainsworth, 1805–1882* (Edwin Mellen, Lewiston, 2003) and *Ainsworth and Friends: Essays on 19th Century Literature and The Gothic*, available at: https://ainsworthandfriends.wordpress.com/

Chapter 4

1. Ainsworth, letter to Crossley, 8 June 1876.
2. Qtd. in Ellis, I, p. 75.
3. Ainsworth, letter to Crossley, 25 March 1825.
4. Ainsworth, letter to Crossley, December 1824, George was Crossley's younger brother.
5. Ainsworth, letter to Crossley, December 1824.
6. During this period, Ebers also published a collection of doggerel verse entitled *Letters from Cockney Lands* by 'Will Brown' (1826) that is widely attributed to Ainsworth, although the author himself made no such claim. In two long poems over 100 pages, ostensibly a humorous guide to London life written by an old soldier to a friend, the anonymous author manages to say next to nothing about

the subject. Compared to the rest of Ainsworth's early poetry, it is difficult to detect any stylistic similarities. There is no mention of the poems in his letters to Crossley, which are instead more concerned with another literary miscellany that he was planning with Ebers but which ultimately failed to launch. While several auction houses and antiquarian booksellers still attribute *Letters from Cockney Lands* to Ainsworth, I am sceptical, this presumed authorship being traceable only to S.M. Ellis's biography, which offers no evidence in support of the claim, and in fact acknowledges that Ainsworth never made it either.

7. Ainsworth, letter to J.P. Aston, 27 November 1825.
8. Ainsworth, letter to Aston, 1 March 1825.
9. Anon. (1826), '*Sir John Chiverton, A Romance.*' *Literary Gazette*, James Moyes, London, p. 422.
10. The closing quotation is from *The Tempest*, 5.1, in which Prospero declares, 'The pine and cedar; graves at my command/Have waked their sleepers, oped, and let 'em forth/By my so potent art'.
11. Anon. (1826), '*Sir John Chiverton; A Romance.*' *The New Monthly Magazine Historical Register III*, Henry Colburn, London, p. 318.
12. Ainsworth, W.H. & Aston, J.P. (1826), *Sir John Chiverton*, John Ebers, London, p. 316.
13. Qtd. in Ellis, I, pp. 134–5.
14. Ainsworth, letter to Crossley, 30 November 1871.
15. Qtd. in Ellis, I, p. 137.
16. 'This work has been generally ascribed to Mr. William Harrison Ainsworth, but in a letter written by Mr. John Partington Aston to Mr. Sutton, author of *A List of Lancashire Authors*, and which was read at the Manchester Literary Club two or three weeks ago, Mr. Aston claims the entire property of the book, for which, he says, he is "solely responsible". In cases of disputed ownership it is always desirable to be perfectly accurate in making a claim, and in order to be correct to the letter he ought to have excepted the lines placed opposite to the Romance: "Eustace, etc.", which I supplied Mr. W. H. Ainsworth with, at his request, as a Motto for the Tale. Mr. Ainsworth, whether the owner or not, evidently took great interest in the work, of which his father-in-law, Mr. Ebers, was eventually the publisher. Jas. Crossley, 15th March, 1877.'

17. Qtd. in Ellis, I, p. 140.
18. This is a questionable memory. As far as I can ascertain, Aston was a clerk at the office of Ainsworth's father, whereas Ainsworth was articled to Kay. Aston went on to work for Kay much later, after Ainsworth had moved to London.
19. Aston, J.P. (1882), 'The Late Mr. Harrison Ainsworth', *The Times*, 6 January, p. 11.
20. *Manchester Guardian*, 13 May 1882, qtd. in Carver, Stephen James (2003), *The Life and Works of the Lancashire Novelist William Harrison Ainsworth, 1805–1882*, Edwin Mellen, Lewiston, p. 417.
21. *Manchester Guardian*, 15 May 1882, qtd. in Carver, p. 418n.
22. *Manchester Guardian*, 18 May 1882, qtd. in Carver, pp. 418–19.
23. Written by Horace Smith in 1826. Ainsworth later described Smith as 'as dull as ditchwater' in a letter to Crossley dated 21 April 1830.
24. Ben Jonson, *Every Man in his Humour* (1616). Bobadil was a soldier who claimed to have survived many great battles and presented himself as an expert military strategist. He is revealed to be a coward and a drunken braggart at the end of the play.
25. Anderson, W.E.K. (ed.) (1972), *The Journal of Sir Walter Scott*, Clarendon Press, Oxford, pp. 213–15. Joe Manton was an innovative Regency gunsmith whose designs paved the way for breech-loading weapons and the modern cartridge bullet. Scott evokes Manton as a much imitated original. He lost a lot of money in litigation against the British Army and died a bankrupt.
26. Marriot, John (1941), *English History in English Fiction*, Blackie & Son, London, p. 9.
27. Sanders, p. 34.
28. 'Even as in a mirror'.
29. A reference to *Twelfth Night*. Like the allusion to Captain Bobadil, this is a strange character with which to compare oneself. Sir Andrew is a rather pathetic figure, a 'foolish knight' who fails to see that his drinking partner Sir Toby Belch is relieving him of his fortune and who is, like Bobadil, shown to be a blustering coward.
30. Paraphrase of *The Merry Wives of Windsor*, I.iii: '"Convey," the wise it call. "Steal"? foh! a fico for the phrase!'
31. From Bruce's address at Bannockburn, 1314.

Chapter 5

1. Ainsworth, 'Dedicatory Stanzas To ——.' *Sir John Chiverton*, pp. v–vii.
2. Ebers, John (1828), *Seven Years of the King's Theatre*, William Harrison Ainsworth, London, p. 306.
3. Ainsworth, letter to Crossley, 'Summer' 1826.
4. Ebers, p. 279.
5. Ainsworth, letter to John Ebers, undated, most likely late August 1826.
6. Ainsworth, letter to Crossley, undated but probably late August/ early September 1826.
7. Egan, Pierce (1869), *Life in London or The Day and Night Scenes of Jerry Hawthorn, ESQ. and his elegant friend Corinthian Tom in their Rambles and Sprees through the Metropolis*, John Camden Hotten, London, p. 167. (Original work published 1821.)
8. Ainsworth, letter to Crossley, 25 November 1826.
9. Ainsworth, letter to Crossley, 3 February 1827.
10. Ainsworth, letter to Crossley, 12 March 1827.
11. Ellis, I, p. 181.
12. Ainsworth, letter to Crossley, 'May' 1829.
13. Moers, Ellen (1960), *The Dandy, Brummell to Beerbohm*, Viking, New York, p. 190.

Chapter 6

1. Ainsworth, W.H. (1849), *Rookwood: A Romance*, George Routledge & Sons, London, p. xxxiii.
2. Ellis, I, p. 230.
3. Ainsworth, letter to Crossley, 7 August 1831.
4. Harman, Claire (2018), *Murder by the Book: A Sensational Chapter in Victorian Crime*, Viking, London, p. 41.
5. Ainsworth (1849), *Rookwood*, Preface, p. xxxviii.
6. Ainsworth, W.H. (1834), *Rookwood: A Romance,* 3 vols, Richard Bentley, London, II, p. 190.
7. Ainsworth, W.H. (1849), *Rookwood*, Preface, p. xxxvi.
8. Ainsworth, W.H. (1849), *Rookwood*, Preface, p. xxxvi.
9. Ainsworth, W.H. (1834), *Rookwood*, II, p. 344.

10. Qtd. in Ellis, I, p. 254.
11. Anon. (1834), 'High-ways and Low-ways; Or, Ainsworth's Dictionary with Notes by Turpin', *Fraser's Magazine*, IX, p. 724. S.M. Ellis believed this to be written by Thackeray, but in a reference to the piece in a letter to John Macrone dated 2 June 1836, Ainsworth attributes it to John 'Jack' Churchill, who had apparently also offered to 'Fraserize' *Crichton.*
12. The Attorney General and the British Ambassador to St Petersburg respectively.
13. Ainsworth, letter to Crossley, 6 May 1834.
14. Qtd. in Collins, Stephen (2012), *James Crossley: A Manchester Man of Letters*, The Chetham Society, Manchester, p. 72.
15. Anon, 'High-ways and Low-ways', *Fraser's*, p. 725.
16. Anon, 'High-ways and Low-ways', *Fraser's*, p. 735.
17. Bulwer-Lytton, Edward (1865), *Paul Clifford*, George Routledge & Sons, New York, p. 219. (Original work published 1830.)
18. Godwin, William (1993), *Enquiry Concerning Political Justice*, Penguin, London, p. 90. (Original work published 1793.)
19. Bulwer-Lytton, *Paul Clifford*, p. x.
20. Maginn, William (1832), 'A good Tale badly Told', *Fraser's Magazine*, V (25), p. 112.
21. Anon. (1834), 'Critical Notices: Rookwood; a Romance, 3 vols', *New Monthly Magazine*, XLI (2), p. 507.
22. Anon. (1834), 'Miss Edgeworth's *Helen*', *Quarterly Review,* LI, pp. 482–3.
23. Qtd. in Ainsworth (1837), *Rookwood*, p. 412.
24. Anon. (1834), 'Dick Turpin's Ride', *New Sporting Magazine*, VII (38), p. 82.
25. Gay, John (1986), *The Beggar's Opera*, Penguin, London, I. p. iv. (Original work written in 1728.)
26. Ainsworth (1834), *Rookwood*, I, pp. 221–3.
27. Ainsworth (1834), *Rookwood*, II, p. 306.
28. Hobsbawm, E.J. (1969), *Bandits*, Weidenfeld & Nicolson, London, p. 24.
29. The historical partnership of William Plunkett and 'Captain' James Maclaine, the original 'Gentleman Highwayman', was similar to that of Dick Turpin and Tom King.
30. Ainsworth (1849), *Rookwood*, Preface, p. xxxvii.

31. For a detailed account of Turpin's life, see *The Lives and Exploits of the Most Noted Highwaymen, Rogues, and Murderers* by Stephen Basdeo (2018).

32. *Read's Weekly Journal*, 8 February 1735, qtd. in Barlow, Derek (1973), *Dick Turpin and the Gregory Gang*, Phillimore, London & Chichester, pp. 78–9.

33. Anon. (1734), 'The persons undernamed are charged upon Oath for committing several robberies in Essex, Middlesex, Surrey, and Kent', *The London Gazette*, No. 7379, 22 February 1734, p. 1.

34. Bayes, Richard & Cole, J. (1739), *The Genuine HISTORY of the LIFE of RICHARD TURPIN, The noted Highwayman, Who was Executed at York for Horse-stealing, under the Name of John Palmer, on Saturday April, 7, 1739*, J. Standen, London, p. 13.

35. Ainsworth (1837), *Rookwood*, p. 408. NB. This was slightly revised from the text of the 1st edition.

36. Ainsworth (1834), *Rookwood*, II, p. 307.

37. Ainsworth (1849), *Rookwood*, Preface, p. xxxiv.

38. Owing to various boundary changes, Dunham Massey is now a civil parish in the Metropolitan Borough of Trafford, Greater Manchester, while Hough Green is a residential area of Widnes in Cheshire.

39. Qtd. in Hollingsworth, Keith (1963), *The Newgate Novel: 1830–1847*, Wayne State University Press, Detroit, pp. 106–107.

40. Qtd. in Elwin, Malcolm (1934), *Victorian Wallflowers*, Jonathan Cape, London, p. 188.

41. Qtd. in Hollingsworth, p. 107.

42. Blanchard, Samuel Laman (1849), 'Memoir of William Harrison Ainsworth', in Ainsworth, W.H., *Rookwood: A Romance*, George Routledge & Sons, London, p. xiv. (Original article published in the *Mirror*, 1842.)

Chapter 7

1. Maginn, William (1834), 'Gallery of Literary Characters. No. L. W.H. Ainsworth, ESQ', *Fraser's Magazine*, X, p. 48.

2. See Michael Sadleir, *Blessington – D'Orsay: A Masquerade* (1933) and *The Last of the Dandies* by Nick Foulkes (2003).

3. Ainsworth, *Mervyn Clitheroe*, p. 129.

4. Kitton, Frederic George (1889), *Charles Dickens by Pen and Pencil; Including Anecdotes and Reminiscences Collected from his Friends and Contemporaries*, Sabin & Dexter, London, p. 19.
5. Forster, John (1872), *The Life of Charles Dickens*, Vol. I., Chapman & Hall, London, p. 86.
6. Forster, *Life of Dickens*, I, p. 96.
7. Forster, *Life of Dickens*, I, p. 122.
8. See Ellis, I, Chapter IX.
9. Ackroyd, Peter (1990), *Dickens*, QPD, London, p. 204.
10. Qtd. in Elwin, p. 182.
11. This refers to Browning's *Strafford*, performed at the Theatre Royal, Covent Garden, in May 1837.
12. Qtd. in Ellis, I, p. 290.
13. Ainsworth (1837), *Rookwood*, Preface, p. xxii.
14. William Makepeace Thackeray, letter to John Macrone, January 1837, in Ray, Gordon N. (ed) (1945). *The Letters and Private Papers of William Makepeace Thackeray*, 4 vols, Oxford University Press, I, p. 328.
15. Ainsworth, letter to Crossley, 29 May 1837.

Chapter 8

1. Ainsworth, letter to Crossley, 8 February 1838.
2. Ainsworth, W.H. (1839), *Jack Sheppard: A Romance,* 3 vols, Richard Bentley, London, I, pp. 147–8.
3. Ainsworth, letter to Crossley, 7 March 1838.
4. Ainsworth, letter to Crossley, 6 September 1838.
5. Ainsworth, letter to Crossley, 25 March 1838.
6. Ainsworth, letter to Crossley, 5 November 1837.
7. Ellis, I, p. 293.
8. Forster, *Life of Dickens*, I, p. 158.
9. Ainsworth, letter to Crossley, 7 April 1838.
10. Ainsworth, letter to Crossley, 25 October 1838.
11. Ainsworth, letter to Crossley, 30 October 1838.
12. Ainsworth, letter to Crossley, 31 October 1838.
13. Ainsworth, letter to Crossley, 11 November 1838.
14. House, Madeline & Storey, Graham (eds.) (1965–2002), *The Letters of Charles Dickens*, 12 vols, Clarendon Press, Oxford, I, p. 485.

15. Ainsworth, letter to Hugh Beaver, 12 December 1838.
16. Ainsworth, letter to Crossley, 22 December 1838.
17. Ainsworth, letter to Crossley, 7 January 1839.
18. Collins, pp. 101–102.
19. Ainsworth, letter to Crossley, 29 January 1839.
20. Dickens, letter to J.P. Harley, February 1839, House & Storey, I, p. 506.
21. Ainsworth, letter to Crossley, 1 January 1839.

Chapter 9

1. Ainsworth, *Jack Sheppard*, III, pp. 310–11.
2. For a full account of the lives of Wild and Sheppard, see *The Thieves' Opera: The Remarkable Lives and Deaths of Jonathan Wild, Thief-Taker, and Jack Sheppard, House-Breaker* by Lucy Moore (1998).
3. Anon. (probably Defoe) (1724), *A Narrative of All the Robberies, Escapes, etc. of John Sheppard* and *The History of the remarkable Life of John Sheppard, containing A particular account of his many Robberies and Escapes*, John Applebee, London.
4. Anon. (probably Defoe) (1725), *The True and Genuine Account of The Life and Actions of The Late Jonathan Wild, Not made up of fiction and fable, but taken from his own mouth, and collected from papers of his own writing*, John Applebee, London.
5. Qtd. in Ackroyd, p. 278.
6. Qtd. in Ellis, I, pp. 387–8n.
7. Qtd in Ellis, I, pp. 386–9.
8. Ellis, I, p. 389.
9. Ackroyd, p. 279.
10. Dickens, Charles (1839), 'Familiar Epistle from a Parent to a Child', *Bentley's Miscellany*, V (March), p. 220.
11. Friswell, p. 263.
12. Vizetelly, Henry (1893), *Glances Back Through Seventy Years*, 2 vols, K. Paul, Trench, Trübner & Co. Ltd, London, I, p. 143.
13. Ainsworth, letter to Crossley, 8 October 1839.
14. Forster, *Life of Dickens*, I, p. 152.
15. Ainsworth, letter to G.B. Davidge, 18 October 1839.
16. Bon Gaultier (William Edmondstoune Aytoun & Sir Theodore Martin) (1904), *The Book of Ballads*, William Blackwood & Son, Edinburgh & London, p. ix.

17. Bon Gaultier, pp. xiv–xv.
18. For more on Ikey Solomon, see Stephen Carver, *The 19th Century Underworld*, Chapter 5.
19. Thackeray, W.M. (1920), *Catherine: A Story*, Caxton, London, (original work published 1840), p. 24.
20. Anon. (1839), '*Jack Sheppard. A Romance*, by William Harrison Ainsworth, Esq', *Athenaeum*, Saturday, 26 October, p. 803.
21. *Athenaeum*, pp. 803–804.
22. *Athenaeum*, p. 804.
23. *Athenaeum*, p. 805.
24. Qtd. in Hollingsworth, p. 142.
25. Forster, John (1839), '*Jack Sheppard. A Romance*, by William Harrison Ainsworth, Esq.', *Examiner.* 3 November, No. 1657, p. 691.
26. Mary Russell Mitford, letter to Elizabeth Barrett, 30 January, 1840, Kelly, P & Hudson, R. (1986), *The Browning's Correspondence*, Vol. 4, Wedgestone Press, Kansas, p. 232.
27. Ainsworth, letter to Crossley, November 19, 1839.
28. Forster, (1839). *Examiner*, p. 691.
29. Blanchard, 'Memoir', *Rookwood*, p. xvi.
30. Cohen, Stanley (2011), *Folk Devils and Moral Panics: The Creation of The Mods and Rockers*, Routledge Classics, London, p. 1. (Original work published 1972.)
31. See also: Martin Barker & Julian Petley (eds.), *Ill Effects: The Media/Violence Debate* (1997); *Youth, Popular Culture and Moral Panics* by John Springhall (1998); and Stephen Carver, *More Weird Tales from the Vault of Fear: The EC Legacy.* (Paper presented at 'Watching the Media' symposium, Edge Hill University, 2011.) Available at: https://ainsworthandfriends. wordpress.com/2016/02/16/more-weird-tales-from-the-vault-of-fear-the-ec-legacy/
32. For a detailed account of the murder, see *Murder by the Book: A Sensational Chapter in Victorian Crime* by Clare Harman (2018).
33. Harman, p. 2.
34. Qtd. in Hollingsworth, pp. 145–6.
35. Qtd. in Ellis, I, p. 377.
36. Qtd. in Ellis, I, p. 378.
37. Ainsworth, letter to Charles Kent, 20 November 1850.
38. Qtd. in Ellis, I, pp. 379–80.
39. Qtd. in Hollingsworth, pp. 146–7.

40. Thackeray, W.M. (1840), 'Going to see a man hanged', *Fraser's Magazine* XXII (128), pp. 154–5.
41. Thackeray, W.M. (1904), *Literary Essays*, Thomas Y. Crowell & Co., New York, p. 233.
42. Thackeray, *Literary Essays*, p. 239.

Chapter 10

1. Dickens, letter to R.H. Horne, February 1840. House & Storey, II, p. 20.
2. Dickens, Charles (1978), *Oliver Twist*, Penguin, London, pp. 33–5.
3. Dickens, *Oliver Twist*, p. 36.
4. Dickens, *Oliver Twist*, pp. 36–7.
5. Thackeray, W.M. (1841), 'Literary Recipes', *Punch*, 7 August, p. 39.
6. Qtd. in Poe, Edgar Allan (1987), *The Science Fiction of Edgar Allan Poe*, Harold Beaver (ed.), Penguin, London, p. 371.
7. Poe, *The Science Fiction of Edgar Allan Poe*, p. 120.
8. Poe, *The Science Fiction of Edgar Allan Poe*, p. 371n.
9. Horne, I, p. 1.
10. Horne, I, p. 13.
11. Horne, 1, p. 14.
12. Horne, II, p. 189.
13. Horne, I, p. 219.
14. Horne, I, p. 231.
15. Horne, II, p. 217. Stéphanie Félicité du Crest de Saint-Aubin, Comtesse de Genlis (1746 – 1830) was a French writer of 'sentimental novels', harpist, educator, and Governess of the Royal Children.
16. Horne, I, p. 220.
17. Horne, II, pp. 219–20.
18. Horne, II, p. 222.
19. Friswell, pp. 258–9.
20. Mayhew, Henry (1851), *London Labour and the London Poor*, Vol I, Office 16, Upper Wellington Street, Strand, London, p. 41.
21. MacKay, Charles (1852), *Memoirs of Extraordinary Popular Delusions and the Madness of Crowds*, 2 vols, Office of the National Illustrated Library, London, p. 260.
22. Thackeray, W.M. (1949), *Vanity Fair*, Collins, London, p. 59. (Original work published 1848.)

Chapter 11

1. Lukács, Georg (1974), *The Historical Novel*, Hannah &Stanley Mitchell (trans.), Merlin Press, London, p. 42.
2. Moore, John (1968), Introduction, in Ainsworth, W.H., *Windsor Castle*, Heron, London, p. 16. (Original work published 1842.)
3. Peacock, Thomas Love (1969), *Crotchet Castle*, Penguin, London, p. 200. (Original work published 1831.)
4. Horne, II, pp. 217–18.
5. Belinskii, Vissarion Grigorevich (1956), *Selected Philosophical Works*, Foreign Languages Publishing House, Moscow, p. 259. (Original work published 1844.)
6. Sanders, p. 37.
7. Ainsworth, W.H. (1840), *The Tower of London, A Historical Romance*, Richard Bentley, London, p. 13.
8. Ainsworth, W.H. (1841), *Guy Fawkes: or, The Gunpowder Treason. A Historical Romance*, 3 vols, Richard Bentley, London, I, pp. 143–5.
9. Ainsworth, *Guy Fawkes*, I, p. 223.
10. Lingard, John (1830), *The History of England from the First Invasion of the Romans to the Accession of William and Mary*, 10 vols, Charles Dolman, London.
11. Ainsworth, *Guy Fawkes*, I, pp. vii–x.
12. Rance, Nicholas (1975), *The Historical Novel and Popular Politics in Nineteenth Century England*, Vision, London, p. 41.
13. Ellis, II, p. 280.
14. Ainsworth, *Guy Fawkes*, I, p. xi.
15. Ainsworth, *Guy Fawkes*, I, p. 224.
16. Reed, John R. (1975), *Victorian Conventions*, Ohio University Press, p. 8.
17. Ainsworth, *Guy Fawkes*, III, p. 345.
18. Ainsworth, *Tower of London*, p. 181.
19. Ainsworth, *Tower of London*, p. 398.
20. Ainsworth, *Tower of London*, p. iv.
21. Ainsworth, *Tower of London*, p. 128.
22. Ainsworth, *Tower of London*, preface, pp. iii–iv.
23. Swifte, Edmund Lenthal (1860), 'Ghost in the Tower', *Notes and Queries*, 8 September, p. 192.
24. Rowse, A.L. (1972), *The Tower of London in the History of the Nation*, Weidenfeld & Nicolson, London, p. 250.

25. Ainsworth, *Tower of London*, preface, p. v.
26. Ainsworth, *Tower of London,* preface, p. viii. The 'infant princess' was Victoria, the Princess Royal and later mother of Kaiser Wilhelm II.

Chapter 12

1. Qtd. in Oliphant, Margaret (1898), *Annals of a Publishing House: William Blackwood and His Sons: Their Magazine and Friends*, 2 vols, William Blackwood & Sons, Edinburgh, II, pp. 260–1.
2. Cruikshank, letter to the Editor, *The Times*, 6 April 1872, qtd. in Cruikshank, George (1903), *The Artist and the Author*, in Grego, Joseph (ed.), *Cruikshank's Water Colours*, A. & C. Black, London, p. xvii. (Original pamphlet published 1872.)
3. Ainsworth, letter to the Editor, *The Times*, 8 April 1872, qtd. in Cruikshank, p. xvii.
4. Ainsworth, letter to Crossley, 7 December 1840.
5. Patten, Robert L. (1996), *George Cruikshank's Life, Times, and Art*, 2 vols, Lutterworth Press, Cambridge, pp. 2, 162.
6. George Cruikshank, letter to Ainsworth, 4 March 1841, qtd. in Ellis, II, pp. 97–9.
7. Ainsworth, W.H. (1841), *Old Saint Paul's; A Tale of The Plague and The Fire*, 3 vols, Hugh Cunningham, London, pp. v–vi.
8. All reviews quoted from the advertisement for 'New Periodical Works Preparing for Publication by Mr. Cunningham, 1, St. Martin's Place, Trafalgar Square', December 1841.
9. Horne, 2, p. 404.
10. When cinema-goers were queuing round the block to see Terence Fisher's *Curse of Frankenstein* in 1957, for example, film critic C.A. Lejeune of the *Observer* described it as 'among the half-dozen most repulsive films I have ever encountered', qtd. in McCarty, John (1984), *Splatter Movies*, Columbus, London, p. 20.
11. Ainsworth, *Old St Paul's*, II, p. 102.
12. Ainsworth, *Old St Paul's*, II, pp. 172–4.
13. Ainsworth, *Old St Paul's*, II, pp. 129–30.
14. Ainsworth, *Old St Paul's*, II, pp. 162–3.

Chapter 13

1. Ainsworth, W.H. (1842), 'Preliminary Address', *Ainsworth's Magazine: A Monthly Miscellany of Romance, General Literature, and Art*, I, 1 (February), pp. i–iii.
2. Ainsworth, W.H. (1898), *The Miser's Daughter*, George Routledge & Co., London, p. vi. (Original work published 1842.)
3. Ainsworth, *The Miser's Daughter*, preface, p. v.
4. Forster, letter to Ainsworth, 27 January 1842, qtd. in Ellis, II, p. 54.
5. Kenealy was the counsel for the 'Tichborne Claimant', a legal *cause célèbre* that captivated Victorian England from 1867 to 1874 in which a man called Thomas Castro (AKA Arthur Orton), a butcher's son from Wapping, claimed to be the missing heir to the Tichborne baronetcy. In the end, he failed to convince the courts, and was sentenced to two consecutive terms of seven years in prison for perjury. During the trial, Kenealy abused witnesses, insulted the Catholic Church, disrespected the judges, and dragged out the trial until it became the longest in English legal history. His conduct became a public scandal and the jury censured his behaviour. He was ultimately disbarred. Kenealy was a diabetic, and his erratic temperament may have stemmed from poor management of the condition.
6. It was Peake, not Shelley, who wrote the famous line, 'It lives!' and contributed the hunchback assistant 'Fritz' to the mythos. His plot inspired the screenplay of James Whale's *Frankenstein*, starring Boris Karloff.
7. Mahony, Francis (1842), 'The Red-Breast of Aquitania', *Bentley's Miscellany*, XI, p. 147.
8. Hughes, John (1842), 'Charles Mathews *not* "at home"', *Ainsworth's Magazine*, I, p. 261n.
9. Mahony, Francis (1842), 'The Cruel Murder of Old Father Prout by a Barber's Apprentice', *Bentley's Miscellany*, XI, p. 468.
10. Ainsworth, W.H. (1842), 'To Correspondents', *Ainsworth's Magazine*, II, p. xxvi.
11. Ainsworth, letter to Charles Kent, 24 February 1880.
12. Anon. (1944), 'The New Gull's Horne-Book', *Ainsworth's Magazine*, V, pp. 318, 324.
13. Ainsworth, W.H. (1843), 'To Our Readers', *Ainsworth's Magazine*, III, p. iv.
14. Ellis, II, p. 33.

Chapter 14

1. Qtd. in Ellis, II, p. 55.
2. Qtd. in Ellis, II, p. 56.
3. Horne, II, p. 402.
4. Ainsworth, W.H. (1844), *Windsor Castle. An Historical Romance*, Henry Colburn, London, p. 205.
5. Ainsworth, *Windsor Castle*, p. 207.
6. Ainsworth, *Windsor Castle*, p. 211.
7. Ainsworth, *Windsor Castle*, p. 26.
8. Ainsworth, *Windsor Castle*, pp. 314–15.
9. Moore, John (1968), *Windsor Castle*, p. 11.
10. Leaning heavily on the Kabbalah, Hermeticism, alchemy, and mystical Christianity, 'Rosicrucianism' was a spiritual and cultural movement that arose in Renaissance Europe after the publication of several anonymous manifestos announcing the existence of a hitherto unknown order 'built on esoteric truths of the ancient past'. Whether or not this was a hoax remains open to debate. Nonetheless, the influence of 'Brotherhood of the Rosy Cross' was strongly felt in the Hermetic Order of the Golden Dawn, itself one of the largest single influences on modern Western occultism. Aleister Crowley was a member.
11. Ainsworth, W.H. (1854), 'Prologue to the Hundredth Volume', *The New Monthly Magazine*, C (January), p. 3.
12. Qtd. in Ellis, II, p. 122.
13. Ainsworth, W.H. (1898), *Auriol; or, The elixir of life*, George Routledge & Sons, London, p. 135.
14. Ainsworth, W.H. (1865), *Auriol; or, The elixir of life*, George Routledge & Sons, London, p. 201.

Chapter 15

1. Dickens, letter to Ainsworth, 29 April 1841, Hogarth, Georgina & Dickens, Mamie (eds.) (1880), *The Letters of Charles Dickens*, 2 vols, Chapman & Hall, London, I, p. 43.
2. Dickens, letter to Ainsworth, 25 September 1842, Hogarth & Dickens, I, p. 92.
3. Ainsworth, letter to Dr Thomas Pettigrew, January 1843.

4. Dickens, letter to Ainsworth, 25 September 1842, Hogarth & Dickens, I, p. 92.
5. Qtd. in Ellis, II, p. 37.
6. Ballantine, Serjeant (1882), *Some Experiences of a Barrister's Life*, Richard Bentley & Son, London, pp. 331–3.
7. Qtd. in Ellis, II, p. 39.
8. Qtd. in Ellis, II, p. 44.

Chapter 16

1. *Reynolds's Miscellany*, First Series, II, 22 May 1847, p. 1.
2. The farmer William Davis (c.1625–1689) was an unusually successful highwayman, active for over forty years before finally being apprehended and executed. He was nicknamed 'The Golden Farmer' by neighbours as he always paid his bills in gold; apparently no one ever paused to wonder where this gold might be coming from.
3. Ainsworth, W.H. (1849), *The Lancashire Witches: A Romance of Pendle Forest*, 3 vols, Henry Colburn, London, I, p. 129.
4. Ainsworth, *Lancashire Witches*, II, pp. 136–7.
5. Crossley, James (ed). (1845). *Pott's Discovery of Witches in the County of Lancaster*. Manchester: The Chetham Society, p. xliv.
6. Ainsworth, letter to Crossley, 15 February 1848.
7. Thackeray, letter to Frances Fladgate, January 1848, *Letters and Private Papers*, pp. 2, 344.
8. Crossley, *Pott's Discovery*, p. 119.
9. Wheatley, Dennis (1971), *The Devil and All His Works*, Hutchinson, London, p. 247.
10. Shelley, Mary (1968), *Frankenstein*, in *Three Gothic Novels* (Peter Fairclough ed.), Penguin, London, p. 396. (Original work published 1818.)
11. Gilbert, Sandra M. & Gubar, Susan (1979), *The Madwoman in the Attic*, Yale University Press, New Haven, pp. 201–202.
12. Milton, John (1997), *Paradise Lost*, (Alastair Fowler ed.), 2nd ed., Longman, London. (Original work published 1667.)
13. Gilbert and Gubar, p. 206.
14. Ainsworth, *Lancashire Witches*, I, p. 169.
15. Ainsworth, *Lancashire Witches*, I, p. 311.
16. Ainsworth, *Lancashire Witches*, II, p. 82.

17. Ainsworth, *Lancashire Witches*, III, p. 4.
18. Ainsworth, *Lancashire Witches*, III, p. 359.
19. Ainsworth, letter to G.P.R. James, 14 November 1849.

Chapter 17

1. Mayhew, I, p. 25.
2. Dickens, letter to W.C. Macready, 30 August 1849, House & Storey, V, p. 603.
3. Mayhew, I, p. 20.
4. Ainsworth, letter to Crossley, 29 October 1847.
5. Thackeray, letter to Mrs Brookfield, 3 September 1849, Gordon, II, p. 584.
6. Mrs Brookfield, letter to Thackeray, 4 September 1849. Gordon, II, p. 585.
7. Thackeray, letter to Mrs Carmichael-Smyth, 23 January 1857, Gordon, IV, p. 13.
8. John Leigh was an old soldier who had lost an arm at the battle of Bunker Hill; he ran a tuck shop opposite the school gates.
9. Ainsworth, letter to Charles Ollier, 3 December 1851.
10. Ainsworth, letter to Charles Kent, qtd. in Ellis, II, pp. 179–80.
11. Ainsworth, letter to Mrs Hughes, 8 January 1852.
12. Ainsworth, letter to Crossley, 4 March 1852.
13. Ainsworth, *Mervyn Clitheroe*, p. 180.
14. Ainsworth, *Mervyn Clitheroe*, pp. 60–2.
15. The house now bears a plaque that reads: 'W. Harrison Ainsworth occupied this house from 1853–1867 and wrote the following romances: The Star Chamber; Lord Mayor of London; The Flitch of Bacon; Cardinal Pole; The Spendthrift; John Law. The Projector; Mervyn Clitheroe; The Spanish Match; Ovingdean Grange; Constable De Bourbon; Constable of the Tower; Old Court. This tablet was erected by C.A. Bleckly, 1910'.
16. Ainsworth, letter to Crossley, 19 October 1854.
17. Ainsworth, letter to Charles William Shirley Brooks, 3 December 1854.
18. Ainsworth, W.H. (1856),. *The Spendthrift: A Tale*, Bernard Tauchnitz, Leipzig, p. 335.
19. Ainsworth, letter to Crossley, 18 October 1869.

Chapter 18

1. Ainsworth, letter to Charles Kent, 12 October 1859.
2. Ainsworth, letter to Charles Kent, 4 August 1859.
3. The house is long gone, but there is a black 'Open Plaque' on the office building now standing in its place – although the date of his death is incorrect – that reads: 'Wm. Harrison Ainsworth 1805–1883 novelist was born in a house which stood on this site'.
4. Ainsworth, letter to Crossley, 21 March 1864.
5. The couple had three children – Francis Minnie Apphia, Frank and John. Frank died in the Boer War, Apphia married two military men, both of whom were killed in action, and John became a captain in the 27th Worcester Regiment, living to collect his pension.
6. Ellis, II, p. 310.
7. Ainsworth, W.H. (1860), 'Epilogue to Volume XLVIII', *Bentley's Miscellany*, XLVIII, pp. 561–2.
8. Ainsworth, letter to Louise de la Ramé, 18 December 1864.
9. Ainsworth, letter to Crossley, 23 November 1869.
10. Ainsworth, letter to Crossley, 18 October 1869.
11. Ainsworth, letter to Crossley, 9 December 1869.
12. Ellis, II, p. 264.
13. Ainsworth, letter to Charles Kent, 7 July 1870.
14. Ainsworth, letter to Crossley, 14 September 1871.
15. Benjamin H. Latrobe, letter to Ainsworth, 4 November 1867 (copy sent to Crossley, 30 November 1871).
16. For a detailed reading of *Merry England*, see Stephen Basdeo's *The Life and Legend of a Rebel Leader: Wat Tyler* (2018), Chapter Six.
17. Ainsworth, letter to Crossley, 25 December 1875.
18. Ainsworth, letter to James George Joseph Penderel-Brodhurst, June 1875.
19. Ainsworth, letter to Crossley, 13 April 1876.
20. Qtd. in Ellis, II, p. 300.
21. Ainsworth, letter to Crossley, 28 July 1877.
22. Ainsworth, letter to Crossley, 30 March 1880.
23. Qtd. in Ellis, II, p. 309.
24. Ainsworth, letter to Dr James Bower Harrison, 22 January 1880.

Chapter 19

1. Ainsworth, letter to Crossley, 4 November 1872.
2. The first edition was nostalgically titled *The Good Old Times*, but it was discovered that a book of the same name was already in print by Anne Manning.
3. Ainsworth, W.H. (1874), *The Manchester Rebels or The Fatal '45*. 2nd ed., Tinsley Brothers, London, pp. vii–viii.
4. Ainsworth, letter to Crossley, 10 October 1873.
5. Qtd. in Ellis, II, p. 288.
6. Ainsworth, W.H. (1873), *The Good Old Times: The Story of the Manchester Rebels of '45*, 3 vols, Tinsley Brothers, London, I, p.184.
7. Ainsworth, letter to Crossley, 21 December 1874.
8. Recently married Society lawyer Charles Bravo of the Priory, Balham died three painful days after taking a massive dose of antimony, used then as an emetic. Despite two inquests, the case was never solved. He may have been murdered by his wife, Florence, her lover, Dr James Gully, or a disgruntled servant. Although conscious enough to make a will, Bravo never gave any indication that he knew what had happened to him, insisting all he had taken was laudanum, leading to another theory that he had been slowly poisoning his wife with tartar emetic and had mistakenly drunk the wrong potion when self-medicating. Because of the grim nature of the death, the social status of the family, the revelations about Florence's private life, and the lack of resolution, the 'Murder at the Priory' was a sensational news story.
9. Ainsworth, letter to Crossley, August 20 1877.

Chapter 20

1. Horne died at Margate on 13 March 1884, aged eighty-one.
2. Crossley & Evans, pp. 1–3.
3. Crossley & Evans, pp. 3–5.
4. 'Say, shall my little bark attendant sail,/Pursue the triumph and partake the gale?' Alexander Pope, *Essay on Man*, 'Epistle iv' (1734).
5. Crossley & Evans, pp. 5–7.

6. *Punch*, LXXXI, 21 September 1881, p. 214. *Ad Multos Annos* means 'to many years' in the sense of 'Many happy returns'.
7. Ainsworth, letter to Crossley, 21 September 1881.
8. Ainsworth, letter to Crossley, 31 October 1881.
9. John Evans was a Manchester journalist and fan who helped Crossley produce the proceedings of the banquet.
10. Ralph F. Ainsworth, MD, FLS, was Chairman of the Council of the Manchester Royal Institution.
11. C.H. Hinde was Ainsworth's solicitor and later the executor of his estate.
12. Ainsworth, final letter to Crossley, 11 November 1881.
13. Ainsworth, letter to Dr James Bower Harrison, 28 December 1881.
14. Ellis, II, p. 342n.
15. Anon. (1882), 'Obituary: Mr William Harrison Ainsworth', *The Times*, 4 January, p. 9.
16. Anon. (1882), 'Funeral of Mr. Harrison Ainsworth', *Daily Telegraph*, 10 January, p. 2.
17. Anon. (1882), 'Obituary of 1882', *Manchester Evening News*, 29 December, p. 2.
18. Anon. (1882), 'From Our London Correspondent', *Liverpool Daily Post*, 5 January, p. 5.
19. 'We (*Manchester Guardian*) understand that the books and MSS, belonging to the late Mr Harrison Ainsworth will be sold by auction by Messrs. Sotherby, Wilkinson and Hodge, in London, at the end of July. Among the books will be found a curious collection of the lives of notorious highwaymen and criminals of various grades, of all times, and all countries. The MSS, some of which are in a pretty complete state, embrace the author's "Rookwood", "Jack Sheppard", "Beau Nash", "Flitch of Bacon", "Mervyn Clitheroe", "John Law", "Old Court", "South Sea Bubble", "Hilary St Ives", "Boscobel", "Manchester Rebels", "Leaguer of Lathom", "Beatrice Tyldesley," "Stanley Brereton," and other fragments. There are, likewise, MSS, in prose and verse, from the pens of Bulwer-Lytton, Lady Blessington, Mrs. Gore, and other brilliant contributors whom the novelist gathered around him during his well-known ventures as editor of *Bentley's Miscellany*, *Ainsworth's Magazine*, and *Colbourn's New Monthly*. Not the least interesting in the collection are a few of those wonderful etchings and tracings by Ainsworth's

great illustrator, George Cruikshank.' Anon. (1882), 'Literary and Other Notes', *Northern Whig*, Monday, 26 June, p. 6.

20. Ainsworth's daughter Emily passed away in 1885; Fanny and Ann both lived until 1908. Ann's family, the Swansons, continues to flourish to this day and are Ainsworth's only lineal descendants. Sarah Ainsworth (née Wells) died in 1901, and Clara, who never married, died in Devon in 1952.

21. *Manchester Guardian*, 2 August 1883, qtd. in Collins, p. 268.

L'envoi

1. Elwin, p. 172.
2. Ainsworth (184), *Rookwood*, pp. xxxvii–xxxviii.

Bibliography

Ackroyd, Peter (1990), *Dickens*, QPD, London.

Ainsworth, W.H. (1822–1882), *Autograph letters of W.H. Ainsworth to James Crossley*, 11 vols, unpublished manuscript, Archives Section, Local Studies Unit, Central Library, Manchester.

Ainsworth, W.H. (1858), *Mervyn Clitheroe*, George Routledge & Sons, London.

Ainsworth, W.H. (1821), 'Horæ Dramaticæ No. 1', *Pocket Magazine of Classics and Polite Literature* VIII, John Arliss, London, pp. 35–9.

Ainsworth, W.H. (1821), 'Horæ Dramaticæ No. III', *Pocket Magazine*, VIII, pp. 314–18.

Ainsworth, W.H. (1821), 'On the Writings of Richard Clitheroe', *New Monthly Magazine and Literary Journal: Original Papers*, I, pp. 123–8.

Ainsworth, W.H. (1821), 'Sir Albert's Bride', *Pocket Magazine* VIII, John Arliss, London, p. 239.

Ainsworth, W.H. (1821). 'The Baron's Bridal'. *European Magazine, and London Review*. LXXX, 537–40.

Ainsworth, W.H. (1821), 'The Dying Laird', *Pocket Magazine* VIII, John Arliss, London, pp. 263–8.

Ainsworth, W.H. (1821), 'To the Editor of the Edinburgh Magazine', *Edinburgh Magazine and Literary Miscellany: A New Series of the Scots Magazine*, IX, p. 589.

Ainsworth, W.H. (1821), *Ghiotto; or Treason Discovered. Pocket Magazine* VIII, John Arliss, London, pp. 181–9, 250–7.

Ainsworth, W.H. (1821), *The Rivals: a Serio-Comic Tragedy. Pocket Magazine* VII, John Arliss, London, pp. 292–3.

Ainsworth, W.H. (1822), 'The Spectre Bride', in Mitsuharu Matsuoka, *Victorian Ghost Stories*, available at: http://www.lang.nagoya-u.ac.jp/~matsuoka/ghost-stories-ainsworth.html (accessed 23 March 2018).

Ainsworth, W.H. (1822), 'What shall I write?', *Edinburgh Magazine*, XI, pp. 38–40.

Ainsworth, W.H. (1823), 'The Half-Hangit', *European Magazine, and London Review*, LXXXIV, pp. 397–404.

Ainsworth, W.H. (1823), *December Tales*, G. & W.B. Whittaker, London.

Ainsworth, W.H. (1834), *Rookwood: A Romance*, 3 vols, Richard Bentley, London.

Ainsworth, W.H. (1837), *Rookwood: A Romance, Revised, Corrected and Illustrated with A New Preface, and Notes*, Richard Bentley, London.

Ainsworth, W.H. (1839), *Jack Sheppard: A Romance*, 3 vols, Richard Bentley, London.

Ainsworth, W.H. (1840), *The Tower of London, A Historical Romance*, Richard Bentley, London.

Ainsworth, W.H. (1841), *Guy Fawkes: or, The Gunpowder Treason. A Historical Romance*, 3 vols, Richard Bentley, London.

Ainsworth, W.H. (1841), *Old Saint Paul's; A Tale of The Plague and The Fire*, 3 vols, Hugh Cunningham, London.

Ainsworth, W.H. (1842), 'To Correspondents', *Ainsworth's Magazine: A Monthly Miscellany of Romance, General Literature, and Art*, II, p. xxvi.

Ainsworth, W.H. (1842), 'Preliminary Address', *Ainsworth's Magazine*, I, p. 1.

Ainsworth, W.H. (1843), 'To Our Readers', *Ainsworth's Magazine*, III, p. iv.

Ainsworth, W.H. (1844), *Windsor Castle. An Historical Romance*, Henry Colburn, London.

Ainsworth, W.H. (1849), *Rookwood: A Romance*, George Routledge & Sons, London.

Ainsworth, W.H. (1849), *The Lancashire Witches: A Romance of Pendle Forest*, 3 vols, Henry Colburn, London.

Ainsworth, W.H. (1854), 'Prologue to the Hundredth Volume', *New Monthly Magazine*, C, pp. 1–5.

Ainsworth, W.H. (1856), *The Spendthrift: A Tale*, Bernard Tauchnitz, Leipzig.

Ainsworth, W.H. (1860), 'Epilogue to Volume XLVIII', *Bentley's Miscellany*, XLVIII, pp. 561–2.

Ainsworth, W.H. (1865), *Auriol; or, The elixir of life*, George Routledge & Sons, London.

Ainsworth, W.H. (1873), *The Good Old Times: The Story of the Manchester Rebels of '45*, 3 vols, Tinsley Brothers, London.

Ainsworth, W.H. (1874), *The Manchester Rebels or The Fatal '45*, 2nd ed., Tinsley Brothers, London.

Ainsworth, W.H. (1898), *The Miser's Daughter*, George Routledge & Co. London. (Original work published 1842.)

Ainsworth, W.H. & Aston, J.P. (1826), *Sir John Chiverton*, John Ebers, London.

Anderson, W.E.K. (ed.) (1972), *The Journal of Sir Walter Scott*, Clarendon Press, Oxford.

Anon. (1734), 'The persons undernamed are charged upon Oath for committing several robberies in Essex, Middlesex, Surrey, and Kent', *London Gazette*, No. 7379, 22 February 1734, p. 1.

Anon. (1821), 'Foscari: A Tragedy', *Edinburgh Magazine*, IX (December), pp. 590–6.

Anon. (1821), 'Hymn to Christopher North, Esq', *Blackwood's Edinburgh Magazine*, IX (49), pp. 60–4.

Anon. (1823), '*December Tales*', *Monthly Review,* CI, pp. 442–3.

Anon. (1823), 'The Maid's Revenge, and A Summer Evening's Tale and Other Poems by Cheviot Ticheburne', *Monthly Review*, CII, pp. 98–9.

Anon. (1823), 'The Maid's Revenge, and A Summer Evening's Tale and Other Poems by Cheviot Ticheburne', *The Literary Chronicle for the Year 1823*, Davidson, London.

Anon. (1826), '*Sir John Chiverton, A Romance*', *Literary Gazette*, James Moyes, London.

Anon. (1826), '*Sir John Chiverton; A Romance*', *New Monthly Magazine Historical Register III*, Henry Colburn, London.

Anon. (1834), 'Critical Notices: Rookwood; a Romance. 3 vols', *New Monthly Magazine*, XLI (2), p. 507.

Anon. (1834), 'Dick Turpin's Ride', *New Sporting Magazine*, VII (38), pp. 82–9.

Anon. (1834), 'High-ways and Low-ways; Or, Ainsworth's Dictionary with Notes by Turpin', *Fraser's Magazine*, IX, pp. 724–38.

Anon. (1834), 'Miss Edgeworth's *Helen*', *Quarterly Review*, LI, pp. 481–5.

Anon. (1839), '*Jack Sheppard. A Romance*, by William Harrison Ainsworth, Esq', *Athenaeum*, Saturday, 26 October, pp. 803–805.

Anon. (1882), 'From Our London Correspondent', *Liverpool Daily Post*, 5 January, p. 5.

Anon. (1882), 'Funeral of Mr. Harrison Ainsworth', *Daily Telegraph*, 10 January, p. 2.

Anon. (1882), 'Literary and Other Notes', *Northern Whig*, Monday, 26 June, p. 6.

Anon. (1882), 'Obituary of 1882', *Manchester Evening News*, 29 December, p. 2.

Anon. (1882), 'Obituary: Mr William Harrison Ainsworth', *The Times*, 4 January, p. 9.

Anon. (1944), 'The New Gull's Horne-Book', *Ainsworth's Magazine*, V, pp. 317–25.

Arliss, John (1821), 'Editor's Note', *Pocket Magazine* VIII, John Arliss, London, p. 36.

Aston, J.P. (1882), 'The Late Mr. Harrison Ainsworth', *The Times*, 6 January, p. 11.

Ballantine, Serjeant (1882), *Some Experiences of a Barrister's Life*, Richard Bentley & Son, London.

Barlow, Derek (1973), *Dick Turpin and the Gregory Gang*, Phillimore, London & Chichester.

Bayes, Richard & Cole, J. (1739), *The Genuine HISTORY of the LIFE of RICHARD TURPIN, The noted Highwayman, Who was Executed at York for Horse-stealing, under the Name of John Palmer, on Saturday April, 7, 1739*, J. Standen, London.

Belinskii, Vissarion Grigorevich (1956), *Selected Philosophical Works*, Foreign Languages Publishing House, Moscow. (Original work published 1844.)

Blanchard, Samuel Laman (1849), 'Memoir of William Harrison Ainsworth', in Ainsworth, W.H., *Rookwood: A Romance*, George Routledge & Sons, London. (Original article published in the *Mirror*, 1842.)

Bon Gaultier (William Edmondstoune Aytoun & Sir Theodore Martin) (1904), *The Book of Ballads*, William Blackwood & Son, Edinburgh & London. (Original work published 1845.)

Bulwer-Lytton, Edward (1865), *Paul Clifford*, George Routledge & Sons, New York. (Original work published 1830.)

Carver, Stephen James (2003), *The Life and Works of the Lancashire Novelist William Harrison Ainsworth, 1805–1882*, Edwin Mellen, Lewiston.

Cohen, Stanley (2011), *Folk Devils and Moral Panics: The Creation of The Mods and Rockers*, Routledge Classics, London. (Original work published 1972.)

Collins, Stephen (2012), *James Crossley: A Manchester Man of Letters*, The Chetham Society, Manchester.

Crossley, James (ed.) (1845), *Pott's Discovery of Witches in the County of Lancaster*, The Chetham Society, Manchester.

Crossley, James & Evans, John (1881), *Specially Revised Accounts of the Recent Banquet to William Harrison Ainsworth, Esq., by Thomas Baker, Mayor of Manchester*, privately printed, Manchester.

Cruikshank, George (1903), *The Artist and the Author*, in Grego, Joseph (ed.), *Cruikshank's Water Colours*, A. & C. Black, London, pp. xvi–xxvi. (Original pamphlet published 1872.)

De Quincey, Thomas (1986), *Confessions of an English Opium Eater*, Penguin, London. (Original work published 1821.)

Dickens, Charles (1839), 'Familiar Epistle from a Parent to a Child', *Bentley's Miscellany*, V, pp. 219–20.

Dickens, Charles (1978), *Oliver Twist*, Penguin, London. (Original work published 1839.)

Drabble, Margaret (ed.) (2006), *The Oxford Companion to English Literature*, Oxford University Press.

Ebers, John (1828), *Seven Years of the King's Theatre*, William Harrison Ainsworth, London.

Egan, Pierce (1869), *Life in London or The Day and Night Scenes of Jerry Hawthorn, ESQ. and his elegant friend Corinthian Tom in their Rambles and Sprees through the Metropolis*, John Camden Hotten, London. (Original work published 1821.)

Ellis, S. M. (1911), *William Harrison Ainsworth and His Friends*, 2 vols, John Lane, London.

Elwin, Malcolm (1934), *Victorian Wallflowers*, Jonathan Cape, London.

Forster, John (1839), '*Jack Sheppard. A Romance*, by William Harrison Ainsworth, Esq', *Examiner*, 3 November, No. 1657, pp. 691–3.

Forster, John (1872), *The Life of Charles Dickens*, Vol. I, Chapman & Hall, London

Friswell, J. Hain (1870), *Modern Men of Letters Honestly Criticised*, Hodder & Stoughton, London.

Galt, John (1821), 'The Buried Alive', *Blackwood's Edinburgh Magazine*, X (56), pp. 262–4.

Gay, John (1986), *The Beggar's Opera*, Penguin, London. (Original work published 1728.)

Gilbert, Sandra M. & Gubar, Susan (1979), *The Madwoman in the Attic*, Yale University Press, New Haven.

Godwin, William (1993), *Enquiry Concerning Political Justice*, Penguin, London. (Original work published 1793.)

Harman, Claire (2018), *Murder by the Book: A Sensational Chapter in Victorian Crime*, Viking, London.

Hobsbawm, E.J. (1969), *Bandits*, Weidenfeld & Nicolson, London.

Hogarth, Georgina & Dickens, Mamie (eds.) (1880), *The Letters of Charles Dickens*, 2 vols, Chapman & Hall, London.

Hollingsworth, Keith (1963), *The Newgate Novel: 1830–1847*, Wayne State University Press, Detroit.

Horne, R.H. (1844), *A New Spirit of the Age*, 2 vols, Smith, Elder & Co., London.

House, Madeline & Storey, Graham (eds.) (1965–2002), *The Letters of Charles Dickens*, 12 vols, Clarendon Press, Oxford.

Hughes, John (1842), 'Charles Mathews *not* "at home"', *Ainsworth's Magazine*, I, pp. 261–2.

Hunt, Leigh (1819), 'A Tale for a Chimney Corner', in Ollier, Edmund (ed.) (1890), *Essays of Leigh Hunt*, Chatto & Windus, London.

Joshi, S.T. (2014), *Unutterable Horror: A History of Supernatural Fiction*, Vol. I, Hippocampus, New York.

Kelly, P & Hudson, R. (1986), *The Browning's Correspondence*, Vol. 4, Wedgestone Press, Kansas.

Kitton, Frederic George (1889), *Charles Dickens by Pen and Pencil; Including Anecdotes and Reminiscences Collected from his Friends and Contemporaries*, Sabin & Dexter, London.

Lukács, Georg (1974), *The Historical Novel*, Hannah & Stanley Mitchell (trans.), Merlin Press, London.

MacKay, Charles (1852), *Memoirs of Extraordinary Popular Delusions and the Madness of Crowds*, 2 vols, Office of the National Illustrated Library, London.

Maginn, William (1832), 'A good Tale badly Told', *Fraser's Magazine*, V (25), pp. 107–13.

Maginn, William (1834), 'Gallery of Literary Characters, No. L. W.H. Ainsworth, ESQ', *Fraser's Magazine*, X (July), p. 48.

Mahony, Francis (1842), 'The Cruel Murder of Old Father Prout by a Barber's Apprentice', *Bentley's Miscellany*, XI, pp. 467–72.

Mahony, Francis (1842), 'The Red-Breast of Aquitania', *Bentley's Miscellany*, XI, pp. 144–7.

Marriot, John (1941), *English History in English Fiction*, Blackie & Son, London.

Mayhew, Henry (1851), *London Labour and the London Poor*, Vol I, Office 16, Upper Wellington Street, Strand, London.

McCarty, John (1984), *Splatter Movies*, Columbus, London.

Milton, John (1997), *Paradise Lost* (Alastair Fowler ed.), 2nd ed., Longman, London. (Original work published 1667.)

Moers, Ellen (1960), *The Dandy, Brummell to Beerbohm*, Viking, New York.

Moore, John (1968), Introduction, in Ainsworth, W.H., *Windsor Castle*, Heron, London. (Original work published 1842.)

Morgan, Peter (ed.) (1973), *The Letters of Thomas Hood*, University of Toronto Press.

Oliphant, Margaret (1898), *Annals of a Publishing House: William Blackwood and His Sons: Their Magazine and Friends*, 2 vols, William Blackwood & Sons, Edinburgh.

Patten, Robert L. (1996), *George Cruikshank's Life, Times, and Art*, 2 vols, Lutterworth Press, Cambridge.

Peacock, Thomas Love (1969), *Crotchet Castle*, Penguin, London (Original work published 1831.)

Poe, Edgar Allan (1840), 'The Signora Zenobia' (AKA 'How to Write a Blackwood Article'), *Tales of the Grotesque and Arabesque*, 2 vols, I, Lea & Blanchard, Philadelphia, pp. 213–29.

Poe, Edgar Allan (1987), *The Science Fiction of Edgar Allan Poe*, Harold Beaver (ed.), Penguin, London.

Popova, Maria (2017), 'The Doom and Glory of Knowing Who You Are: James Baldwin on the Empathic Rewards of Reading and What It Means to Be an Artist', *Brainpickings*, available at: https://www.brainpickings.org/2017/05/24/james-baldwin-life-magazine-1963/ (accessed 7 March 2018).

Rance, Nicholas (1975), *The Historical Novel and Popular Politics in Nineteenth Century England*, Vision, London.

Ray, Gordon N. (ed.) (1945), *The Letters and Private Papers of William Makepeace Thackeray*, 4 vols, Oxford University Press.

Reed, John R. (1975), *Victorian Conventions*, Ohio University Press.

Rowse, A.L. (1972), *The Tower of London in the History of the Nation*, Weidenfeld & Nicolson, London.

Sanders, Andrew (1978), *The Victorian Historical Novel, 1840–1880*, Macmillan, London.

Shelley, Mary (1968), *Frankenstein*, in *Three Gothic Novels* (Peter Fairclough ed.), Penguin, London. (Original work published 1818.)

Smith, The Rev. Jeremiah Finch (1874), *The Admission Register of the Manchester School*, Vol. III, Chetham Society, Manchester.

Swifte, Edmund Lenthal (1860), 'Ghost in the Tower', *Notes and Queries*, 8 September, p. 192.

Talfourd, Thomas Noon (1849), *The Letters of Charles Lamb*, Edward Moxon, London.

Thackeray, W.M. (1840), 'Going to see a man hanged', *Fraser's Magazine* XXII (128), pp. 150–8.

Thackeray, W.M. (1841), 'Literary Recipes', *Punch*, 7 August, p. 39.

Thackeray, W.M. (1904), *Literary Essays*, Thomas Y. Crowell & Co., New York.

Thackeray, W.M. (1920), *Catherine: A Story*, Caxton, London. (Original work published 1840.)

Thackeray, W.M. (1949), *Vanity Fair*, Collins, London. (Original work published 1848.)

Vizetelly, Henry (1893), *Glances Back Through Seventy Years*, 2 vols, K. Paul, Trench, Trübner & Co. Ltd., London.

Wheatley, Dennis (1971), *The Devil and All His Works*, Hutchinson, London.

Worth, George J. (1972), *William Harrison Ainsworth*, Twayne, New York.

Index